Library of
Davidson College

*Juridical Positivism
and
Human Rights*

This volume was prepared and published
under the auspices of

The Center for the Study of Ethics and Public Policy
Department of Political Science

Queens College
City University of New York

Juridical Positivism and Human Rights

by MIECZYSLAW MANELI

HIPPOCRENE BOOKS   NEW YORK

List of Author's Previous Books

War of the Vanquished 1971

History of Political and Juridical Ideas (5 vols.) 1963-1968

Foundations of Political Science (Contributor and Editor), 3 volumes, 1967-1968

Machiavelli: A Monograph 1968

Art of Politics 1967

The Functions of the State 1963

The Activity of a Socialist State 1957

Forthcoming:

Freedom and Tolerance

ISBN NUMBER: 0-88254-449-7
Copyright © 1981 by Mieczyslaw Maneli
LIBRARY OF CONGRESS CARD NUMBER: 80-9063
PRINTED IN THE UNITED STATES OF AMERICA

For my Children

Elizabeth and Les

Contents

	Preface	i
I.	Introduction	1
II.	Jeremy Bentham	9
	1. Theory of Law and Legislation	14
	2. The Greatest Happiness Principle and the Limits of Sovereignty	17
	3. The Codification and Interpretation of Law	21
	4. Freedom of the Press	30
	5. Freedom of the Press and Bureaucratic Privileges	33
III.	John Austin	39
	1. Definition of Law and Legality	40
	2. "Unconstitutional" and "illegal" Acts of the State	48
	3. Juridical Rights	55
	4. Utilitarianism, Juridical Positivism and Resistance Against Oppression	59
IV.	Rudolf von Ihering	67
	1. Ihering's Dynamic Concept of Jurisprudence	67
	2. Theory of Law	69
	3. In Praise of the Struggle for Law	82
	4. Shylock as the Hero of our Time	92
	5. Beyond Liberalism, but still Positivism	94
V.	The Positivist Theory of the Interpretation of Law	97
VI.	Communist Juridical Positivism and Polish Neo-Positivism	115
	1. The Evolution of Communist Jurisprudence	115
	2. The Formation of Polish Juridical Neo-Positivism	132
	3. Stefan Rozmaryn—A Classic of the Communist Neo-Positivism	138
	4. Recent Developments in Communist Legal Theory	149
VII.	The New Theory of Argumentation and American Jurisprudence	165
	Preliminary Remarks	165
	1. Where Holmes and Dewey Stopped	167
	2. The Origins of the New Rhetoric	176
	3. The New Rhetoric and Pluralism	180

	4. Logic, Rationality and Pluralism	185
	5. Dialogue, Rhetorical Arguments, Truth	200
	6. Rhetoric and Politics	215
VIII.	Human Rights: Philosophical and Juridical Problems	223
	1. A Most Controversial and Fashionable Topic	223
	2. Human Rights and Sovereignty	227
	3. The Notion of Human Rights: Historical Approach	233
	4. The Notion of Human Rights: Philosophical Background	238
	5. Law and Rights	246
	6. Human Rights and Freedom	257
	A. Kant's Philosophy of Autonomous Freedom	258
	B. Hegel's Dialectic of Freedom	261
	C. Marx's Dialectic of Liberation	264
	D. Dewey's Great Synthesis	268
	E. Freedom and Privacy	273
IX.	Juridical Positivism Reconsidered and Updated	279
	1. A New Phase in the Evolution of Juridical Positivism	279
	2. Juridical Mythology and Demythification of Juridical Positivism	284
	3. Interpretation of Law and Modern Values	297
	4. Kelsen's Pure Theory of Law—A Travesty of Juridical Positivism	318
	5. Ronald Dworkin's Criticism of Juridical Positivism	327
	6. Legal Realism	339
	7. Does Antigone Need "Natural Law"?	345
X.	Conclusion: Towards Positivist Realism	363
	References	373
	Index	403

PREFACE

Successive waves of immigration from Europe and Asia during the twentieth century have greatly enriched American legal scholarship. Wars, revolutions, and dictators have driven schlolars from their homelands to settle in Canada and the United States with the expectation that the freedom of expression there would permit them to develop their ideas without the restraints to which they would not conform. Most of those who have crossed the seas have been reared in what is now being called the "Romanist" tradition with its high regard for generalizing practice in theory, and not a few have felt that the common lawyers need to be introduced to theory. There is widespread belief among the Romanists that the comparatists at their first congress in Paris in 1900 were right when they received the sole common lawyer, Sir Frederick Pollock, as if he were a representative of a legal system that should be characterized as "folkloric," to use the expression of Professor René David of Paris in his review of the history of comparative law.

In the view of the Romanists the pragmatists of the common law have not yet matured philosophically, even though they have been receptive to Romanist philosophers and have, in several cases, offered the newcomers chairs in their universities. Hans Kelsen, Ernst Rabel, Josef Kuntz, Albert Ehrenzweig, N.S. Timasheff, Vladimir Gsovski, Max Rheinstein, John C.H. Wu from China, and numerous younger men and women still in graduate schools prove the point.

The most recent group to arrive in the U.S.A. includes legal scholars from Eastern Europe. Mieczyslaw Maneli is one of these. He belongs to a far different school than the Russians like Timasheff and Gsovski who fled the Bolsheviks after 1917, or the Germans and Austrians who fled Hitler, Maneli was a member of the legal elite of his native Poland, teaching successive generations of students at the University of Warsaw. His was a dream of a new society that would replace what seemed to him to be the tyranny of the past with a new humanism, stemming from what is now called the early or young Marx and the socialist philosophers of the nineteenth century.

The dream of Maneli and of many of his colleagues was lost as the wheel turned. They found themselves enmeshed in a system unavoidably influenced by the pressure of Soviet jurists who were developing theories seemingly with no purpose other than to justify the tyranny of Joseph Stalin and his cohorts. Maneli began to wonder what had gone wrong with an approach from which he had expected so much. He asked himself what could be done to reestablish the humanism which, as a younger scholar, he had found in some Marxist-inspired writing. This volume represents conclusions at which he arrived after he had made his home in the West and found a prominent place in a great university, where he is teaching American youth what he thinks they need to know about the philosophical foundations of humanistic thought.

As with his predecessors from Europe and Asia who have reached North America, Maneli is in considerable measure a product of the environment in which he matured. He differs from his émigré predecessors in that his environment was created by men and women who called themselves "communists." This means that he had not felt the natural law influences so prominent among many of those who had arrived before him. Maneli's new convictions had no place for natural law explanations of human rights. They also had no room for theories based upon any kind of "pure theory of law." They could not separate legal and sociological scholarship, for law was clearly a social instrument. Further, all phenomena were studied historically; nothing was seen as immutable, as static.

Maneli's former colleagues were revolutionaries. They did not expect society to roll on slowly and inevitably toward a new day. They felt a need for radical change, for breaking or at least speeding the course of history. Maneli was one of this generation, and in this volume the Western reader may sense a certain continuity of thinking between the Warsaw and New York eras. Maneli obviously reveres the "positivists," and he begins with Jeremy Bentham to explain what they mean to him. It is the positivists whom he chooses to analyze in brief perceptive essays in which he is determined to set straight the record of what they thought and said. Scores of others have summarized the thinking of these monumental figures, but Maneli adds something generally unfamiliar to Western readers, namely the approach of an educated Eastern European nurtured in dialectical thought. Liberated from the strictures that still limit imaginative development of Marxist-oriented thought in the USSR and, to some extent, in the rest of Eastern Europe, he does not have to write in parables or with veiled hints. He states clearly what he wants Americans to know about a Polish scholar's assessment of positivists. Simultaneously, he gives a clue as to what those who have remained behind may be thinking as they attempt to restore a more compatible balance between the state and the individual.

After leaving his heroes, the classical positivists, Maneli turns to Stalin's legal henchmen and to contemporary Polish legal scholars. Stalin's lawyer, A.J. Vyshinsky, the arch-simplifier of Marxist doctrine on law, earns nothing but his contempt. His former colleagues in Warsaw and Cracow who attempt to break out of the confining restraints of the simplistic Stalin era to a pluralistic explanation of law, while remaining sufficiently orthodox to keep their professional chairs, merit his sympathy.

Maneli has been carefully following the evolution of legal philosophy among Soviet academics. He finds their position to be a sharp departure from the legal thinking prevalent during Stalin's rule. Indeed, in some cases he reveals "earthshaking" developments, in that they recognize man's rights as natural, inborn, and inalienable.

In attempting to rationalize the cause of this trend, Maneli presents some arresting explanations, focused on a utilitarian approach. Soviet jurists taking the new position are not, in his view, embracing the influence of natural law, but are concluding that governing increasingly requires, even in the Soviet Union, the consent of the governed. Rulers—even Communist-oriented—cannot any longer close their eyes to what is becoming evident in their own countries, as well as in many of the awakening populations of the newly-established countries: that rulers must gain a measure of popular support for what they do. They cannot rule with armies and police alone, and their legal philosophers must find a rationale for the new approach. The rationalization cannot be validated in terms of natural-law argumentation, but it can be validated in positivist terms if positivism is understood as its pioneer thinkers intended it to be.

Perhaps, above all else, Maneli shows himself to have been influenced by his own revealing experience. In his view, the Easterners, in response to political pressures to conform to positions taken by tyrannical leaders, have overlooked the humanistic restraints which Bentham and his successor positivists placed upon sovereigns. Maneli points out frequently that there is no need to espouse natural law to support demands for respect of human rights on the part of sovereigns, for he finds that the great positivists have never accepted the positions that all commands are legal. The right of mass opposition and even of revolution against tyrants has always been perceived by positivists to be inherent in their position.

Maneli presents a compelling argument based upon what he sees as the annihilation of the confining boundaries of nation states as the world community replaces them with the concept of one world. To Maneli the United Nations, with all its limitations of competence to prevent its becoming a superstate, is increasingly developing into an instrument of expression for world-wide attitudes, reaching even to the level of positivistic commands issuing from the peoples of the world as the new sovereign. In this new expression of mass views, taking the form of Declarations and Covenants, Maneli finds a limiting factor which the leaders of nation states no longer can ignore. Human rights have become, in Maneli's view, subject to the protection of a new world jurisdiction. It is, therefore, not meddling in the internal affairs of a sovereign state to require that its rulers adhere to the new popularly created norms of the world community. Sovereigns who have signed and ratified the Covenants on Human Rights have, in Maneli's view, exercised their sovereignty to bind themselves, and Maneli believes the great positivist philosophers would agree.

Maneli coined a new expression for his approach to positivist thinking. He calls it "Positivist Realism." His is an interesting concept, not entirely new in all of its aspects, but clearly articulated. For internationalists, or one-worlders, it will be heartening to read that what they have hoped might eventually result from the slow and undramatic placing of brick upon brick in the humanistic effort to create a legislative basis for worldwide recognition of the rights of man is reaffirmed by Maneli. Those who follow official Eastern European statements of views will know that Maneli treads an uphill road in his effort to influence them, for he has gone well beyond any position currently acceptable to East European leaders. These leaders still resist appeals to conform to what many Westerners are prepared to accept as norms of international law. But, if Maneli is right, the Communists can expect in the future a demand that they justify their positions. For Maneli those demands can be made in positivist terms which Communist leaders can understand. There is no need to ask them to take the unacceptable jump into natural law.

One cannot expect Maneli's thesis to be acceptable in the foreseeable future by leaders who do not feel threatened by their own masses, but Maneli notes that of late dictators have been toppled in several countries in spite of efficient security police forces and a pampered army. When they refused to accept humanistic demands, even their armies deserted them. In Maneli's view, the events of the recent past foreshadow the near future.

The sad fact needs to be noted that when the masses have risen to topple a dictator, the new leaders, in their zeal to create the society of their dreams, often revert to methods of rule no less onerous than those they fought to replace. Perhaps the process of revolt will have to be initiated again and again over generations before the lesson is learned everywhere that dictatorship, for whatever reason, breeds mass anger destined eventually to oust the dictator.

Perhaps Maneli is right that the masses can be educated if given explanations by legal philosophers that seem reasonable to them, rather than starkly rational ones, and that the audience for ideas must be kept clearly in mind when the explanations are made. Maneli asks that philosophers study the art of persuasion, and he commends to the persuaders Chaim Perelman's techniques of dialogue, expounded in that popular philosopher's *The New Rhetoric*. Maneli expects that it will be possible to gain the adherence of average people by making use of such techniques. It may be that if these methods are followed in support of international lawmaking in the sphere of human rights, the process of persuasion can be speeded so as to require would-be reformers to adopt democratic techniques soon after seizing the palace rather than persisting in dictatorial methods which they should shun in their own interests, for the newly-liberated masses can be expected to turn against them before they have established themselves.

Whatever the American reader's conclusion as to the practicality of Maneli's proposals, it will become evident as he proceeds through this volume that important ideas are put in words by a scholar educated in an environment unfamiliar to that of the reader. Maneli has opened a window to the East, and that is a major contribution of his study.

John N. Hazard
Columbia University

I.
INTRODUCTION

Juridical positivism is not the favored philosophy of our day; in fact, it is a chief target of criticism. It is held responsible for many of the vices which beset modern political regimes. There are governments and unimaginative ideologues, unable to cope with their real problems, who constantly look about for a scapegoat. Legal positivism has been re-named the philosophy of Creon. As such it is regarded as one of the sources of the corruption of power and justice, of authoritarianism and totalitarianism.

In communist countries, on the other hand, juridical positivism is accused of being a bourgeois ideology, supportive of capitalistic regimes, that endangers socialism and "socialist legality."

Let us remember that only a few decades ago, almost every jurist on the European continent claimed to be a positivist — even if he did not use this word. Today most are reluctant to admit such affiliation.

How did it happen that the situation and moral climate connected with juridical positivism has changed so radically?

It would appear that all the important political and ideological forces of this world have united to fight against legal positivism: the Thomists and existentialists, the neo-Kantians and phenomenologists, the rationalists and the personalists, the adherents of various natural law theories, the dogmatic communists and revisionists, the "official" Marxists and the "opportunists," the liberals and the conservatives, the spokesmen for the juntas and the African presidents, scholars in Moscow and in Washington, in Peking and at the Vatican.

What has caused such antipathy toward such a formerly respectable doctrine? Political interests? Ignorance? Social antagonisms? Philosophical objections? Memories of recent crimes and abuses of power?

It is the purpose of this study to explain the historical tradition of legal positivism, its genuine meaning and the role it has played in society. We also intend to analyze its distortions and misinterpretations.

It is not easy to explain the passions aroused by politics and ideology with regard to juridical positivism. Notwithstanding the difficulties, it is necessary to analyze the source and forms of ignorance, the strange amnesia which seems to have overcome the most ardent critics of the doctrine; such critics pretend to have forgotten the important progressive role which positivistic jurisprudence has played in the development of the rule of law and democracy, of social stabilization and *habeas corpus*, of social security and individual rights.

Parliamentary liberal democracy, which developed in the Western world in the nineteenth century, was accompanied by juridical positivism. The one has always been inseparable from the other. Each supports and strengthens the other. Liberal Western parliamentary political systems have undeniably been connected with juridical positivism, its concepts of rights and legality. They constitute one organism, one body and soul. They are condemned to coexist, to develop together and to adjust to new social conditions.

During the last century, of course, democracy underwent a series of changes and evolution. One can say the same of legal positivism: it too has changed and it is necessary that it continue to change, consciously and deliberately, in the spirit of freedom and democracy. In this study we will analyze topical issues in the light of old but basic principles of jurisprudence, as elaborated throughout the centuries. To achieve this goal we must return to the basic writings of the individual positivists and correct the misunderstandings which have arisen around them.

Since WW II new political and juridical phenomena have appeared. The war criminals who had been held responsible for the crimes committed against humanity were tried and sentenced. Almost all the nations of the world signed the Charter of the United Nations and accepted the principles of the Universal Declaration of Human Rights. Aggression, racism, colonialism and torture were outlawed. The covenants based on this Declaration were adopted, if not ratified, by the United Nations.

The principles laid down in these documents not only became part of international law, but also in various ways, of internal positive law. This development deeply affected the systems of municipal law. It changed the public's outlook and approach to legal questions to such an extent that philosophers of law were compelled to take into consideration the new situation. We are dealing with new bodies of law, we face new legal systems. The original doctrines of legal positivism cannot continue to be supported or rejected uncritically.

Instead of being dropped, juridical positivism must be modernized, while preserving its spirit and quality as an instrument that promotes democratic thought, security, certainty, and order. The *aggiornamento* of many old ideas and institutions is high on the agenda of our century. Updating juridical positivism is also an urgent cause.

The philosophy of juridical positivism never has been an uncritical "establishment" theory preoccupied with gilding and supporting the existing law and regimes. But today's philosophy of juridical positivism can and should promote the creation of new legal provisions and institutions as well as new interpretations and applications of existing laws.

Some religious believers are convinced that there is no salvation outside their church. A genuine jurist who adheres to the principles of freedom, certainty, justice, order, and legality, must express a similar conviction: there is no salvation for legality, democracy, constitutional order, the preservation of individual rights and liberties, except through the positive legal system expressed in the principles of law of all nations. The theory of juridical positivism, when correctly understood, interpreted, developed and applied, constitutes an indispensable part if not the keystone of the complicated edifice of the legal order, justice, and freedom.

Our analysis of juridical positivism is based on the works of the most representative authors who contributed to its genesis. Since this is not a historical treatise,

Introduction

our excursions into the past will be limited to the barest minimum.

The origins of juridical positivism can easily be detected in the writings of the great ancient philosophers. Beginning with Democritus, the Sophists, through Aristotle to Cicero; they all understood that the practically applicable provisions of law are the rules enunciated or at least supported by a government. They also understood that the provisions of law may be just or unjust, can tend to achieve the common good, or serve a particular interest only. All those thinkers, although their approach and findings diverge basically, declared that there is an undeniable, unavoidable, and necessary link between law and the exercise of political power. Many at the same time argued that there are eternal laws which are higher and more important than any laws of a Creon. The most important fact is that when some of the ancient authors adhered to natural law theories, they endeavored in that way to find a remedy for the exigencies of official, governmental law, remedies against the laws which they regarded as unjust, tyrannical, and contrary to the public good. The concept of norms which are above existing legal rules has the same origin as the ideas of justice from the philosophical and sociological viewpoints: when people feel uncomfortable with the existing social conditions they describe them as being unjust and wish therefore to change them. Since the idea of justice can be regarded as a reaction to a condition which is perceived as unjust, the concept of a natural or higher law can also be regarded as a reaction to the existing positive law as enforced by a government.

In order to demonstrate this point, let us analyze the

famous passage from Cicero's *De Legibus* (On the Laws).

Cicero of course was familiar with the writings of the Greek philosophers and therefore his way of thinking is especially characteristic:

> ... the origin of justice is to be found in law, for law is a natural force; it is the mind and reason of the intelligent man, the standard by which justice (jus) and injustice are measured. But since our whole discussion has to do with the reasoning of the populace, it will sometimes be necessary to speak in the popular manner, and give the name of law to that which in written form decrees whatever it wishes, either by command or prohibition. *For such is the crowd's definition of law.* (Emphasis supplied). But in determining what justice is, let us begin with that supreme law which had its origin ages before any written law existed or any state at all had been established.[1]

Cicero makes an observation which could be repeated in any historical epoch: the crowd understands that law is what the legislator decrees in written form, either by command or prohibition.

According to Cicero the "crowd" (the man in the street) intuitively adheres to the philosophy of legal positivism without any philosophical analysis. Laws, for the average man, are rules which are applied and enforced by governments. For the average man law is one of the instruments of government which uses it sometimes freely, sometimes reluctantly, and sometimes overzealously.

One can argue that the feelings and perceptions of an uneducated and often illiterate crowd should not be regarded as the standard for what law really is. Although this argument is usually correct, it is wrong here. The people know what law is because day after day in all important events of their lives they are affected by the activity of law enforcement agencies. The people do not and cannot understand many social and psychological processes which take place when law is formulated, promulgated, interpreted, applied, and enforced. But the people, "the crowd," are able to perceive and understand what is basic: the laws command and prohibit and whoever opposes them will be punished by the government. This is a theory of law, which, let us remember Cicero's words once more, "has to do with the reasoning of the populace."

Juridical positivism embraces this simplest, most obvious, and most appealing *meaning* of law. This epitome is not the *whole theory* of law; it is only one of the elements, but this key element must not be overlooked in any acceptable theoretical formulation.

Almost two thousand years later, the same manner of reasoning can be found in the opinion delivered by Justice Story (*Swift vs. Tyson*, 41 U. S. (16 Pet.) 1, 1842):

> In the *ordinary use of language* it will hardly be contended that the decisions of Courts constitute laws. They must, at most, only be evidence of what the laws are; and are not of themselves laws. They are often reexamined, reversed, and qualified by the courts themselves, whenever they are found to be either defective, or ill-founded, or otherwise incorrect. The laws of a state are *more usually understood* to mean the rules and enactments promulgated by the legislative authority thereof, or long established local customs having the force of laws.[2] (Emphasis supplied).

Once more an eminent author and practicing jurist describes what law is "in the ordinary use of language" and expresses the theory of juridical positivism. Even more characteristic is the fact that Story, one of those who actively adhered to the idea that English common law should remain valid in the United States, stressed that the decisions of the courts do not constitute laws "in the ordinary use of language." The decisions of the courts are only evidence of the existing laws. A continental juridical positivist could not have expressed this positivistic idea more clearly.

Once more we return to our former question: are the feelings of the "crowd" as expressed in the ordinary use of language, misleading? Should a genuine juridical scholar beware of them? We do not think so. If people have felt and thought along the same lines for thousands of years in various social, political, and juridical systems, these perceptions and reflections must have been founded on similar circumstances. Ordinary language expresses the collective wisdom and the collective historical experience of mankind. One can, of course, change the terminology and arbitrarily introduce terms which are alien to experience, alien to our knowledge and to the intuition of the people. Such terminology would be understood by specialists, but the "crowd" would remain estranged and thousands of scholarly treatises would not induce ordinary people to believe what is contrary to their daily experience and to their common sense.

We expound in this volume another approach to legal theory: *positivist realism*. This doctrine is a philosophical amalgam of juridical positivism and American jurisprudence, international and municipal norms on human rights, and the philosophy and methodology of the New Rhetoric. Positivist realism emerges not as a timeless theory, but as a theory adjusted to the social realities at the end of the 20th century.

II.
JEREMY BENTHAM

Jeremy Bentham was one of the founders and classic exponents of modern juridical positivism. Like every classic thinker he expressed at once the strongest and the weakest aspects of this theory and presented it in the clearest possible way. Like other classic thinkers he has had his admirers who were prepared to *iurare in verba magistri*, but also his detractors who would gladly have assigned to him Johann Goethe's opinion that he was a *"hoechst radikaler Narr"* and found it inconceivable that a thinker as wise as Etienne Dumont (editor, friend, and populizer of Bentham's ideas) could *se declarer le disciple et l'admirateur constant de ce fou de Bentham*.[1]

Among Bentham's most ardent adversaries may have been Karl Marx who nevertheless in a thoughtful manner spoke of him as a genius of bourgeois stupidity.[2]

In this way Marx released Bentham from personal responsibility for the limitations, inconsistencies, and contradictions to be found in his volumes, shifted the responsibility on to the social system and held capitalism responsible for the deficiencies of Bentham's works. Whatever Bentham's contribution to the capitalist "super-structure" may have been, Marx attributed it to the work of genius. Let us note in passing that Marx knew only some of Bentham's books, especially *The Introduction to the Principles of Morals and Legislation*, which always has been the best known work of Bentham although it was one of his first and lacks the subtle reflections and critical remarks which one finds in his later published and unpublished writings. Had these works been available to Marx, one could speculate that he would have quoted him as another example of Hegel's dialectic: Bentham had gone so far in his defense of bourgeois society that he had reached the frontiers of apology. And whoever reaches the limits, Hegel observed, has already crossed beyond them. Although typical members of the bourgeoisie, such as Granet was (described by Balzac very realistically), thought that Bentham's every idea was balm for their souls, neither he nor other believers in capitalism, nor its radical enemies (including Marx and Marxists), were able to establish that many of Bentham's ideas were akin to a time-bomb which might explode when least expected and foster new radicalisms. Bentham is not appreciated in the twentieth century among the new ideological conservative right, and he is still anathema to the radical left.

Radicals on both sides have good reason to loathe Bentham: he stood for unlimited political liberties, he criticized opulent rulers who thought only of happiness for the minority, and he spoke out for free competition.

During his lifetime, one of the most important British politicians, Alexander Wedderburn (among others he held the posts of Solicitor-General, Attorney General, and Lord-Chancellor), commented that Bentham's greatest happiness principle was "dangerous," and that it was "dangerous on certain occasions to consult it."[3]

Wedderburn made his remarks shortly after Bentham's publication of the *Fragment on Government* in 1776. Bentham's attention was drawn to them and he therefore immediately added the following rebuff to the first edition of *An Introduction to the Principles of Morals and Legislation*: "This is as much as to say . . . that it is not consonant to utility, to consult utility: in short, that it is *not* consulting it, to consult it."[4]

Bentham's response to political criticisms of his principle was somewhat restrained in the decade of the 1780's, since he wished to confine his counter-criticisms within the framework of scholarly, logical discussion.

While preparing the second edition of *An Introduction to the Principles of Morals and Legislation*, Bentham decided to give a political answer to the political criticism of his philosophy. There are many indications in the 1820s that his writings became more forceful, courageous, and radical.

In July 1822, Jeremy Bentham wrote an "addition" which revealed his understanding of the various, deeply ingrained, and to some extent "hidden" political implications of his principle of utility. He wrote that what Wedderburn had observed was indeed "strictly true," because the greatest happiness principle must unquestionably be dangerous to every government which "has for its *actual* end or object, the greatest happiness of a certain *one*, with or without the addition of some comparatively small number of others . . . *Dangerous* it therefore really was, to the interest — the sinister interest — of all those functionaries, himself included, whose interest it was, to maximize delay, vexation, and expense, in judicial and other modes of procedure, for the sake of the profit, extractable out of the expense."[5]

Bentham often stressed (see below) that the interests of a government's bureaucracy differ from those of the greatest number of people. Even more, he claimed that there was an antagonism between them. Never before had Bentham combined so explicitly an attack on the privileges of upper-class bureaucracy and the greatest happiness principle (to the best of my knowledge based on Bentham's writings published to the present day).

In 1780 Bentham failed to mention the name of his critic, Alexander Wedderburn, but by 1822 he had become more open, less diplomatic, more politically conscious, and "class" oriented. With passion and acerbity, rare in his writings, he criticized the former high-ranking courtier: "In a Government which had for its end in view the greatest happiness of the greatest number, Alexander Wedderburn might have been Attorney General and then Chancellor: but he would not have been Attorney General with £15.000 a year, nor Chancellor, with a peerage, with a veto upon all justice, with £ 25,000 a year, and with 500 sinecures at his disposal, under the name of Ecclesiastical Benefices, besides *et ceteras*."[6]

There is no doubt that Jeremy Bentham, an ardent and gifted proponent of private property, of free capitalist competition which according to him should remain free of governmental restrictions, and even included usury in the domains which should remain unregulated by government, became an acid critic of the then new, post-feudal privileges. He no longer criticized Wedderburn for not caring about the greatest happiness of his subjects, but criticized him for symbolizing and benefiting from the governmental system of privileges. The higher the position one maintained in the hierarchy, the greater were the benefits and advantages which were dispensed at the expense of the greatest number. It would be easy to find striking similarities between Bentham's and Marx's criticism of bourgeois society and of the bureaucratic system of immunities and privileges.

There are many indications which point to Marx's unfamiliarity with these aspects of Bentham's writings. But those who claim to be Marx's disciples have had an opportunity to study and become familiar with "Bentham the unknown" and quote him for their own benefit. But the "left" will not do so because Bentham was radically anti-bureaucratic and consistently attacked the privileges enjoyed by governmental functionaries; he was for unlimited personal freedom, for strict legalistic guarantees; he opposed every legal, political, religious, or philosophical fiction.

That is why he is unpopular among contemporary "rightists" and "leftists" alike. That is why his juridical positivism became one of their favorite targets.

Bentham was an unusual author. David Baumgardt writes of him in his brilliant monograph:

> Did any other European of the eighteenth century do as much as Bentham did for the clarification of great issues which are still vital in 1949? He contributed to the organization of a permanent international peace, as well as to social and economic reforms of manifold types, to the emancipation of the colonies, to the creation of a league of nations and of a noncoercive arbitral tribunal for settling of international disputes, to the codification of English and American Law, to the improvement of prisons, to the limitation of capital punishment, to the exclusion of corporal punishment from

school discipline, to the prevention of cruelty toward animals, to the enlargement of public health legislation, to the emancipation of women, to the establishment of savings banks, to the creation of an international language, to the theory of language and analysis of its impact on philosophical thought in the sense of modern semantics, to the founding of one of the greatest institutions for higher secular learning, to the promoting of encyclopedic education and, last but not least, to the laying of a new, critical foundation of ethics. I know of no one, particularly of no one on the European continent, who could in this respect rival the greatest reformer of English Law[7]

Bentham was, as Stendhal observed, the Epicurus of his time. But Bentham was better versed in law and jurisprudence than the ancient philosopher.

1. Theory of Law and Legislation

Legislation and private ethics should go hand in hand, Bentham wrote. He differentiated between general ethics and private ethics. Ethics in general is the art of directing men's actions to the production of the greatest possible quantity of happiness for those whose interest is in view.[8]

Ethics as the art of directing a man's own actions can be called the *art of self-government*, or *private ethics*.[9]

Both private ethics and legislation should have the same end: the greatest happiness of the greatest number. Every individual ought to perform what he believes will maximize his happiness, but he should not impose his opinion or his will on other individuals; he should not even try to compel them to do something or nothing. There are situations, however, when the legislator can and ought to compel people to act or to desist from action in order to insure maximum happiness.

The legislator acts by promulgating legal norms, otherwise known as laws.

Law, or *the law*, Bentham writes, is an abstract and collective term meaning "the sum total of a number of individual laws taken together."[10]

Every law is a command or its opposite; law can have either a coercive, or discoercive nature; discoercive law is a revocation, in whole or in part of a coercive law.[11]

Every law in one way or another is connected with force or coercion.

In *Of Laws In General*, we find Bentham's fully developed definition of law: "A law may be defined as an assemblage of signs declarative of a volition conceived or adopted by the *sovereign* in a state, concerning the conduct to be observed in a certain *case* by a certain person or class of persons, who in the case in question are or are supposed to be subject to his power: such volition trusting for its accomplishment to the expectation of certain events which it is intended such declaration should upon occasion be a means of bringing to pass, and the prospect of which it is intended should act as a motive upon those whose conduct is in question."[12]

This definition of law is clear, classic, and positivistic. It rejects the ideas of natural or divine laws, and concentrates on what according to Bentham is real and realistic: law is the will of the sovereign in a state. He, or his agents, are the authors, and guarantors, of every legal provision. But the legal norm separated from the entire legal corpus cannot properly be understood or observed. The sovereign is the author of the body of laws.

Bentham wrote: "A body of laws is a vast and complicated piece of mechanism, of which no part can be fully explained without the rest. To understand the functions of a balance-wheel you must take to pieces the whole watch: to understand the nature of a law you must take to pieces the whole code."[13]

Bentham's assertion that only the legislator is *sovereign*, and that no one else can be a genuine lawgiver, became anathema to every adversary of legal positivism. From that assertion the famous conclusion was drawn that Bentham, Austin and all other positivists promoted the idea that "law is law," that *Ordnung ist Ordnung* and that whoever opposed "the law" should justifiably be punished.

Point by point we will prove that the moral and political conclusions allegedly drawn from Bentham's definition are not Bentham's, but those of his adversaries.

Bentham's theory, although magnificently elaborated, is simple and limited as far as the definition itself is concerned: law without force behind it has no meaning; a sovereign who has real power can promulgate any norm, but this does not mean that the people will really observe whims or caprices. The sovereign is legally unlimited, but de facto, his power, arbitrariness, and caprice do have bounds. Bentham gives the following example: Let the sovereign attempt to prohibit the imbibing of alcoholic beverages and fornication. Will he suceed? "Not all the tortures which ingenuity could invent would encompass it . . . "[14]

Bentham warned that even the most powerful sovereign-legislator should not exceed the limits of necessity. There is no need to limit the liberty of the subject if there is not profit to society. If passion or prejudice inspire a legislator (as was the case with Louis XIV's laws against the heretics) hatred and disobedience will result, disappointment ensue, which in turn produces ill will towards the author of the laws. The result will be that the legislator will defeat himself and stultify his own end.

All other explanations by Bentham in the sphere of jurisprudence are logical, positivistic derivatives of his fundamental definition of law.

What is an offense? It is "an act prohibited," or, what amounts to the same thing to Bentham, it is an act "of which the contrary is commanded by law."[15]

2. The Greatest Happiness Principle and the Limits of Sovereignty

The end of any law, and especially of a Pannomion, as Bentham referred to an all-comprehensive code of Law, should be the greatest happiness of the whole community, by which is understood the governors and the governed together.[16] From this fundamental principle Bentham deduced his next principle which already has a closer bearing on law, the happiness-numeration principle. According to this rule, one should prefer the happiness of the greater number to that of the lesser number in the event of a conflict. More specific ends of the all-comprehensive legislation were elaborated by Bentham in the following way: maximizing universal security; securing the existence of sufficiency and subsistence of all the members of the community; maximizing abundance; equality-maximizing and inequality minimizing. Bentham mentioned specific principles concerning penal law, e.g. the positive pain-preventing principle. This means among others, let no one produce pain for no other purpose than the pleasure derived from the contemplation of that pain. In the sphere of civil law Bentham gave various axioms concerning property.

Other specific ends can be deduced from Bentham's voluminous writings with recommendations and principles outlined for legislators to keep in mind. The above enumerated principles (ends) are relatively general, but when Bentham tried to be more specific, he remained within the realm of generalities which cannot be mechanically applied even if desired. Every end, principle, maxim, or axiom needs to be interpreted and evaluated in order to be embodied into codes or practical life. And there is always the possibility that a different conclusion will be drawn from the general rule by a different interpreter.

Whatever the concrete meaning of either the most general or the most specific principles may be, they still constitute a viable and insurmountable limit upon the activities and functions of the sovereign legislator. He cannot, and should not disregard them and act capriciously or arbitrarily, according to Bentham. He is bound, not by positive law, not by the chimera of natural law, but by the greatest happiness principle and its concomitants. If the sovereign legislator violates these requirements he will sooner or later feel the consequences which Bentham also analyzed. He even mentioned the possibility of resistance (which should not be confused with the notion of right) against oppression. Such opposition would be justified not by "inalienable rights" but by the utility principle.

How can, and should, the Bentham principles practically be applied and embodied into everyday life? He himself understood that one can draw contradictory conclusions from the same general principles: "In each of the axioms, the antagonizing, or say competing, interests of two parties are conjointly brought to view . . . in those which relate . . . to subsistence, abundance, and equality, *they are the parties whose interests stand in competition, no blame being supposed to have place on either side.* By the legislator, preference should be given to that interest by preference to which the happiness of the greatest number will be most augmented."[17] (Emphasis supplied).

The legislator should also act in the following capacity: he should be an honest broker or mediator among antagonistic groups and interests, and he should especially attempt to avoid inequality-maximizing. The result can be a compromise with each party continuing to defend its own interests.

In the event of competition between interests, there is indeed no possibility to determine who is right. Here one can sense the influence of Aristotle's *Rhetoric* with "no blame being supposed to have place on either side" (See the above quotation).

One of the completely forgotten ideas of Bentham's theory of politics and morality is this: In case of competition and antagonisms, both sides can represent legitimate and morally justifiable interests. There is no reason to blame either for defending and promoting its own. The interests of both sides should be reconciled insofar as possible and a compromise should be reached by the legislator.

If no one should be blamed for the diverse interpretations of the greatest happiness principle, that also means that all interpretations may be right. Such a conclusion does not conform to Cartesian logic, but it is admissible from the rhetorical viewpoint. Bentham more or less consciously took a step toward a rhetorical revival. The legislator, in the final analysis, must be persuaded which solution proposed by the competing, antagonistic parties is the better at any given time.[18] More discussion of this problem will be found in subsequent chapters.

Power, Bentham wrote, can be either limited or unlimited. When it is unlimited, "the condition of the servant (i.e., citizen of the state—M.M.) is styled *pure slavery*."[19] Slavery takes place according to the mere rules of the language, Bentham argued further, wherever "the limitations prescribed to the power of the master are looked upon as inconsiderable."[20]

Bentham's idea here is fundamental to an understanding of legal positivism: the unlimited power of the sovereign is the source of pure slavery, and law does not apply to the slave. That simply means that where the power of the government is unlimited, laws are not applicable to the "subjects" (they are slaves); for there can be no genuinely *legal relations* between a master and his slave; there can be no legal order in such circumstances.

What happens when the power of the "master" is limited? "Whenever any such limitation is prescribed, a kind of fictitious entity is thereby created, and, in quality of an incorporeal object of possession, is bestowed upon the servant: this object is of the class of those which are called *rights*: and in the present case is termed, in a more particular manner, a *liberty*: and sometimes a *privilege*, an *immunity*, or an *exemption*."[21] Those limitations on the one hand, and those rights, immunities, and exemptions on the other, may be as various as the acts, positive or negative, which the master may or may not perform, in order to oblige his servants. Corresponding to the infinitude of these "liberties" is the infinitude of the modifications which are admitted by the condition of mastership. "These modifications, it is evident, may, in different countries, be infinitely diversified."[22]

The power of the legislator, according to Bentham, is limited by its nature, by the genuine process of legislation. Law creates obligations (duties) on the one hand and rights on the other. Law does not bestow upon the master arbitrary, capricious privileges, but imposes on him an infinitude of duties which he must perform (by positive or negative acts) in order to respect the privileges, immunities, and exemptions of the subjects. A country with unlimited power (mastership) would be "a spot upon the earth so wretched as to exhibit the spectacle of pure and absolutely unlimited slavery;"[23] in such a place everything would be legal and illegal; the uncertainty would be a part of the general terror.

Unlimited slavery would correspond to unlimited governmental power: that is the essence of Bentham's thought. Hence positive laws (as the only "true" laws) must bestow not only power but also rights, privileges, immunities, and exemptions.[24] Their complexity limits the sovereign and precludes his becoming — to use modern terminology — a totalitarian dictator.

3. The Codification and Interpretation of Law

Bentham drew many far-reaching, radically democratic conclusions from the greatest happiness principle. In the introduction ("Advertisement") to the publication of the letters addressed to Count Toreno for the use of the Spanish Cortes (1821), Bentham wrote that the principle of the greatest happiness for the greatest number required the drafting of a new Penal Code with the following rules to be observed:

—there should be many competing authors, every draft, if possible, should be the work of a single hand and the name of the author should be disclosed;
—all foreigners should be admitted to the competition with the local authors, and they should even enjoy preferential treatment;
—the test of the ruler's aptitude to rule and legislate should be his willingness to establish an all-comprehensive code.

There is a certain pattern to Bentham's conclusions. They reveal his "democratic," "populist" attitude. None of his specific proposals can be regarded as inherent in the principle of the greatest happiness of the greatest number. There is even the possibility that an enlightened and sophisticated conservative could draw from the utility principle conclusions contrary to Bentham's.

The import of Bentham's "Advertisement" to the "Letters to the Conde de Toreno" lies in the fact that he himself directly connected the specific, not so general principles of legislation with his basic ethical and political principles. He demonstrated *ad oculos* the direct and immediate role which the greatest happiness principle can play in politics and legislation.

Bentham's assertion that a foreigner can be a good, if not better legislator in a given country is one of the most visible elements in his writings of the eighteenth century: all people are equal, according to him, apart from social and national origin. The basic conditions of life and human nature are everywhere the same, therefore any enlightened philosopher, well versed in the problems of government, can be an advisor to any ruler and legislator. After all, Bentham himself, and his other great predecessors such as Voltaire, had been advisors to the Russian czar and his legislators. It was quite normal for Bentham that a Spanish legislator should turn to him for advice.

This is one of the reasons why the Germans, who had already been deeply nationalistically oriented and believed in the singular union between the *Geist der Nation* (Spirit of the Nation) and the spirit of the laws, were so critical of Bentham. Bentham, they believed, was more worldly, more international and supra-national than their countrymen. Even Goethe, perhaps the most humanistic and cosmopolitan of them used to insist: *Wer den Dichter will verstehen, muss in Dichters Lande gehen.*

Here we will find one of the reasons for the devastating opinion Goethe held of Bentham. Whereas Bentham believed that he could advise any legislator all over the world while living in London, the Germans felt that neither they, nor anybody else, were prepared to elaborate and institute a new code for Germany. Codification, they argued, was an accomplishment that requires years of study of law and of the "spirit of the nation." It is simply irresponsible, the Historical School believed, to draft a new code before all the necessary studies had been undertaken. Codification, they asserted cannot be "elaborated," "imposed," or "legislated," it must grow from the national soil and soul.

Whereas the Germans studied the philosophy "in depth," and preferred to wait, Bentham viewed it as conservative, anti-democratic absurdity (apart from his reverential remarks about Savigny himself, who after all was not only a philosopher, but a great historian as well)[25] and he would advise anyone who was willing to listen that any nation without a code of laws or with obsolete ones should immediately begin preparations for a new code, an all-comprehensive one, because partial codification would not solve any problems, but rather add to the existing doubts and disputes. One should strive to reach the stage of legal certainty as soon as possible, and should relinquish unnecessary excursions into the past, into the pre-industrial age of darkness. This ideal, Bentham believed, could be achieved through a thorough, innovative codification only.

It was Bentham's opinion that the laws which existed in England and in other countries did not secure certainty because they bristled "with a certain science as repulsive as it is inexact and useless, and which owes its obscurity to its own absurdity . . . "[26]

That is the reason it is necessary to codify the laws and to issue one code which will encompass, as Bentham recommended, all the laws, civil and penal, internal and international, political and constitutional. Concerning substance and procedure, he wrote that they should be grouped around four notions upon which everything turns in a code of laws: offenses, rights, obligations, services.[27]

This monumental work should, and must be, accomplished by the legislator who will be able to abolish all other legal, quasi-legal, or so-called legal norms and unclear customs (mores) which have the force of law.

These recommendations by Bentham constitute one more important social, political, and juridical aspect of juridical positivism: it is a theory which is a reaction against the complexity and uncertainty, obscurity and sheer absurdity of the laws inherited from previous epochs, predominantly the feudal, or preindustrial. Throughout hundreds of years, legal, or quasi-legal, norms, institutions, and privileges grew. They were accumulated in a disorderly fashion and finally created a web of norms which, as it was once observed, according to the expression of Solon himself, can be penetrated by a strong being, but will strangle a weak one. Juridical positivists, beginning with Bentham, were strongly in favor of an all embracing code like the Napoleonic Code which, according to their reasoning, would modernize their society and their legal systems. No one would be able to accomplish such a task other than a sovereign legislator who would be able to elaborate and promulgate an all-comprehensive collection of laws which would be "*rules* expressive of the will or wills of some person or persons belonging to the community . . . with whose will insofar as known, or guessed at, all other members of that same community in question, whether from habit or otherwise, are regarded as disposed to act in compliance."[28]

The concept of the sovereign supreme authority being a power and a legislator, is presented in the works of Bentham in many ways. One of them is the capacity of a ruler who puts an end to the political and juridical disorder caused by the accumulation of rules throughout the ages and supported by various vested ("sinister," as Bentham describes them) interests. "I have endeavored to throw the burden upon the legislator, that the yoke may be lightened for the people. I have given the labour to the strong, that the repose of the weak may be better secured."[29] The heaps of diverse norms, written and unwritten, precise and vague, legislative, juridical and customary, could be removed only by the iron broom of a sovereign legislator and be replaced by the positive, legal norms promulgated in due form by the government and sanctioned by it. No other alternative was available and Bentham was right.

The concept of codification as recommended and represented by the juridical positivists also has other aspects: historical, and theoretical.

Historical: positivists favor an immediate codification in order to put an end to the intolerable situation when one does not know for sure what the law is, how it can be interpreted and how the norms are to be applied which are dubious, uncertain, and unclear.

Theoretical aspect: Codification should be attempted once and for all and all subsequent laws should be of a legislative nature — neither judicial, nor customary — and should clearly be incorporated by the legislator himself into the body of the code in order to avoid the return of the feudal experience with its web of incoherent and often inconsistent rules. The laws should be constant, the code permanent. "The code of laws having been thus prepared, it will be desirable to preserve it from the injuries to which it is liable . . . once in a hundred years, let the laws be revised for the sake of changing such terms and expressions as by that time may have become obsolete — remembering that this will be more needful in regard to the language of the legal formularies in use, than that of the text of the laws themselves."[30]

This recommendation represents modernity and realism with a mixture of two utopias: eighteenth and nineteenth century illusions and wishful thinking. The thinkers of both centuries dreamed of something stable. The "natural law" partisans dreamt of an ideal system of law, based on immutable requirements, which could last forever.

Bentham's aspirations were more modest: he wanted a code which might survive without substantial changes for one hundred years. He also referred to human nature and the immutable principles of political economy[31] and therefore thought that a legislator should observe his very simple, yet basic recommendation to "*Be quiet.*"[32]

If the government does not do too much, then it will avoid mistakes and there will be no reason to correct the minimal set of laws.

But Bentham understood that the principle of the official "changelessness" of the code is only one of the possible "injuries" to which the code can be liable as "to its matter and as to its form."[33]

Although a legislator can officially be inactive, there could be attempts to introduce unwritten laws. This should be forbidden; the head of the hydra of this type of norms should be cut off, and the wound cauterized. In order to achieve this end one principal rule of interpretation and application of law should be applied which Bentham put into the following words: " . . . the text of the law should be the standard of the law."[34]

This sentence at first glance appears to be some kind of a definition *per idem*, but indeed it contains a very important indication and instructions. It means first of all that it is the text of the law and nothing else which determines whether a given case falls within the law. It is the text of the law which should be decisive to establish whether there is a gap, whether a new case is not provided for by the code. A judge can, and should, indicate a remedy in the case of a "gap in the code" but no decision of a judge, or of any other individual ("expert," "professor"), "should be allowed to be cited as law,"[35] until the legislator himself has embodied the new norm in the code.

It may well be that a particular provision "appears at first sight to be repugnant to one more general;" these two provisions should either be reconciled, or, if this be impossible, the particular provision should prevail over the general.[36]

Bentham understood that there may be contradictions even in the best of codes. In such a case the first reaction of a jurist should be that the contradiction is only apparent, an illusion, of "first sight," due rather to the weakness of our, and not of the legislator's mind. The interpreter's premise should be that the legislator had been reasonable and had been striving to achieve the greatest happiness for the greatest number. For this reason, among others, he does not want any contradictions. This presumption should be regarded as one of the principal maxims determining the method of interpretation. If after all attempts at reconciliation, contradictions are still found to be irreconcilable, and it is established beyond any reasonable doubt that the given case had not been provided for in the code, then the judge should present the case to the legislator and should not even try to create a precedent.

One can here ask another simple and logical question: Can the law be explained? Bentham was unable to give a consistent answer to this question and he hesitated between a fully negative and a positive one. His difficulties in this respect are methodological and philosophical.

In the same chapter (No. xxxiv: "Of the interpretation, conservation and improvement of a code") of his essay "General view of a complete Code of Laws" he gives two, not identical, answers.

When Bentham stressed that the text of the law should be the chief object of attention he added: "the examples which may be given being designed only to *explain*, not to *restrain*, the purport of law."[37]

In the next sentence he already withdrew partially from the concept of explanation: one should not pay attention, he warned, to any commentaries on the code, nothing should be allowed to be quoted in the court that points to the sense of the text.

As if this warning were insufficient, Bentham added the following phrase at the end of his pamphlet: "When, however, a passage appears to be obscure, let it be cleared up rather by alteration than by comment."[38]

Let us recapitulate Bentham's commentaries:
—when the text is clear, one may give examples in order to *explain* the text;
—explanations should be exemplifications only, but not explanations of the text, and all commentaries should be regarded as unnecessary and useless;
—what is in fact obscure should not be explained, but referred to the legislator.

Bentham misunderstood one of the basic philosophical questions in the sphere of interpretation: nothing is clear *eo ipso* or *per se*. Bentham was under the illusion, partially caused by the Cartesian *Discourse on Method*, that one could see the essence clearly and distinctly even without a rhetorical discussion prior to the process of *understanding*. We will deal extensively with these problems in the subsequent chapters of this book.

Bentham, as far as possible, wanted to avoid the process of interpretation in order to achieve one of the guarantees of the greatest happiness principle: maximizing universal security.

4. Freedom of the Press

Bentham also deduced a constitutional requirement for freedom of the press from the principle of the greatest happiness for the greatest number. Freedom of the press meant for Bentham, specifically, the freedom to criticize the government as a whole with its general policy and particular activity, and the freedom to criticize the government's functionaries. The situation in the United States should prevail everywhere, Bentham pointed out, that is: "no more restriction upon men's speaking together in public, than upon their eating together in private."[39]

Bentham's praise for freedom of speech and the press is one of the most magnificent and most forgotten, in history. The government should care no more about men speaking together in public than about their eating in private, because both functions are natural for the human being. Why single out freedom of speech? As Bentham pointed out in many other writings, the liberty of the press should not be granted or given, it should exist by itself. No permission should be necessary. The exercise of the natural gift of speaking and writing should simply be unrestricted, be it in private or public. We are not granted the right to eat and sleep by the government; we simply exercise these faculties; we should just exercise the human ability to speak. Any restrictions upon this ability and natural gift are artificial, *contra naturam*, and oppressive.

Bentham interpreted the First Amendment of the American Constitution. According to his philosophy, the U.S. Constitution does not confer liberty of the press upon Americans. It simply affirms its existence and prohibits anyone, especially the Congress from restricting the human faculty and potential of speech and writing.

In this connection one should remember that Bentham usually distinguished clearly between the concept of liberties and of rights. Liberties, as for example freedom of the press, simply exist, and they should not be impeded in their existence or exercise because they were not created by any government. Obligations are connected with rights, and they both result from laws.[40] Their existence depends on the force of government. Liberties depend on the government in a negative sense only: they are exposed to encroachment by the government, and the state should, according to Bentham, desist from all such restriction.

Bentham was not alone in this respect. All the classic, true juridical positivists of the nineteenth century favored unlimited freedom of speech and the press. They all believed that there could be no more powerful limitation upon the power of the government than unrestricted criticism of its activity. They all agreed with Bentham that freedom of speech, the press, and publication, contribute to the betterment of the moral standards of society, consequently people are happier.[41]

Bentham mentioned that freedom of the press could cause certain inconveniences. But the evils of censorship and suppression far surpass the minor evils of freedom, he insisted. The alleged advantages of censorship lag far behind the blessings of freedom.[42]

The genuine evils of the elimination of freedom of thought are immeasurable: they can stop the entire progress of human thought, because every new and important truth must have its enemies. Why? " . . . For the single reason that it is new and important . . . If the advance of the human mind had depended upon the good will of those in authority, where should we be today? Religion, legislation, morals, the physical sciences, all would be in darkness."[43]

Bentham understood the basic truth about bureaucrats: whenever they are authorized to say yes or no, their answer will by preference be no.[44] There is only one remedy for society if it wishes to avoid these negative effects of bureaucratic activity. It must limit the bureaucrat's power to a minimum. Especially the power to make arbitrary decisions without being held responsible for blocking initiative.

Every form of censorship is dangerous to society. Censors must operate in secrecy, and every shadow over governmental operations is a danger to society, its rights, liberties, and security.

Secrecy about any procedure, criminal, civilian, political, administrative, is the "greatest of abuses . . ."[45]

All governmental procedures should be open to scrutiny: "The procedures which are arbitrary without public hearings and the possibility of appeal, are unfair, unjust, in and by themselves."[46]

Bentham is not far from Kant's assertion, that the degree of openness in governmental operations is a measure of a government's morality. The point of departure for both is different, the conclusions the same; darkness, says an old French proverb, gives birth to crime.

5. Freedom of the Press and Bureaucratic Privileges

Bentham wrote that one of the greatest differences between the American constitutional system and all other forms of government is the fact that American officials enjoy no special privileges or immunity from criticism. Their reputations are not protected by special laws, usually known as libel laws. Let us put aside the question to what extent Bentham's interpretation and presentation of the American legal and political system is correct. Important are his legal and political ideas which he decided to illustrate by using American examples.

Such a method had already been applied by Montesquieu and Voltaire, who used to present the British political system and the spirit of tolerance not as it was, but as they wanted it to be, or rather, as they wanted to present it to the French nation, as examples to emulate. The good faith of these political philosophers is irrelevant here. It is quite possible that they really believed in their visions, that they accepted wishful thinking for reality, or, it is also possible that they assumed that for various reasons they were serving a good cause when they stressed that their political and legal concepts were in force and confirmed by practical results.

Bentham wrote that there were people who believed that the state would be "helpless" without special protection from criticism; that its reputation and even its existence would be endangered. Bentham's response to such objections was: "Look to the *United States.*

There you see government, do you not? Well: there you see government, and no *libel law* is there: the existence of the supposed deficiency you shall see; and where libel law is the article, you will see how much better *deficiency* is than *supply*."[47]

Bentham was not a utopian thinker, however, and he understood the practical problems that could arise if the government and its administrative institutions were irresponsibly or viciously attacked. The principle of the greatest happiness also might be violated. Should the respective employees suffer for the sake of the "greater happiness" of others? Would the interests of the "greatest number" really be served in this way?

Every criticism of the government, Bentham argued, conveys "an imputation on *reputation*" of a person taking part in the government and also "on the reputation of the persons at the head of the government." An innocent criticism, a victimless criticism does not exist. Bentham accepted this fact, but still defended the liberty of the press and criticism, taking into account all the social circumstances and political implications.

Bentham did not limit his analysis to general philosophical considerations, but moved on to more specific legal analysis of the libel law. He distinguished two kinds of criticism which according to various laws could be punishable: defamation, and vituperation.

Defamation was described by Bentham as imputation which to a certain degree is particular, more or less defined, and concrete; this implies an imputation of an individual act which is legally punishable, or at least disreputable.

Vituperation is an imputation which is vague and general, at least to a certain degree.

What should the legislator's attitude be regarding such acts; should he treat them as offenses when the person offended is a public functionary? In legal practice all over the world (with the exception of the United States — he stressed), the offense is regarded as mischievous and demands a stronger repressive force when the rank of the person offended is higher. The forms of procedure applied to such offenses differ from those normally followed.

A reverse practice should take place, according to Bentham. And here once again he referred to the American experience. There should be no punishment for *vituperation*, "how gross soever."[48]

No punishment should ensue for defamation, unless the imputation be false and a result of "wilful mendacity" accompanied by "the consciousness of its falsity" or with "culpable rashness."[49]

Only under those circumstances could the criticized public functionary prevail in an action for defamation. The critic nevertheless should preserve all possible privileges and rights of a defendant; he should even enjoy the privilege of a presumption that he, the *critic of the government, is right and innocent*. This is the philosophical standpoint and background of Bentham's constitutional doctrine and juridical interpretation.

The court should judge the case in the usual way: no special tribunal and no *special* form of procedure should be applied. Even more: Bentham understood how difficult it is to win a case when the government as a whole, or even one member of the establishment supported by the whole power of the centralized bureaucracy, is the plaintiff and has practically unlimited resources to support his case. Bentham therefore recommended: ". . .

the defendant should be at liberty to make proof of the truth of the imputation; and, for that purpose, to extract evidence from the person who is the subject of it, as he might from any other person at large."[50]

Bentham understood and took into account the *code d'honneur* of the establishment and understood that it will be fighting tooth and nail to protect its "reputation" and its own interest. He therefore recommended that the defendant should have the right to "extract evidence" from it. It is not without significance that Bentham used the word "extract" instead of the more polite expression "obtain" or "have access to" the available evidence. He knows that especially where an agency of government is complaining, a defendant must "extract" evidence he needs from it.

The heart of freedom of the press is the unlimited power to criticize the government including the famous "sovereign" legislator, who should not have the privilege of protecting his "official reputation." His exemption from criticism would be the death knell of a free press: "For these notions, speaking in general terms, my reason is — that to place on any more advantageous footing the official reputation of a public functionary, is to destroy, or proportionately to weaken, that liberty, which, under the name of *the liberty of the press*, operates as a check upon the conduct of the ruling few; and in that character constitutes a controlling power, indispensably necessary to the maintenance of good government."[51]

Bentham never believed the illusion that it was the "people" or the "majority" who really exercised power. In any state the "ruling few" exist. They rule, but it is the press that should constitute and exercise the "controlling" "supervisory" power, or the government will be a bad one. There can be no good government, no efficient executive and legislative branches, without the liberty of the press to criticize them, to vituperate, and to a certain degree, to defame them without punishment. Why these special privileges for the critics of the government, for the press? Bentham wrote: "Speaking more particularly, whatsoever evil can ever result from this liberty, is everywhere, and at all times, greatly outweighed by the good."[52]

Bentham deliberately chose between two conflicting values: the dangers caused by the unlimited liberty of the press with the unlimited possibilities of vituperation and even defamation, on the one hand, and the special protection of the good name of the establishment on the other.

Bentham harbored such a deep distrust of the good will and innocence of the "ruling few," who constitute the establishment, that he was inclined to believe that they would "cover up" whenever they had the chance, at the expense of the entire population.

Bentham went so far that he even distinguished between the defamation of a private person and that of a public functionary. In the latter case it is up to the functionary who was criticized to prove that the insinuations were the result of the "wilful mendacity" of the critic accompanied with "consciousness of its falsity." Here Bentham delineated some important aspects of the modern Constitutional doctrine of the U.S. Supreme Court. It seems that — according to Bentham — the critic of government enjoys the presumption of good faith whereas the government is always "suspected" and has to prove its innocence. The government has no right to withhold from the public the documents which could damage its reputation. Even more, officials are obliged to make available everything that might support the allegations of the critic.

Bentham in this way drew the most consistent and logical consequences from the principle that the end the government should aspire to is the greatest happiness of the greatest number.

The government, according to him, should have no special interests that differ from the good of every individual and therefore law should protect the individuals but not the special, "sinister" (Bentham) interests of the public functionaries.

III.
JOHN AUSTIN

John Austin developed and systematized utilitarianism in the sphere of jurisprudence. Although he lacked the innovative spirit of his master and teacher, Jeremy Bentham, he was a more precise jurist. He was a practical lawyer while his contemporary and countryman, John Stuart Mill, followed a broader humanistic path. Due to his knowledge, facility in communication, and excellent qualities of mind, Austin was able to produce a well-conceived, clearly written treatise which for good reason gained the reputation as a classic in modern jurisprudence.

Austin's lectures on *The Philosophy of Positive Law* represent much more than an expanded, modernized version of the simplistic ideas that had been attributed to Thrasymachus and Hobbes. Austin's book is in fact a philosophical and political study of the essence, the origins, the functions, and ends of law in modern society. The author also undertook to explain the main political implications of his doctrine, including implications which have become especially topical after his time: may the people take up arms against an oppressive government? How can such resistance be justified within the framework of a legal order and by the philosophy of juridical positivism? What is the source and nature of individual legal rights? How are they protected? By whom, and against whom? By what means?

John Austin became after Jeremy Bentham, the principal English juridical positivist. To this day he has been underestimated for the original thinker and gifted author that he was.[1] Although he was able to present his juridical and political philosophy with brilliance and at times unusual force and passion, he never ceased to think as a jurist and he continued at the same time to be a well-versed, up-to-date philosopher of morality and politics.

In presenting Austin's ideas we will concentrate less on his well-known definitions of law and sovereignty, but rather on the unknown, forgotten, or misinterpreted Austin, such as Austin the proponent of individual rights *erga omnes,* including the state; we will concentrate on Austin the author and realist, rather than the limited pragmatist; the author who tried to define not only the sources and scope of law but analyze the legality and morality of resistance to oppression and civil disobedience.

1. Definition of Law and Legality

Austin defines the boundaries which distinguish positive law, the only sort that is properly called law, from all the confusions surrounding it, in the first part of his work. Hence he called the first six chapters of his book "The Province of Jurisprudence Determined."[2]

John Austin

Austin asserts that every determination, including that of jurisprudence must be positive and negative at the same time. Positive determination concerns the "matter," the "essence," or the "nature," of law.[3] Negative determination concerns the distinction between what appropriately concerns jurisprudence and all other objects with which it might be confounded.

In order to determine the scope of jurisprudence one should first define the nature of law itself; he formulates the classic positivistic definitions of law: "... law strictly so called, that is, law set by political superiors to political inferiors ... may be defined as a rule laid down for the guidance of an intelligent being by an intelligent being having power over him."[4]

Norms, without power underpinning them, cannot be legal norms. There are many norms also established by men which are improperly called legal rules, because they are not written by political superiors who have the power to sanction violations.

Whoever calls these non-legal norms laws is using the term as a figure of speech only because he is not speaking of *positive law,* which is the only appropriate matter of jurisprudence. He is either speaking of positive morality or he is using an analogy or metaphor. One figure of speech is the phrase, "Law of Nature," which is in large measure responsible for much "muddy speculation" introduced into the field of jurisprudence and morals.

The above general definition of law requires clarification which Austin supplies.

Every law is a command, he writes, but not every

command is a law. The term "command" comprises the term "law." Command expresses a wish, but it is distinguished from other significations of desire not by form or style, but by the power and the purpose "of the party commanding to inflict evil or pain in case the desire be disregarded."[5]

Even though it be expressed in the imperative mode, a wish is not a command if it lacks behind it the power and the purpose to inflict evil or pain upon violators. Once one is vulnerable to evil caused by a commander, one is under "duty" to obey the "command."[6] One may conclude therefore that command and duty are *correlative* terms; they are correlated by the idea of incurring evil. Some sanctions can be called punishment.

Austin openly disagrees with Locke and Bentham who considered "sanction" or "enforcement of obedience" could be extended to "a conditional good" as a reward. Rewards may help, Austin agrees, to evoke motives to comply with a commander's wishes, but a command is sanctioned by the possibility of suffering evil or pain and, as he argues further, the extension of the term, "sanction," in the spirit of Bentham's utilitarianism, would be "pregnant with confusion."[7]

The next characteristic feature of law, according to Austin, is that legal commands are *general*; they oblige "generally to acts or forbearances."

The command which obliges to a "specific act or forbearance" is a command which we call occasional or particular and such a command should not be called a law. Austin himself realizes that it may be difficult at times to distinguish between what is "general" and what is "specific," but this weak point of his theory is truly unimportant. The confusion over the distinction between general and particular does not affect the substance of his definitions, however, but bears only on the problems of the classification of the peripheral phenomena which loosely affect the essence.

In order to illustrate his theory, Austin quoted an example which was to become a classic in works on jurisprudence.

A lawgiver determines a class or description of acts which are prohibited generally and indefinitely (e.g., stealing), and then commands a general punishment for transgressions (e.g., thieves shall be hanged). A judge commands that a specific thief shall be hanged for a specific theft. The command of the lawgiver is general; it is therefore a law (or legal rule). The command of the judge, on the other hand, is occasional (or particular) and should therefore not be called a legal rule (norm) although that does not accurately square with the established forms of speech,[8] Austin pointed out.

The next characteristic feature of legal norms is the fact that norms are the commands given by a superior. Superiority in this context is not to be confused with precedence or excellence, as is usually done. Political superiority is determined by might. This term should be interpreted and applied as literally as possible: "the power of affecting others with evil or pain, and of forcing them, through fear of that evil, to fashion their conduct to one's wishes."[9]

A true legal norm is a sanctioned norm. Law can establish rewards and appeal to pleasure, but these motives do not suffice for the enforcement of legal rules.

Law, therefore, exists only within the state, through the state, and is sanctioned by the state. When political superiors decide to enforce a law, they can put the entire power of the state into motion in order to compel compliance with the law which they have promulgated.

The sovereign is interested in the observance of the law by everyone; this is another of Austin's contentions concerning jurisprudence. Whether, and to what extent, this typically postivistic dogma is correct, is another question which for the time being is irrelevant to our considerations. But this positivistic "truism" is a philosophical component of the positivistic theory of legality.

Austin is a proponent of legality as conceived in the most traditional, obvious, and distinctly "conservative" way: strict observation of the law — what exactly it means should be explained by jurisprudence because the science of law should be in the service of legality. Austin comprehends jurisprudence as "the science of law, or at most the science of law combined with the art of applying it."[10]

When Austin expounds his theory of jurisprudence in the direction of "the strict notion" of legality, he is more consistent, more logical, and more positivistic than many of his Roman grandmasters, Ulpian, Gaius, and Celsus. He believes, for instance, that Ulpian was great as long as he seized the principles of the Romans and presented them with an admirable logic, clarity, and penetration. Ulpian reduced the positive system of Roman law to a "compact and coherent whole." But, according to Austin, Ulpian displayed "pitiable . . . contemptible imbecility when he borrowed his general philosophy from the Greeks and generally tried to define jurisprudence as: "... *divinarum atque humanarum rerum notitia, justi atque injusti scientia ... Juri operam daturum prius nosse oportet, unde nomen juris descendat ... nam, ut eleganter Celsus definit, jus est ars boni et aequi.*"[11]

These well known, classic lines of Ulpian, elegant, poetic while down to earth, became the target of Austin's fury. Why? Because, according to Austin, Ulpian compared the science of legislation with deontology, because he did not see that law itself is "the standard of justice: and whoever opposes justice to law, or vice versa, and alleges for example that law is an immediate creature of justice, is as logical as a man who says of someone else that he is the child of his own offspring. If one dislikes a given law and deems it unjust, one should have the courage to say that this law conflicts with the "law of God," or conflicts with a law of another "superior authority." Whoever deviates from the law in force, is "unjust with reference to that law." Whoever violates a law is not generally unjust, but is unjust with regard to that law.

"The judge who habitually talks of equity or justice—the justice of the case, the equity of the case, the imperious demands of justice, the plain dictates of equity—forgets that he is there to enforce the law of the land, else he does not administer that justice or that equity with which alone he is immediately concerned."[12]

A judge should be the administrator of the given law, of the given equity, and justice. Although he should be more than *la bouche des lois* (the mouthpiece of the laws, as Montesquieu used to say), he should not assume the role of a legislator and should be prohibited from introducing any element *contra legem* or even *extra legem* into the process of enforcing the law. These are Austin's assertions.

Austin is especially vehement in condemning the covert, cowardly way of changing the law in the process of its interpretation and application. Changes can be made by innocent substitution of the legal norms with moral maxims. It is at times even difficult to discover such little frauds. He quotes the example of a decision rendered by "so great a man" as Lord Mansfield.

According to English law, a promise is not binding usually unless accompanied by actual consideration. Lord Mansfield overruled this distinction, according to Austin, by asserting that moral obligation was sufficient consideration. What is a moral obligation? Austin asks. It can be, he argues, an obligation imposed by a group's opinion, by God, or by any other precept of positive morality. All those are sources of moral obligation, but the obligation itself is disputable. Introduction of such a dubious notion into juridical judgments enables the judge to enforce his own, personal concept of morality, "enables the judge to enforce just whatever he pleases,"[13] Austin concludes.

In this way we approach John Austin's principal concern that every positive law should be definite and should not be interpreted and applied as if it were indefinite, or simply absurd. Austin consistently combined his theory of law with the theory of the division of powers. He did not pay lip service to this theory, but drew definite conclusions from it: the legislator should remain a legislator; the judge should enforce the law, should regard justice like a perfume that emanates from the law, and he should anticipate that legal provisions are concrete, full of content, and not an empty jar.

"I do not blame Lord Mansfield," Austin writes, "for having assumed the office of a legislator. I by no means disapprove of what Bentham has chosen to call by the disrespectful, and therefore, as I conceive, injudicious, name of judge-made law. My censure refers to the timid, narrow, and piece-meal manner in which judges have legislated, and for legislating under cover of vague and indeterminate phrases, such as Lord Mansfield employed in the above example, and which would be censurable in any legislator."[14]

There is something prophetic in Austin's tirade against "vagueness" in the law and in his battle against attempts to introduce "vague and indeterminate phrases" into the system of law, and into the system of the enforcement of law. Austin writes as if he had foreseen the criticism which would be voiced against him by his future powerful adversaries from the school of *Freie Rechtslehre*.

If the authorities of a given country want to change the laws, let them do so openly—that is Austin's admonition and recommendation. It is an "injudicious" and "disrespectful" show when the judges make law in a "timid, narrow, and piece-meal manner." Such cowardly methods evoke in Austin a just contempt and he is deeply appalled by them because he understands that the "little" "quantitative" changes in the corpus of the law can be, as Hegel once observed, treacherous and *"hinterlistig"* (deceitful, cunning): one overlooks them for a while but is suddenly confronted eventually with a qualitatively new system. He demands safeguards against such wayward procedures. Once we proclaim that we want to live within a system of law because it is necessary for the benefit of our society, then we should adhere to our philosophy and strictly observe the provisions of law; this after all is the nature and substance of legality. There is no legality aside from one based on positive law, and let us not fool ourselves, argues Austin, that we can invent another kind of legality and security. And let us not deceive ourselves into believing that equity and justice can practically be separated from law. If we do not like the system of equity and justice which we have, let us change it, but let us not take short cuts to circumvent legal obstacles which can properly be surmounted only by the legislator.

2. "Unconstitutional" and "illegal" Acts of the State

Austin's tribute to positive law, legality, and juridical positivism is well known and one can find the description of this part of Austin's theory in nearly every textbook on the history of juridical doctrines and the philosophy of law. It is important however, that the Austinian ideas presented above are not his entire theory on the subject. So far we have only considered the beginning of his treatise, which he called "Definitions." In explaining the title of his work, "The Province of Jurisprudence Determined," Austin stressed that he had found it "necessary" first of all to distinguish positive law from various similar phenomena.[15] The chapter(s) in which the author presented determinations and distinctions must necessarily be his own ideas but documented in a special light, in a deliberately oversimplified manner. Many presentations are similar. In order to avoid ambiguity one must over-simplify the definition, reserving time and space later for more specific elaboration to overcome and prevent possible misunderstandings and simple errors. Nearly every serious author must first clear the decks to prepare for the future battle of ideas.

Spinoza understood the dangers of definitions better than any of his contemporaries when he observed that *omnis definitio perniciosa est.* In the case of John Austin this remark became painfully true: his university successors and the politicians in the field of jurisprudence simply went no further than the threshhold between the long entrance hall and the living space of his thoughts. From the perspective encountered at the corridor they announced that the positivist Austin favored absolutism and other heresies. We now intend to prove that this image of Austin has been a distortion, that instead he is a defender of a democratic parliamentary system which guarantees juridical rights and legality based on clearly defined legal norms.[16]

The most important philosophical and political question which any theory of law must answer is: can the sovereign body act unconstitutionally and/or illegally?

John Austin's answer, forgotten either by chance or design, is affirmative.

Austin distinguishes, perhaps not precisely enough for the standards of the last quarter of the 20th century, between the notions, "unconstitutional" and "illegal."

In every society (depotism is excluded from these considerations, see below) there exists a set of principles or maxims which are accepted or adopted, tacitly, or openly by the society and the sovereign. Austin writes that they are habitually observed by the sovereign. What is the source of these principles or maxims? It may be a belief in God, deference to utility, or some other source which is not even worth mentioning. When the sovereign promulgates laws which conflict with those principles or maxims, they may be called "unconstitutional, though they cannot be called illegal."[17] In the broadest sense, the expression "unconstitutional" means the following: the violated principle(s) had been usually observed by the sovereign; they had been conformable to the opinions and the sentiments of the community which was shocked by the given act of the government because they regarded the principles in question as useful and the government's decision pernicious. The notion, constitutional law, was here used by Austin in the sense of positive morality or in the sense of "the compound of positive morality and positive law."[18]

Austin uses the expression, "unconstitutional activity," not in the sense of a violation of a written constitutional act, but in a broader, rather a moral, social, political sense, but also in a quasi-legal sense: behavior of the sovereign which shockingly diverges from the legitimate expectations of the society is regarded by the people as unconstitutional and could cause political, social, and quasi-legal trouble for the sovereign.

Austin, like Jeremy Bentham, does not live by legal norms alone. He understands that law operates within a given social and political environment, it is effective in one political situation, but fails in another. (Let us note, by the way, that Bentham and Austin both are much closer to the ideas of American realists than is usually supposed).

Austin writes about the violation of constitutional

law (as a system of positive morality) by a "sovereign," be it, as he explains, a "monarch" or a "sovereign number," acting in its or their "collegiate and sovereign capacity."[19] In their character as "sovereign" (monarch, or sovereign number), they cannot be legally constrained. The situation changes dramatically, however, when the "sovereign number" is not considered "collectively," in its corporate character, but severally. It then loses its quality of being incapable of legal limitation and it is, as individuals (or a smaller aggregate that is part of the sovereign number) *subject* to the supreme body of which it is a component. These individuals, or an aggregate of individuals, let us here quote *in extenso* the forgotten or underestimated conclusion of Austin, "may be legally bound by laws of which the [sovereign] body is the author." If a law set by the body to its members "is clothed with a legal sanction, or the means of enforcing it judicially are provided by its author, it is properly a positive law."[20]

The subsequent conclusion is a logical syllogism: whoever, including of course members of the sovereign body, violates the positive law, is acting illegally. "The breach of law is unconstitutional, inasmuch as the violated law regards the consitution of the state ... The breach of law is also illegal, inasmuch as the violated law may be enforced by judicial procedure."[21]

Austin must have been aware of many practical, political, and juridical deficiencies in his theory. But do the proponents of "natural" and "inalienable" rights and justice have a stronger case when it comes to blaming the sovereign for illegal acts? Were they on stronger ground when they condemned violations which were committed by George III against his subjects in the

American colonies, than those who depend upon positive morality "compounded by positive law?" The triumph of certain ideas presented as "natural law" or "natural justice" was finally secured in France, Poland, and in America, in the 18th century, not by the inherent force of ideas called "inalienable rights" but by the physical and political power of those who claimed that they represented self-evident truths, against the rule of despots and tyrants. John Austin considered that his theory would give the victims of persecution firmer basis to resist oppression because he appealed to positive morality compounded with positive law and judicial means.

Every sovereign, Austin continues, and every member of the sovereign body (including the king-in-parliament) enjoys only a restricted freedom from legal constraints for two reasons: 1) Moral restrictions, i.e., the opinions and sentiments of the existing community. One could argue that under the guise of opinions and sentiments, Austin brings in through the back door, the concept of moral or natural law which he says he despised. That is not so. There is a substantial difference between the notion of eternal, constant, unchangeable, moral, or natural (divine) law and the notion of opinions and sentiments current in a particular community.[22] Such opinions and sentiments are not constant and are not welded on to granite; they are historically, economically, and socially determined.They are, in essence, political and as Austin understands it, they exercise a political influence which even the most powerful authorities must take into account if they do not want to put their power in jeopardy. Austin is neither a blind "positivist" nor an "absolutist" wearing blinders who reads the text of the laws only. He is a political realist who understands that power and the laws are exercised in a given society which has its prevailing opinions and sentiments; these latter may be so powerful that even a well-entrenched emperor can be hurt if he disregards them. The difference between Austin and the natural law theorists can be boiled down to this simple, but clearly elaborated concept: let us not deceive ourselves with notions of eternal justice, let us be practical; power can be lost when a ruler tries to rule for long against the sentiments and opinions current in his community; they impose limits on everyone's power. How? Austin's answer to this question is the second point in his enumeration of the restraints upon the unconstitutional exercise of statutorily unlimited power by a sovereign. 2) A command opposed to the constitution will not, Austin declares, be "legally binding."[23] Austin deliberately uses the word "command" to describe unconstitutional norms which are not "legally binding." The author of such norms usually pretends that these norms are legal rules, but his effort to make them legal according to Austin, will be vain. The consequences of making commands which are not "legally binding" are so grave and are so colorfully described by Austin, that every proponent of the natural right to resist government oppression would delight to read them.

Austin argued that first of all, those who are commissioned to execute an unconstitutional command should refuse to obey, because otherwise they "would probably be amenable to positive law if they tried to accomplish their mandate."[24]

And if they decided to follow the mandate and execute "the pretended statute" (Austin's term),[25] what would the result be? They "would be liable civilly or criminally, if they attempted to execute the order,"[26] is Austin's contention.

Austin theorizes that one should disobey illegal orders even if they are issued by the highest authorities, such as the king or the house (parliament) or both together. One should also refuse to obey illegal commands by any lower-ranking officer.

What John Austin is recommending is called "disobedience" in political language. He knows the term and uses it consciously: "If the king or either of the houses, by way of proclamation or ordinance, affected to establish a law equivalent to an act of parliament, the pretended statute would not be legally binding, and disobedience to the pretended statute would therefore not be illegal."[27]

The Prince of Juridical Positivists wrote that disobedience to an unconstitutional, illegal, "pretended statute," (notwithstanding that it has been issued by a king or parliament) would be legal. Even more: disobedience in such circumstances would be a legal duty and whoever executes the illegal order of the sovereign would be civilly and criminally liable. Here John Austin is nearly more Rousseauist than Rousseau himself and more Thomas Paine than Paine himself, with one basic difference, however. Austin avoids Rousseau's and Paine's inflamatory terminology. Their terminology may have been appropriate before and during revolutions, but Austin lived during a period about which Napoleon said these memorable words: *Le roman de la Revolution est fini!* Positivist John Austin fights for the rights of individuals against the encroachments of government during a period of bourgeois parliamentary stability. Instead of calling on his countrymen, the industrialists, merchants, shopkeepers, and bankers to *"formez vos bataillons,"* he simply advised them: do not carry out illegal orders, the sovereign will be forced to back down and eventually will have to ingratiate himself to regain lost popular confidence.

From the philosophical and sociological viewpoints, Austin's jurisprudence should be described as a theory of law which attempts to protect the rights of individuals to a maximum degree against any illegal acts committed either by fellow countrymen, or by the governmental authorities, even the highest authority, the sovereign himself, during a period of relative stability.

3. Juridical Rights

These reflections lead us to one of the principal problems of legal theory, the origins and substance of legal rights. Austin gave a classic positivistic definition: "Every legal right is the creature of a positive law; and it answers to a relative duty imposed by that positive law, and incumbent on a person or persons other than the person or persons in whom the right resides."[28]

Let us briefly observe how precise Austin was: he wrote about legal rights, but not about rights in general. He was aware that philosophers, theologians and politicians use this word in many senses; he knew that this is an expression which has been confused deliberately and therefore has been misleading.

In order to avoid any misunderstandings concerning his juridical, and broadly speaking, his philosophical views in this matter, he added an explanation which really could have been omitted because it was already contained in the definition already given: "To every legal right, there are therefore three parties: namely, a party bearing the right; a party burdened with the relative duty; and a sovereign government setting the law through which the right and the duty are respectively conferred and imposed."[29]

The perennial problem of law in the objective and subjective senses, the question which is one of the most confused in European jurisprudence, was approached by Austin in the classic positivistic way: rights (known also as subjective rights) are offspring of the laws (known also as law in the objective sense) but not vice versa, and they exist thanks to the might of the sovereign and his legislative activity. As long as the two sides, the one representing rights and the other representing duties, are peacefully cooperating, the sovereign *tacet*; he remains silent, observing vigilantly; this sovereign is not active although he is watching everything. The sovereign begins to act when "voluntary" cooperation fails. Then he reminds his subjects that he is the final author of the given rights and duties which are guaranteed by his might.

From this viewpoint, but in a limited sense only, one might say: "right is might," and vice versa.

This expression is indeed paradoxical; it is, as Austin points out, either a truism, "affectedly and darkly expressed," or even worse: it is "thoroughly false and absurd."[30]

From the juridical point of view the substance (essence, nature, fabric) of rights is a "faculty" which "resides in a determinate party or parties, by virtue of a given law ... and avails against a party ... other than the party in whom it resides."[31]

When Austin used the word "faculty" he indicated his understanding of the controversial importance of the problem which surpasses the sphere of jurisprudence, since it is rather the subject of social, political, and economic theories: if right is a faculty only, then there must be a long way from faculty to reality, and a long way for the transformation of possibility to actuality. The sovereign can be helpful chiefly, as Austin indicates, to protect against a person other than the one who is entitled to the given right. But is the notion of "right" negative only? Negativity cannot exhaust a notion which is basically positive. This problem of "reality" or "positivity" of the rights remained without deeper analysis by Austin and other positivists. This does not mean, however that they completely ignored its importance. During the nineteenth century they preferred to concentrate their efforts on the fight for rationalistic, "non-ideological" concepts of rights; they tried to explain their contents and find the simplest juridical means for their protection.

Austin, more consistently than Bentham, combined the theory of legal rights with the principle of utility. His point of departure is utilitarian: once we accept the theory that the proper end of governments should be "the greatest possible advancement of human happiness" then we should also agree that political institutions should cooperate in order to achieve these ends.[32]

Austin, at the same time, warns that this end, the advancement of human happiness, should not be identified simplistically in a one-sided manner, with the growth of national wealth and with the preservation of property.

"If that were the paramount purpose, the end might be the advancement of misery, rather than the advancement of happiness."[33] And further: "... wealth ... is not the weal of the community ... it is one of the means."[34]

In order to advance the happiness or common weal of a people, a government "must confer on its subjects beneficent legal rights, or such legal rights as general utility commends ... [it] must preserve those rights from infringement, by enforcing corresponding sanctions."[35]

The concept of rights in Austin's theory is not only juridical but also economic and political. The legal rights are instituted in order to advance the greatest possible happiness; their nature is juridical, their end is moral and political. Among existing legal rights, property rights have a special place. They should be protected, not because they are sacred, but because they are necessary to attain happiness. They are not morally absolute. They should be subordinated to the end of the common weal. But wealth, Austin argues, is not the only source of the common weal. Whoever forgets that political power may promote the weal of the community through checking the growth of its wealth, does a grave disservice to the people, Austin asserts. Although the general and particular ends rarely conflict, it can happen in the case of property laws that the political institutions may hinder the advancement of the common weal by quickening the growth of the community's wealth.[36]

These general remarks by Austin are not only deeper than the ideas of the "economists" and the unimaginative followers of Smith, but they are also prophetic: it happens more often than not in our century that the rights of property conflict with other rights and with the furthering of the greatest happiness of the greatest number. The left-wing and Catholic critics of juridical positivism charge that this philosophy defends the absolutism of property rights; yet it was John Austin who anticipated the possibility that restrictions should be put on this right for utilitarian purposes.

These remarks by Austin should also be applied to his theory of the interpretation and application of law.

4. Utilitarianism, Juridical Positivism and Resistance Against Oppression

Sovereign power cannot be limited by statute, but this does not mean—as we already pointed out in the previous chapter—that the supreme power is absolutely unlimited and that it should be regarded as irresponsible. Austin even recommended "active resistance" when the sovereign does not fulfull his duties, but acts instead, against the interests and reasonable expectations of the citizens. In order to substantiate these ideas, he connects his general theory of politics and law with the principle of utility (also known as the principle of maximum happiness). This principle is the basis of all the restrictions and duties to which, according to Austin, might is subject.

The political, and juridical conclusions which Austin drew from the principle of utility present another chapter which the critics of juridical positivism usually forget, or simply ignore.

Austin wrote that no human might or superiority is absolute. Only God's superiority is simple and absolute. But in "all or most cases"[37] of human superiority the relationship between superior and inferior is reciprocal; the superior might be viewed from another aspect as the inferior. He presented two extreme examples.

A monarch is superior to the governed; he can enforce compliance with his will. But the governed, collectively or en masse, are superior to the monarch, because they are able to "check . . . the abuse of his might by his fear of exciting their anger; and of rousing to active resistance the might which slumbers in the multitude."[38]

It is quite natural to Austin that the governed should resist and find a way to vent their anger when their monarch abuses his might. Austin did not examine all the aspects of the problem of the legality or non-legality of resistance by the governed, but he stated, as clearly as Jean Jacques Rousseau himself would have, that the governed (the people or masses—in the phraseology of the Jacobins, or Marxists), can indeed be superior because they too have might and can inflict evil or pain on the monarch-lawgiver.

Austin's second example is: a member of a sovereign assembly is superior to the judge who is bound by the law of the sovereign body. But the legislator is also a citizen or subject, and in this capacity he is inferior to the judge who has the power to enforce the law.[39]

Once more Austin expresses what is evident to any legalist and democrat, without verbosity: a judge should be independent of the legislator, but he is the underling of the latter's law nevertheless. Even the legislator, once he has promulgated his law, is himself bound by his own product. He therewith becomes inferior to the judge who enforces the norms established by his former superior, the legislator. Without issuing any political manifestos, Austin takes for granted that the law creates rights and duties for everyone. He took the division of powers for granted along with checks on the monarch and the legislators.

Austin went further: he accepted tyrannicide. The assassination of a ruler who is a tyrant, can be a mischievous act even if supported by the majority unless, Austin stressed, "guided by a perfectly sound judgment."[40]

The verdict of a sound judgment, according to Austin, is the only justification for tyrannicide. This, according to him, is a justification, but not a juridical legalization. At any rate, a "perfectly sound judgment" supersedes the official law when there is a struggle against tyranny.

Once Austin had reached this conclusion which is beyond the normally accepted interpretation of juridical positivism, he tried to solve the following problem: when can the governed become justifiably so "angry" that their "active resistance" would be justified? His general answer was: "the perfectly sound judgment" can be reached only in harmony with the principle of utility.

One should act in accordance with the principle of utility, understood as "the measure or test" but not as a "motive or inducement." This distinction determines that the Austinian principle of utility in politics and jurisprudence is very far from any moralistic approach, be it the Judeo-Christian, or the Kantian.

His considerations in this respect are so important that they must be quoted in full:

"1. General utility considered as the measure or test, differs from general utility considered as a motive or inducement.
2. Our conduct, if truly adjusted to the principle of utility, would conform to rules fashioned on the

principle of utility, or be guided by sentiments associated with such rules. But, this notwithstanding, general utility, or the general happiness or good, would not be in all, or even in most cases, our motive to action or forbearance."[41]

The sovereign's activity should accord with the principle of utility, but this does not mean, Austin wrote, that every private individual should consider the good of his neighbor or the "general good" when making decisions. Austin was a consistent individualist and today's nationalists would have many good reasons to accuse him of lack of patriotism or an "anti-state" attitude.

General utility should be considered as the measure or test of human conduct, but not as a motive or inducement.[42] The final source of the principle of utility in human creatures is God himself. One should follow His disclosed commandments; His undisclosed commands can, and should be, deduced from the principle of utility.

In order to be certain that one is acting according to this principle one should simply act, without entertaining second thoughts or reservations, according to one's own interests. One should be an enlightened, conscious egoist. In this way one will do one's best in the service of the interests of others and for the "general" "public" interest. Austin's reasoning in this respect is simple, open, and without constraint.

Every individual is the best judge of his own interests; he knows best what produces for him the greatest pleasures and pains. If he were to neglect his own interest it would mean that he is managing his interests unskillfully. Consequently, the general sum of pleasures will be diminished, the sum of pains will increase. How can a person skillfully serve the general good when he is unable to take care of his own interests?

The notion of "common," "general," or "public" interest or happiness, Austin interprets in the nominalistic spirit: it is the "aggregate enjoyments of the individuals."[43] Such words as public, family, country, mankind, are only "concise expressions for a number of individual persons considered collectively or as a whole."[44]

If one would like to use the well-known expressions of Jean Jacques Rousseau in *The Social Contract*, one could say that Austin interprets the common good simply as the sum of individual goods determined by the *volonté de tous;* the mere concept of the *volonté générale* is for him either identical with the *volonté de tous,* or it is humbug.

The idea that a person ought to sacrifice his own good for the sake of the general good is regarded by Austin as an absurdity. Every individual sacrifice partially destroys the general good: "The general good would be sacrificed to the name of the general good:—an absurdity when broadly stated . . ."[45]

If the criterion of morality were the public or general good, then "the lover should kiss his mistress with an eye to the common weal."[46]

The only restriction which Austin imposes on the free pursuit of one's own interests is the following: one should never pursue his own peculiar good "by means inconsistent with that paramount object" (that is, the common good of the greatest number).[47]

It may at times happen that we should take the common good into consideration, that benevolence should be our motive, but then our decisions should be determined by "partial" rather than "general" benevolence: ". . . by the love of family, rather than by sympathy with friends or acquaintance, rather than by patriotism; by patriotism or love of country, rather than by the larger humanity which embraces mankind."[48]

Austin's consistently individualistic approach leads to conclusions which would be condemned by every contemporary patriot or nationalist: individual interest should take precedence over the interest of one's country, not to mention the good of humanity. "An enlightened regard for the common happiness of nations, implies an enlightened patriotism; whilst the stupid and atrocious patriotism which looks exclusively to country, and would further the interests of country at the cost of all other communities, grossly misapprehends and frequently crosses the interests that are the object of its narrow concern."[49]

Austin was a consistent individualist, a consistent liberal for whom the personal happiness of the individual is the paramount objective. The mere concept of general or common good as opposed to the individual is for him so unimportant that he hardly discusses it. He does not much value such notions as the "good" of the country or nation; he is a forceful exponent of the individualistic, and cosmopolitan traditions. Virtue, the Stoics used to teach, *nuda homine contenta est*. Similarly, his kind of philosophy disregards "atrocious" patriotism, does not allow the patriots to motivate you, but insists that you think about your own interest and pleasures; when you and your neighbors are happy, the fatherland will be happy too. Any other understanding of the happiness of the country or humanity is, for Austin, a hoax.

This type of individualistic philosohy, this consistent personalism, as Austin's approach might be called in the twentieth century, hardly can be interpreted as an abandonment of human freedom, or individual rights to the caprice of the legislator. On the contrary: the legislator is restricted by the powerful, reasonable, rationalistic and, last but not least, *divine* principle of utility and individual happiness.

IV.
RUDOLF VON IHERING

1. Iherings' Dynamic Concept of Jurisprudence

Rudolf von Ihering combines in his philosophy of law the traditions of Roman law with the positivistic philosophy of August Comte, the utilitarianism of Bentham, the liberalism of John Stuart Mill, and the juridical theory of John Austin. He became one of the best known and most influential authors in the field of jurisprudence and civil law in the second half of the nineteenth century in Europe.

Like all great representatives of juridical positivism, he was not only a professional philosopher but also an eminent specialist in specific branches of law. He began as a student of civil and Roman law (*Abhandlungen aus dem Roemischen Recht*, Leipzig, 1844; *Zivilrechtsfaelle ohne Entscheidung*, Jena, 1847). During the years 1852-1865, his monumental *Der Geist des Roemischen Rechts auf den verschieden Stufen seiner Entwicklung* (4 vols.) was published. In 1852 he also became one of the cofounders and editor of the *Jahrbuecher fuer die Dogmatik*, which in a very short time became one of the leading legal periodicals in Germany, and *eo ipso*, in

Europe. The word *"Dogmatik"* became synonymous with the strict, rational, interpretation of the law. Ihering's own articles, published in this yearbook, contributed heavily to the development of this specific branch of the science of law known as the "Dogmatik." In this way Ihering perhaps more than anyone else helped to blend juridical positivism as a philosophy of law with the theory and practice of the interpretation of law. He contributed enormously to fostering the image of the German *Rechtslehre* and its practice as the world leader. His great talent of being able to combine utilitarian philosophy, economic and political liberalism, with the philosophy of law and the theory of interpretation and application of the law fully justified the American lawyers' famous opinion that Ihering was the German Bentham.[1]

Ihering's *opus magnum*, his life's work, had been completed when he reached his sixties: *Der Zweck im Recht* (vol. I, 1877; vol. II, 1883). Perhaps even more characteristic for the positivistic approach to law is his relatively small pamphlet, *"Der Kampf ums Recht"* (Regensburg, 1872). The pamphlet enjoyed the publication of seventeen editions in the German language during a thirty-year period. It was a juridical best-seller. Bentham's ideas of *"The Defense of Usury"* were combined with the American ironical challenge, "sue me." The book was written with a passion unique among German scholars and unusual even for the jurists of other nations. Because of the contents of his writings and the style of the presentation, Ihering became known all over the world as the herald of legality and of legal rights.

2. Theory of Law

According to Ihering's theory, law is a totality of norms enforced by the state to secure the interests of a society, and of every person individually. The most general purpose of law is to preserve the conditions of social life by use of the coercive power of the State.

Ihering defines the interests of law in a utilitarian spirit: everything that diminishes pain, maximizes pleasure. The *end* or purpose of law is pleasure. Pleasure, therefore, is the creator of law. Hence the motto of Ihering's treatise was: *"Der Zweck ist der Schoepfer des ganzen Rechts."*

Ihering's argument is that human beings always try to achieve pleasure. Pleasure is the end purpose, the energizer, and generator of human activity. Law results from human activity. Since every human action is purposeful, the end or purpose must inevitably be regarded as the creator of law.

Everyone wants to achieve what is pleasant; each may have his own ideas of what happiness is, and people try to achieve their own goals, very personal, often egoistic ones. If everyone looks to his or her own business, society as a whole will gain, according to Ihering. This concept of liberal political economy was one of the dogmas of Ihering's philosophy. Individual interests converge and result in a cooperative development of exchange, industry, commerce, art, and public welfare.

People are not only egoists, Ihering asserted, they also are motivated by altruism; when so motivated Ihering called the motives moral. Motives abetting egoistic performance are those of reward (profit) and coercion;

altruistic (moral) motives manifest themselves as feelings of duty and love. These four elements: profit, coercion, duty, and love, are combined in one unit, egoism and altruism. They convert efforts into socially useful activity. They form the intellectual basis of law.

According to Ihering, the end of every society should be the fulfillment of individual needs. From the juridical viewpoint these needs can be divided into three categories:

a) non-or-extrajuridical needs. These can be met without the help of social or juridical activity. Nature itself creates conditions to take care of them.

b) needs of a mixed character, juridical and extrajuridical. Their fulfillment depends on social activity such as labor, industry, and the security of life. Immediate juridical intervention (coercion) is not necessary in order to achieve these ends, but the existence of a legal order is indispensable to its proper functioning.

c) needs whose fulfillment depends directly on coercive legal norms. Not all people would voluntarily pay their debts or taxes, but no norms or coercion are necessary to require eating, drinking, and procreation.

Ihering wrote that law was a necessary means for the preservation of society and of individual human life. This does not mean, however, that the contents of law are unchangeable. Law changes intermittently,[2] but the method of securing its effectiveness is always the same: the exercise of coercion.

The ends of society change gradually. They diversify at various stages of social evolution. Legal norms therefore must be adjusted to the new ends, to the new needs, and the new levels of civilization. Hence, Ihering argues, the concept of eternal natural law is an absurdity in itself. One can compare the idea that natural law is immutable with the concept that all patients always should be treated with insulin.

The object of legal regulation is the behavior of people. It does not matter that particular legal norms pertain to private, penal, or public law. They all influence the behavior of individuals. People are always "private" individuals who simultaneously are members of society. A man is not simply an "isolated" human being, a closed "monad," separated from the environment; he is also a social being, a member of many social groups, including the state, the church, various parties, clubs, and organizations. A jurist has to take into consideration not only the individual but also the social aspects of the human being. He needs to remember that the state, although composed of individuals, is above the individuals. The individual, due to his dual character of existence and activity, when trying to satisfy his needs, has to strive to achieve not only his very personal, egoistic ends, but also his social ends.

Under the influence of Bentham, Ihering wrote that society is "nothing more than the sum of the individuals."[3]

This statement can be misleading when taken out of context.

Ihering really disagreed with the "atomistic" theory of society according to which society is only an aggregate of sovereign individuals (the philosophy ascribed to Kant among others). He argued that legal norms assure the realization of individual ends, transform them at the same time into the means necessary for the weal of the whole society. Of course, whatever the interests of society are, it is the individual in the final analysis upon whom legal limitations are placed. The real problem is whether, and to what extent, the individual is compensated for the limitations to which he is subjected and what advantages are offered to him in exchange.

Ihering's answer to this question is unequivocal: the limitations upon the individuals are necessary and it pays to be subjected to them in a state with a good legal order.

How does the miraculous transformation from private into common interests take place?

Ihering did not discuss this question nor was it answered by Bentham, or Mill.

Whatever the description of the purposes and the objectives of law may be, legal guarantees, according to this philosophy, exist not only for the sake of the individual, as for instance, property rights, but for the benefit of the whole society. Law should harmonize the individual and the general interests. It is therefore at times permitted to expropriate property from its owner, or to impose other restrictions on him for the common good. Ihering deliberately analyzed this view.

These considerations constitute the philosophical background of Ihering's definition of law in the broadest sense.

Ihering's famous positivistic definition of law is:

"... law is the sum of the *compulsory rules* in force in a State ... Only those rules laid down by society deserve the name of law, those which incorporate coercion or, since, as we have seen, the State alone possesses a monopoly of coercion, those which have political coercion behind them ... *the State is the only source of law.*"[4]

Ihering avoids ambiguities which are present in the

various schools of natural law, customary law, or such foggy philosophies as that of the Historical School. Not the Spirit or the Soul of the Nation, but the State is the only formal and real source of law, Ihering stressed. Philosophers and politicians can, of course, say whatever they wish about the variety of the sources of law, but, Ihering stressed, the jurist who does not want to lose "all firm ground under his feet," should not speak of the law in such a manner; he must stick to the positivistic notion . . . " For him there is no other criterion of law than the recognition and realization of the same by the force of the State."[5]

It happens that in society there are norms which are effectively imposed upon their members by various nongovernmental organizations. The Church, for instance, uses moral and religious persuasion to induce its members to observe the Commandments. The Church in modern times cannot use external coercion, and so long as the State does not lend its support to these norms, the Commandments are not laws. Ihering admitted, however, that practically speaking they "exercise the *function* of legal norms."[6]

But there is a distinct difference between the nature of things and their functions; the essence and the forms of existence, wrote Ihering, should not be identified. There are many organizations which effectively impose their rules on their members. In a given organization such rules function as if they were laws, but they are not. Even more, the existence of particular organizations (like a band of robbers) can be prohibited by the State and observation of their rules be punished. Therefore Ihering concluded that laws are only those rules which are backed by the State which is the sole and the only source of laws with the capacity to enforce them in various ways.

Legal norms are not merely "coercive"; they are the rules which are enforced by the State. "Coercion carried out by the State forms the absolute criterion of law; a legal rule without legal coercion is a contradiction in terms, a fire which does not burn, a light that does not shine."[7]

Immediately after that statement, Ihering attacked Puchta and the Historical School. He wrote with contempt that "one of our most famous jurists" has not yet "recoiled" from the "monstrous idea" of a legal rule without coercion. Citing Puchta's opinion expressed in *Pandekten* (para II, e) that custom rejected by the legislator as a source of law still continues to exist, although deprived of its effect upon the judge, Ihering remarks with biting irony: "You might as well say, when fire is extinguished by water, it still remains fire, only it does not burn. Burning is no more essential for fire than the judge's enforcement of its observance is for law."[8]

Ihering's main target remained the Historical School. Whereas Bentham and Austin concentrated their criticism on natural law supporters, Ihering concentrated the critical powers of his mind and wit on his German enemies, Savigny, Puchta, Hugo, and others. It was their school which in Germany was held intellectually responsible for the slow progress of legislation and for hampering the process of complete unification of law. All liberals, socialists, progressives and the enlightened elements in Germany who longed for a new progressive codification and for the final rejection of ancient barbarian customs supported Ihering's fight against the Historical School even if they were not prepared to embrace his philosophical and political credo.

Every legal norm, Ihering wrote, is a *norm,* that is, it designates a direction for another's behavior. Briefly: every legal norm expresses a *command*; it is negative when it expresses a *prohibition.*

The question which now logically arises is: to whom are the imperatives of the State addressed? Reflections on this problem open a new chapter in Ihering's juridical positivism and his philosophy in general. "The answer can only be: to the organs which are entrusted with the management of coercion...."[9] The norm is legal when the organs of government are obliged to carry them out by means of external coercion.[10]

In the bare expression that the government is obliged to enforce legal norms, the idea is implicit that the organs of state have no choice: they *must act* in the direction prescribed by the sovereign legislator.

From the viewpoint of Ihering's total philosophy, this reasoning is rigorously logical and it contains within it the nucleus of an answer to a central political question: does the State bind itself when it publishes laws and obligations for its organs to carry out by means of external coercion? The answer to this question, as we already suggested, is of paramount importance for the assessment not only of Ihering's theory, but of any modern juridical and political philosophy.

Ihering wrote that the State can, of course, issue laws which are not binding in themselves, but it can also issue a "legal norm with the object and the assurance of binding itself thereby. With this form only, if it is actually observed" Ihering stressed, "the law reaches its complete stage, *viz.*, the certainty of an unfailing realization of the norm is at once laid down."[11]

The law reaches its "complete stage"—let us note this expression—only through those legal norms which bind the State. Only then does the law become a genuine law, because only such legal norms assure the "certainty" of unfailing enforcement.

It was one of the most important political and philosophical statements which constituted an inseparable part of Ihering's positivistic juridical theory. A genuine law is not simply a norm enforced by the State's coercion, but it is a norm which binds the State itself, which coerces the sovereign to use his monopoly of coercion. To bind—from every philosophical or political viewpoint—means to restrict. Hence we reach the conclusion: a genuine law, enforced by the State, is a law which at the same time restricts the sovereign power of the State.

The sovereign (legislator) cannot be limited by any superior or external force because, as Hobbes had observed many times, that force would then be the superior which would really be the sovereign. But the sovereign can promise to restrict himself and can set into motion a self-propelling mechanism which, let us repeat this paradox, will coerce itself to act coercively and restrictively, that is, legally.

Ihering stated: the State is "the social organization of coercive force."[12] Strictly speaking, it is coercive and self-coercive—and this is the *essence of the positivist concept of law, right, state, and legality.* If one removes one brick, the whole philosophical edifice falls down.

Let us note that according to Ihering it is the nature of law that it should refrain from pushing its own power and the use of force too far. This self-restraint makes the entire difference, according to him, between the use of force in the animalistic and in the human world. In the animal world the stronger lives at the expense of the weaker and it is the former who, in the event of a conflict, annihilates his opponent. In the human world the weakest and the poorest have an "assured existence . . . by the side of the strongest . . . ."[13]

Mankind developed from the world of animals, therefore force must be important throughout history. If the world's history "were renewed a hundred and a thousand times, humanity would always come to the same point where it finds itself at present: under the law, for man cannot but establish such conditions as make community life possible."[14]

Force ultimately arrives at law. When the defeated enemy is not killed but transformed into a slave, he is already regarded a human. Later, when servant, worker, and maid come under certain protection, which can only be legal, we have entered into a period when law officially has become the successor of the blind, passionate rule of force, that law is an enlightened substitute for force, without losing its organic connection with force. Law is introduced in order "to induce force to maintain the right measure,"[15] to reduce the excess of pressure, because excess can "arouse" the "opponent" to desperate acts. The only motive and entirely sufficient reason why force "arrives at law" is the self-interest of force itself. No other factor is necessary. "Force thus sets a limit to itself, which it desires to respect; it recognizes a norm to which it intends to subordinate itself, and this norm approved by itself is *Law*."[16]

Ihering thereby substantiated the next principle which, we must repeat, usually is overlooked by all critics of juridical positivism: Law, according to Ihering, is not just an expression or product of force; it is not merely a form enabling legally unlimited use of force according to the will of the legislator and the law enforcement agencies; law is a force which "sets limits to itself." Law which sets no limits to force is not law! Such law would be another name for force which may be useful to some politicians and rulers but their "law" is not law.

This very simple theoretical point is so prominent in Ihering's books that it is difficult to believe that it has been overlooked by the adversaries of juridical positivism. Ihering does not regard as law every norm which is presented by the government as law. Is it necessary to have recourse to the law of nature in order to reject rules imposed by the legislator as legal norms? No. It is sufficient to state that the given law does not set limits to itself. It therefore defies the idea of law and legality.

The mere fact of the existence of law does not guarantee its observance. The positivists did not live in the world of illusions and they understood as well as any reasonable man today does that the authorities can trample law under their feet, but law nevertheless will remain in existence once it "has been placed in the world ... this fact can never be undone."[17]

Authorities who trample law under their feet should be regarded as primitive, prelegal, force. The mere emergence of law created a new dialectic of oppression:

"...it is no longer *force* that does this, but *despotism*—which is force qualified by opposition to law."[18]

That is the essence of Ihering's juridical positivism. Sheer force which "arrived at law" changed the situation of mankind to such a degree that the mere nature of unlimited, passionate force, had reached a fork in the road once and for all. Whoever deprives the "weakest and the poorest" of the protection of the law, is a despot. Despotism, according to legal positivism, can be defined as a political system which has such a name due to the existence of law: despotism is force opposing law. Prelegal force could not be called despotic because no point of reference yet existed. Despotism is a legal and a political phenomenon, because it implies the existence of a political process which helps to maintain the right measure of force—law. The mere concept of despotism is legalistic; it is a denial of law. Its existence is conditioned by the existence of law. Ihering here translated the Hegelian concept of the unity of contradictions into juridical language: they constitute a unity and they are in a state of permanent struggle, but their existence depends on one another.

What happens when the government, especially on the highest level, violates the law? What happens when the monarch fails to realize his duties either within a constitutional or an absolute monarchy? Ihering answered that in the event of a violation of international law or public law (i.e., constitutional), the people may harbor feelings which are tantamount to the popular reaction that their own rights were violated. What can the people do in such a case? Ihering's response was very simple: the people must take the law into their own hands. "War and uprising, which are the means used, are the forms of *self-help* in *public law* which, in default of legal protection, the people in defense of their rights take into their own hands, as the individual did for a similar reason in former times in defense of his *private rights*."[19]

Let us set aside for the time being the problem of international law and let us concentrate on the public, i.e., constitutional internal law. What Ihering wrote was a clear justification of a popular uprising or revolution against a despotic government. When we say that Ihering "justified" uprising, we do not mean a legal justification, because it could lead us eventually to the concept of natural or divine law and its defense of resistance to oppression. Ihering's "justification" is a political, practical, factual, perhaps even moral, justification. One can explain his attitude in the following way: Ihering made a statement of fact when he claimed that an uprising is a normal means of self-help or self-defense. Ihering simply stated a fact, which could almost be called non-ideological: the people use various means of self-help (including an uprising), when and where the authorities fail to carry out their duties (by commission or omission). One does not need any legal or legalistic "excuse" or "justification" for an uprising against a despotic government which represents, as already stated by Ihering, force which is in opposition to law. One can, of course, claim that an uprising against despotism (as defined by Ihering) is indeed a fight for the restoration of the rule of law. But Ihering does not seem inclined to write or justify what is obvious. The possibility of an uprising against a disregard of law by the highest authorities is an integral and, at the same time, an essential part of the positivistic concept of law (at least to the understanding of its classic representatives).

The problem is controversial from every viewpoint: philosophical, juridical, and political. Ihering was aware of this and he wanted to make it as clear as possible that his legal positivism was not *carte blanche* for despots, but he was not prepared to reintroduce any of the rejected natural law theories in order to find a juridical justification for resistance to oppression. He accepted the idea of an uprising against despotism as something natural for society, a simple matter of fact.

There are in Ihering's writings, nevertheless, elements which indicate that he was an authentic German writer, influenced by the Prussian tradition, who finally recognized that "Ordnung" is a value in itself. He compared despotism with anarchy and concluded that if one had to choose between those two evils, despotism would be preferable: "Even in a state of delirium, *despotism* still remains a political form, a mechanism of social force. But *anarchy, i.e.*, impotence of the State force is no longer a political form, it is an absolutely antisocial condition, the decomposition, the dissolution of society. Everyone who puts an end to it, in whatever way it may be ... does a service to society ... for an intolerable form of political system is nevertheless better than no system at all."[20]

Condemning anarchy unequivocally, Ihering nevertheless proved that he understood revolution to be inevitable in certain circumstances and not to be confused with anarchy. Revolution, instead, should be accepted as a reality, a political and juridical fact.

> *Revolution* bears quite a different character from anarchy. Although outwardly quite similar to it, . . . because it does not negate order *in general*, but only the *existing* order. It desires order, but a different one from the one existing hitherto. If it succeeds we call it a *revolution*; if it does not succeed, we call it a *rebellion, insurrection*. In the success of the first lies the sentence of condemnation of the political powers, in the failure of the second lies in its own doom.[21]

Ihering concisely expressed the whole attitude of the juridical positivists toward revolution in the above paragraph. The positivists are not revolutionaries, but they are prepared to accept a new political reality provided that the revolutionary government institutes (or reinstitutes) an effective *legal order*. Revolution is a successful insurrection, rebellion is a defeated revolution.

Ihering even understood that the period immediately following a revolution may be harsh, that every sudden change of government must be difficult in the life of the nation. Following the period of horror, inhumanity, and bloody orgies, "moderation makes its appearance."[22]

In Ihering's vocabulary, moderation signifies one thing above all: the rule of law. After the sentence condemning the old power, the revolutionary government institutes laws, creates rights, binds itself. And the jurists continue their work. Their expertise in legal methods is indispensable to the new regime as well, and the new post-revolutionary government sooner or later starts to perceive this fact. To be a jurist means to be a professional; this is another one of Ihering's principal theses.

3. In Praise of the Struggle for Law

In a short pamphlet, *Der Kampf ums Recht*, Ihering

tried to prove with amazing consistency and courage that although the purpose of law is peace, the means by which law operates, nevertheless, is struggle. Struggle is eternal because there must be an eternal fight by law against the encroachments of lawlessness. The life of the law within a country coincides with a struggle among individuals and social groups. The existence of international law consists in the struggle among nations and governments.

Every law and legal right, everywhere in the world, Ihering wrote, is a law and right fought for; all were created from inimical forces. There is no legal maxim or principle which has not been opposed by a contradictory maxim or principle which had to be fought against and overcome. When a law is finally promulgated and established, it does not become an inert phantom, phenomenon, or idea. It does not become separated from life or society, but it lives its own new life; it exists as a product of a continuing struggle of social forces. Law exists under the condition and to the extent that it is fought for. Law and rights are kept alive only as forces in perpetual tension. That is the reason, Ihering wrote, why the goddess of justice, Themis, is presented as a woman who holds a balance in one hand and a sword in the other: "The sword without the balance would mean brute force; the balance without the sword, impotence. One is joined to the other: the state of perfection exists only where the power of the sword justly responds to the precision of the balance."[23]

In every epoch, law emerges from the entire population of a given state and from the activity of its government. Law is the result of the endless process of tension among the changing and interchanging economic and moral interests. Every individual constantly defends his rights while taking part in the social process of labor within the nation. While fighting for his rights, every individual simultaneously contributes to the realization of the ideals of justice.

People who usually live in peace and quiet do not realize that law is not something static, given once and for all, but that it represents a process of constant struggle for its existence and realization. The people, Ihering argued, live under an illusion that they live under conditions of peace and order; their misconception is the same as that of a rich landowner who is so accustomed to profit from the fruits of the labor of others that he doubts that his wealth is the result of labor.[24]

Ihering wrote that in reality property and law consist of many elements which are socially divided so that there always will be people in the same society who enjoy peace and material wealth, while others have to fight for their peace and their rights. Law like property is compared by Ihering to Janus, the god who has two faces; one group of people sees one face, the second group, the other. There are people who have to fight, and there are people who live in relative peace; these latter live under illusions; they are deeply mistaken because they believe that the temporary peace they enjoy is a sort of paradise on earth. Peace cannot be preserved without a struggle for it. History teaches us that the mere preservation of life and peace results from the constant vigilance and uninterrupted difficult strife. The relationship which exists between struggle and life is more or less the same as the relationship that exists between work and property, Ihering concluded.

Ihering attributed two meanings to "law," objective

and subjective. Objectively, law is the totality of legal norms. They determine the existing public order and the legal state of affairs. Subjectively, right, like law, constitutes the application of general, abstract norms to the specific, singular conditions and circumstances of life of particular individuals.[25] Both forms of law have to fight against resistance in order to survive, as living rules of life must always defend themselves in order to preserve their "mastery over force."

Once we decide that the existence of law depends on victorious struggle, we can also conclude that the state must continue its struggle for legality and legal order against lawlessness and all similar forms of nihilism which tend to destroy the existing order and the existing state of affairs.

Ihering threw one of his poisoned darts in this connection against the historical school and especially against Savigny and Puchta, its leaders. Ihering found it ridiculous to assert that the law develops in a peaceful, painless, evolutionary way, as Puchta for instance claimed, comparing it to the development of language. According to the principles of the Roman law a creditor was entitled to sell his debtor as a slave, or an owner had the right to retrieve his things from an illegal possessor: it is absurd to consider that principles such as these have developed with as little turbulence as the rule that "cum" is followed by the ablative case, Ihering wrote sarcastically.

The similarity between the development of law and that of language is superficial. They both developed invisibly. Many judicial principles have been invisibly formed throughout the centuries. They developed as precedents in deciding diverse, individual cases, but ultimately they became the raw material of juridical rules. When the legislators, consciously and deliberately, transformed these rules into legal principles backed by the force of the state, these rules finally became laws, generally acknowledged by civilized nations.

Every change in the existing corpus of laws, Ihering wrote, affects various private interests, sometimes substantially, often painfully. As long as certain laws are in force, the interests of various people are connected with their existence. Sometimes the very existence of certain social, economic, and professional groups depends on these laws. Every change of law, Ihering argued, is *sui generis causa belli*. The existing interests must resist the introduction of any adverse changes; they are conservative.

The struggles between the groups supporting legislative and opposing changes are inevitable. The outcome of the struggle will not be decided by the power of persuasion but, in the final analysis, by the balance of political power of the contending parties. Ihering did not believe in the existence of the mystical power of inertia; if there are laws and institutions in a society opposed by the major portion of public opinion, that means that they are desperately supported by the social groups which have vested interests in the preservation of these laws. This conclusion, Ihering wrote, is of paramount importance for his theory and methodology: the constant rivalry and competition of interests exist in every society, including the sphere of objective and subjective law; everything lives because it is supported by certain social forces and is opposed by other social forces. Every new concept of law has to fight its way through a jungle of conservative traditions and finally just prior to the changes, when the new ideas are already on the verge of adoption, the struggle is narrowed down to two parties: one party cites sacred historical privilege and respect for tradition while the other claims that it represents creativity, undeniable rights to happiness, and a peaceful future. In this struggle of ideas and interests, Ihering stressed, the essence of law reveals itself, and who is to prevail in this controversy must be left to the decision of history.[26]

All great historical accomplishments, social, political, and juridical, are the product of struggles: the abolition of slavery and serfdom, the modern anti-feudal rights of property, freedom of conscience and speech, freedom of choice in the exercise of one's profession, all these political and juridical ideas became incorporated into constitutions and laws on the ruins of old laws. They are all tainted with blood; the law is like the god Saturn, who, acording to Roman mythology, devoured his own children. The law in the process of devouring its children (obsolete laws) is reborn; it has its future because it destroys its outworn past. Every new law claims eternal validity, but this claim is against the very nature of law and against the ground and reasons which gave birth to the new law itself. Ihering concluded, in the dialectic spirit of Heraclitus and Hegel: whatever is born is predestined to die.

The history of the evolution of law, he continued, is full of drama, conflict, fruitless effort and triumph. The people who were dissatisfied with a given legal order searched for new paths; they did not even realize what they really were looking for. But they did search for something new and better. In the spirit of the Hegelian philosophy of history, Ihering wrote that the history of law is the history of a bloodbath, of strain, effort, waste, and heroic accomplishment. Should we regret that the history of politics and justice has been so? No, Ihering continued in the Hegelian spirit; it is inevitable that the better and more reasonable should be the result of a new struggle against old, outdated forces. The fact that the birth of the new law was so strenuous and accompanied by birthpangs, creates a special affinity between the law and the society that engendered it like the bond between mother and child.

Ihering's subsequent description of the relations between law and society is less clear and contains oversimplifications. One may agree with Ihering that law is the product of struggles among various social forces and, even more, that within the groups of the sponsors every law is the result of struggle and of compromise. But why does Ihering think that once a law is accepted, enacted, promulgated, and enforced, its strict observation comes to be in the interest of all of society, or at least of the majority?

There is a deep gap between Ihering's presentation of the historical evolution of law and his presentation of its role in an existing society. One might compare this internal contradiction with one of Hegel's: everything in history is imperfect; it is only one moment in the eternal dialectical process of the struggle of contradictions; and finally the absolute idea returns to itself in the form of the Prussian monarchy and thus reaches its peak of perfection.

It could be argued that neither Hegel nor Ihering was as simplistic and naive as their adversaries would have us believe. The facts nevertheless remain: the two highest-ranking German philosophers in their respective fields were unable to cope with the existing reality anywhere nearly as critically and deeply as they dealt with the past.

Ihering needed this projection of the past for very practical and important reasons: in order to substantiate and expound his idea that it is a moral duty to struggle for one's own legal rights whenever and wherever they are being impinged upon.

The legal rights of the ordinary members of society, of the proverbial man in the street, often are considered unimportant, without genuine value, like the right of a peasant who sues his neighbor because the latter threw a few stones into his field. It may be that the conflict between the two peasants could have been resolved very simply; the offended party could have removed the stones from his field and could have continued to enjoy the use of his property. But this solution would not be right, socially or morally, Ihering argued. The wrong had to be avenged, damages awarded, justice restored, and the wound healed. One should not reason or argue under the illusion that since the material value of the damage was so low, it was insignificant. When rights are violated, material considerations should not dim our perspectives, they should not diminish our perception of the gravity of the wrong inflicted.

Ihering suggested that we draw the following comparison: Let us suppose that one nation annexed to its territory one square mile of the territory of its neighbor. This square mile is empty, dry, with poor vegetation, without practical value. The nation from whom the property was taken started a war to recover the lost territory. Who would condemn the nation that resorted to arms in order to retrieve its land? Everyone would sympathize with the nation that had to fight, because everyone understands that there are higher values here, the honor of the nation and the conviction that once you let your neighbor take an inch of your territory wrongfully, next time he will take all.

Why do people who sympathize with the nation in the second example condemn the peasant in the first example who went to court for protection and to demand restitution?

Comparatively speaking, the peasant's loss is greater than the loss sustained by the nation. Why not support the right of the peasant to sue, to fight, to get satisfaction, and compensation? Because people apply two different standards to situations, one to nations, and another to ordinary people; one to higher-ups, and another to the lower classes. Does this imply that in practice people agree with the Roman proverb: *quod licet Jovi, non licet bovi?*.

Ihering wrote that it is highly improper, immoral and unreasonable to underestimate and discourage the struggle of the simple peasant for his rights and his duty to use all legal means at his disposal. Not only are general and particular property rights at stake, but the personality of the owner, his dignity, his feelings of law and legality, and his self-esteem. Once we feel that the nation which was injured in this second example ought to start a bloody war, that it ought to sacrifice the life and property of thousands of its subjects, then one should not tell the peasant in the first example to refrain from fighting to vindicate his rights. The defense of one's rights should not be regarded as the result of a personal inclination to be quarrelsome. To fight and sue in the courts is a legal, moral, and social duty. We should praise those who turn the other cheek, the Bible tells us, and those who do not sit in judgment so as not to be judged themselves. The Holy Scripture is incorrect! The category of people who prefer peace over struggle, who are prepared to relinquish their rights rather than to fight, that category of people should be ostracized, according to Ihering!

One who gives in to others, or gives up his just struggle for his violated rights is a coward and a social misfit. Whoever flees from the battlefield against lawlessness, disorder, and anarchy is a coward. The truly virtuous will fight against the violators of laws and rights to a victorious conclusion. The duty to struggle is one of Ihering's most important contentions in *Der Kampf ums Recht*. It is a duty toward the self, and it is a duty toward the whole society because society as a whole is interested in the realization, the *actualization of law, and of each person's rights individually.*

Society's interest lies in the defense and the full realization of its law. Without that it cannot survive for any length of time. The State creates laws for practical aplication and not for study by scholars only, Ihering argued. The life of the law depends on the vitality of personal rights. Whoever stops fighting for his own rights strikes a blow at law generally. Ihering compared the relationship of law and right and reminded us that it is akin to the circulation of the blood: it starts with the heart and ends at the heart. The law, like blood, has to flow through various vessels. These vessels along the road of the law are the legal, subjective, and personal rights. These rights were created by the State in order to defend its own law, in order to let the law "flow." Everyone who is entitled to a legal right immediately becomes a defender of the whole legal order; by defending and protecting his own interest in that order, he protects the entire system of law. An individual who defends his own, personal, "egoistic" rights to the bitter end, acts like a knight defending sacred ideals; he participates in a noble and ennobling struggle.

Let us suppose, Ihering continued, that an employer ceases to demand that his employees work for their pay, that the creditor forgives his debtors, that the customer does not mind being cheated by a dishonest salesman. Who will suffer as the result of such unpunished wrongs? Not only the immediate losers, but society as a whole. Respect for the law would be undermined generally and the whole social and legal system would become the spoils of the law-violators.

The fate of the defenders of law in such a deplorable situation, the status of the private citizens and of the civil officers, would be unfortunate indeed. Those who would continue to fight for their rights and the realization of law would become martyrs; they would be cursed by those who ought to be their allies. Instead of receiving thanks and rewards, they would be sneered and laughed at. Decomposition of society and anarchy would be in progress.

4. Shylock as the Hero of our Time

Every customer, shopkeeper, artisan, employer, landlord, and tenant who fights for petty, trivial interests, receives Ihering's blessing. He is proclaimed a knight of the great legal order and of highly praised ideals. He becomes a hero.

No wonder then, in order to dramatize his point, that Ihering chose a very special person to champion: Shylock, of the *Merchant of Venice*. Why did he select a usurer as his hero and the promoter of his ideas? Shylock, after all, rightly or wrongly, enjoys the worst reputation. He is the symbol of an overriding love of money which has generally been despised and denounced.

Classic writers, and Ihering doubtlessly belongs to their number, gain their reputations because they have the courage to draw final, logical, scholarly, and moral conclusions from their own theories no matter how startling the results. All these authors who defend what appears to be their weakest point, gain respect and manage to put their real message across by surprising and then persuading. Ihering seemed to think that by rehabilitating such a controversial figure who demanded his rights even when they included a pound of flesh, he would be able finally to convince everyone that there was really something noble and even heroic about suing anyone who broke his contract.

The philosophical meaning of the apology for Shylock is far-reaching. Ihering stressed the importance of every individual in society. He maintained that every single person has "inalienable" rights which really exist and can and must be defended by each member of society. According to Ihering, even Shylock performed a socially essential role. Therefore, and this is the moral, let us not hang back, let us fight for what is due us. We, the individual human beings, are the final judges of what is good and moral. Law is an instrument in our hands, our sword and our shield.

5. Beyond Liberalism, but still Positivism

Comparing the political and social significance of the writings of Bentham, Mill, and Austin, on the one hand, and of Ihering on the other, it becomes evident that Ihering favored much more government intervention than they. He believed that law can and should impose on individuals more restrictions and more duties towards society.

Ihering's views about property laws are especially significant in this respect. "Jurists and laymen agree that the essence of property consists in unlimited control by the owner, and every restriction is essentially an encroachment upon it, which is incompatible with the idea of the institution."[27]

Ihering's comment: "My view is that this conception is fundamentally wrong."[28] Why? Because society could not tolerate some actions by a proprietor, such as abandonment of his land or buildings or withdrawing of land from cultivation and giving it over to hunting when the fruits of the land are scarce.

It is obvious that once society starts to limit private property through legal provisions, the gate to further intervention will be opened widely.

Ihering understood this fact and welcomed it; the other three condemned, and sought to avoid as much as possible more government intervention in the life of society.

The administrators of public revenue, he wrote, make all persons and things tributary "to the purposes of society."[29] One must contribute taxes as compulsorily as one must pay all the costs of production of every cup of coffee or a cigar.[30] The State compels its citizens to pay taxes; this fact can be expressed in legal terms in the following way: "The expense budget of the State or municipality resolves itself into as many *legal rules* as it has *items*. Everyone says to you, contribute to this item. It is your duty to support the army and the fleet, to build streets, to provide for schools and universities, etc. With every new purpose which arises in the system of administrative authorities you get a new obligation...."[31]

We must participate in these increasingly numerous and expensive ventures, but everything beyond these legal duties, Ihering stressed, is private, personal, and we preserve our rights which should be protected by the State. Ihering went beyond the first phase of liberalism, but remained strictly positivistic. "Society cannot interfere in the sphere of my private rights; here her empire ends and mine begins. Here is the point where I can say to her, so far and no further."[32]

Here begins the new and forgotten, or at least underestimated, function of juridical positivism. When liberalism with its concept of the State as "watchman" was slowly and inevitably pushed aside, positivism entered as the main ideological champion of private rights which "remained" after the expansion of the functions of the modern, post-liberal state.[33]

This specific work was revived—let us anticipate the ideas of the next chapters—by the new breed of legal positivists in socialist countries during the process of de-Stalinization.

V.
THE POSITIVIST THEORY OF THE INTERPRETATION OF LAW

The positivist theory of the interpretation of law is directly connected with the social and political ends of juridical positivism itself: the preservation of legality and of the legal order, the strengthening of social certainty and the predictability of the behavior of public authorities, respect for individual (subjective) rights.

Positivists would willingly subscribe to Montesquieu's idea that law should not be interpreted at all but simply applied, that a judge should be only the mouthpiece of the law. Positivists nevertheless were sufficiently experienced and professionally oriented to understand that these ideas in *The Spirit of the Laws* were only utopian dreams. Positivists at that time reasoned since once the law needed to be interpreted, such interpretation should be subject to scientifically elaborated rules. That, according to them, was the only way to secure a uniform system of interpretation and application of law; it was a basis for realizing the ideals of the rule of law and the *Rechtsstaat*.

The problems of the interpretation and application of law are important in the theoretical writings of all juridical positivists. The more advanced the theory, the more sophisticated the theories of interpretation.

The new, modern wave of criticism of juridical positivism, on the other hand, began as a criticism of the juridical dogmatism, that is, of the principles of the strict, almost mechanical interpretation and observation of the provisions of law. Critics of juridical positivism, who had already appeared at the end of the nineteenth century, still adhered to the basic tenets of juridical positivism. They only wanted to relax its rules, to make law more responsive to the new requirements of life. Under Francois Geny, the "young French school" initiated the attack. They were later joined and superseded by adherents of various new concepts of interpretation which stressed anti-dogmatism. The new theories represented the viewpoints of teleology (Kohler), of sociology (Eugen Ehrlich), of the *Interessenjurisprudenz* (Heck), and of the *Freie Rechtslehre*[1] (Kantorowicz).

It is one of the ironies of history that when Western European authors sought a way to retreat from the strict understanding and application of juridical positivism and its philosophy of interpretation, new, gifted, and important representatives of the traditional positivistic theory of interpretation emerged in Central and Eastern Europe, and in Russia and Poland in particular.

The Russians and the Poles, who took over the best and most creative elements of positivist theory of interpretation, announced that the traditional theory was a common heritage of mankind. They consequently began to develop, systematize, and formulate it into a system which they claimed with typical zeal was the only true and correct method of interpretation. They defended the positivist theory of interpretation against its Western critics.

At the beginning of the twentieth century, East Europeans became the most ardent proponents of this theory which they declared to be indispensable, for both political and philosophical reasons.

In the nineteenth century, constitutionalism and legality had become a way of life in Western Europe. The division of powers, a respect for law and individual rights, had become a part of normal social and political life. The system of justice worked. The rules of interpretation inherited from the Romans, combined with the improvements introduced especially by John Stuart Mill, were sufficient to meet the basic requirements of society and of its jurists. Empirical knowledge and the maxims of interpretation largely sufficed, permitting jurists to verify their positions, conduct successful litigation, and substantiate conclusions with supportive reasoning. The law and its application was for them their daily fare. No philosophy is needed to consume one's daily bread.

For East Europeans however, including the Russians and the Poles, who had to live under the semi-barbarian czarist regime, a struggle for decent laws and their honest application was a necessity. The czarist government was, after all, willing to observe the legal rights and liberties of individuals only when it was politically expedient to do so.

For the Russian, Polish and other jurists in Eastern Europe the development of prinicples of interpretation founded on sound theory became a part of a practical program tending to "civilize" the Russian empire, helping it to catch up with the West.[2] Although their endeavors were interrupted by the October revolution and their great theoretical contribution practically forgotten, their efforts had not been in vain.

There were also philosophical motives which contributed to the East European's desire to embrace a Western theory of interpretation. Every Russian, Pole, and Czech who aspired to prominence in the legal profession had to study law in the West, especially in Germany. They were all under the influence of the German theoretical schools and the German tendency to combine practice with fundamental philosophical considerations. The craving for philosophy, so far removed from Anglo-Saxon empiricism and pragmatism, was a feature of the Slavic mentality.

The tendency to "philosophize" combined with German studies and the aspiration to secure the rule of law in the vast territories subjected to the lawlessness of the Romanovs and the Hapsburgs, all fostered the evolution of a theory of interpretation.

Nevertheless, the East European jurists did not want to limit their work merely to absorbing scientific ideas from the West. They wanted to know what the West was doing; they wanted to learn and keep abreast of the Western *"Kulturtraeger,"* surely; but they also wanted to go beyond their masters. No Polish or Czech jurist could have been regared as a true scholar unless he demonstrated a full command of the latest Western theoretical literature. An ability to discriminate between the various trends and theories was also *de rigueur*.

These remarks have been made to introduce our analysis of an unusual treatise in the world of juridical literature, *Theory of the Interpretation of Civil Law* by Professor Eugene Waskowski. The author was a Pole, but he started his scholarly career as a professor of law at a Russian university. After WW I and the October Revolution, when the free Polish state re-emerged, Waskowski returned to Poland and continued his scholarly activity there.

The first edition of Waskowski's monograph was published in Russian under the title: *Utchenje o tolkvanii i primienienii grazhdanskich zakonov* (The Science of Interpretation and Application of Civil Laws, in *Utchonyje Zapiski Novorossijskavo Universitieta*, 1901, as vol. 8, and then separately). Twelve years later he published a handbook especially for students, the *Rukowodstwo k tolkovaniju i primientieniju zakonov* (1913) (A Guide to the Interpretation and Application of Laws).

Between 1933 and 1936, a Polish version of the book was published (in *Palestra*, then separately). The monograph was revised, expanded, and an analysis of new legal material was added, but primarily the book contained an updated critical survey of the latest trends in the jurisprudence of Western Europe.

Waskowski was a consistent juridical positivist and a strict observer of the principles of legality from the beginning of his career. Although, to the best of my knowledge, he never wrote about political affairs directly, his theory of interpretation always contained a political meaning; he wrote in favor of legality at a time when the czarist bureaucracy was attempting to eliminate laws which might have tied their hands. Later he stuck by his scholarly and moral principles during the rising wave of fascist terror and lawlessness which had begun to inundate his second fatherland, Poland. The last edition of his *Theory of Interpretation* appeared in 1936, a year after the semi-fascist April Constitution (1935) was promulgated.

Generations of Russian and Polish jurists were educated with the help of Waskowski's writings. His monograph is a compendium of conclusions derived from West and East European juridical experience and the latest achievements of European theory. Juridical positivism, which had begun as a West European philosphy, was elevated to a higher stage by Eastern scholars, a stage in which a consistent, well-elaborated theory of the interpretation of legal norms was added to the existing philosophical foundation.

Waskowski did not claim originality. On the contrary, he stressed that he was presenting the traditional Western therory modified according to the demands of modern life. Such modesty on the part of the Russian-Polish scholar was typical and had its political motive.

Waskowski knew that a theory presented as Western would have greater weight with his Eastern countrymen than a theory presented as his own. He also knew that it would be more difficult for the government to ban "imported" ideas than domestic coinage.

Waskowski's monograph really is original compared not only with Eastern but also Western judicial literature. He presented, elaborated, and developed Western theories, and applied them to the new Non-western social, cultural and political situations. The Eastern adherents of juridical positivism and of the traditional method method of interpretation could have quoted Pushkin when he was accused of following in the footsteps of Byron and imitating him: "I am not a

Byron," Pushkin wrote," although I wander with my songs all over the world, as Byron used to do; I am a different poet."

The Russian-Polish positivists were like their Western predecessors, but they differed from them, too. Pushkin added that he was a Byron with a "Russian soul." A Russian scholar and jurist of Polish origin was still another thing—a West-European thinker who was able to adjust to the Eastern soil and soul.

We mentioned earlier that the criticism of juridical positivism began with an attack on its theory of interpretation. Clearly, there were many elements either obsolete or not fully elaborated in the positivist theory of interpretation. The positivists preferred to use a legal fiction rather than open the door to unscrupulous distortion of law. It may be that if judged in terms of their political intentions it would be improper to blame them; but from the scholarly viewpoint they were at fault because they inadvertly opened other avenues for a successful attack against them. Whatever the shortcomings of the positivists may have been, one thing seems to be undeniable: hostility toward the theory of interpretation has many European antecedents. We do not intend to go too far into the past. Let us only remember that two most influential schools of law developed an almost nihilistic attitude toward the theory of interpretation—the natural law doctrines, and the historical school.

The hostility of natural law theorists was of course politically motivated. With their rejection of the former autocratic legal systems, opposed to the people, they also rejected the existing precepts for interpreting the law. They all wanted to replace the complicated feudal system of privileges based on birth by a system of law which would be clear and simple enough so that decent, reasonable people would be able to understand it, observe it, and apply it. The most radical of all (Winstanley, Mably) looked upon the juridical profession itself as a gang of professional deceivers. Beaumarchais expressed the same sentiment in *The Marriage of Figaro*.

The nihilist's attitude toward the existing legal systems and the juridical profession showed that the natural law theorists had not even bothered to develop any serious arguments against the theory of interpretation. To them it was obvious that such a theory was unnecessary. The obvious does not require demonstration.

The historical school, on the other hand, opposed the elaboration of the theory of interpretation for philosophical and ideological reasons. They tried to justify their convictions.

Let us remember that the historical school included eminent jurists, scholars, and historians who enjoyed great prestige even among those who disagreed with them about basic political and philosophical issues. People listened when they spoke. This is at least a partial explanation why the opposition of the historical school, particularly that of Savigny and Puchta, toward the positivst theory of interpretation and application of law impeded the development of that branch of jurisprudence. According to Savigny, interpretation is an art, beautiful examples of which were created in ancient times and can still be helpful. However, according to him no theory exists. Even if one were to be developed, it would still be doubtful that it would be of any use. The charming, classic examples, Savigny wrote, of the art of interpretation can develop our taste, our "feeling": *(Rechtsgefuehl)* for law, but art, as usual, can give us no recipe for avoiding errors.³

Puchta was even more categorical: the science of "juridical hermeneutics," or the science of critical evaluation and interpretation of law, does not exist at all. And Puchta added, this superficiality that is presented as something, is in reality nothing; it should not even be taken into consideration. What a jurist needs is common sense; the rules of interpretation are needed for feeble heads only; but a person whose mind is weak should not seek to be a member of the judicial profession.⁴

Even at the end of the nineteenth century there were philosophers of law who doubted that a theory or science of interpretation was necessary. They wondered if it existed at all. Belime wrote that *"les lois s'interprètent par le bon sens, faculté native, incommunicable, rebelle à l'analyse, indocile à tous les préceptes."*⁵

Belime was echoed in Germany by Wurzel who claimed: *"Keiner juristischen Wissenschafts Name ist so verschollen wie der juristichen Hermeneutik. Keine Regel begegnet man mit solchem Misstrauen als einer Auslegungsregel."*⁶

The great Russian and Polish scholars did not doubt that the *"bon sens"* and *"faculté native, incommunicable"* were too obscure and uncertain advisors and that jurists needed a more reliable guide.

One of the pillars of pre-revolutionary Russian jurisprudence, Shershenevitch, in his *Course of Civil Law,* ridiculed this irrational approach; he favored a conscious effort to elaborate general rules of interpretation.

After a series of experiments, Shershenevitch wrote,

"a painter finds out a paint of a special color and sufficient durability. A physician, observing the effects of medication in many cases slowly finds, step by step, the most effective dosage. The evolution of the sciences, better knowledge of nature, comparisons and systematization of the rules already discovered are putting aside this slow process of finding norms, rules which were theoretically deduced from empirically confirmed scientific data are becoming more and more important."[7]

Waskowski wrote that interpretation is an art and a science. He used the word, "art," in the same sense as Savigny (and sometimes John Stuart Mill) that is, a practical ability to achieve a certain end. He admitted that the art of interpretation in its first stages was empirical. From practical experience one can deduce empirical rules which are not universally valid. They are useful, nevertheless. Later on, juridical interpretation entered its second stage of development; rationalistic or truly scientific generalizations were made upon which jurists started to build a scientific theory of interpretation. In this phase, mankind was able to develop (here Waskowski used John Stuart Mill's English term in his Polish text) "approximate generalizations."[8]

Waskowski tried to present the most complete list possible of the "approximate generalizations," in this way presenting a fully developed art and science of interpretation.[9]

According to the authors of Russian and Polish origin, interpretation of law is a science which can be compared with the rules of grammar and logic. One can of course speak correctly without a knowledge of grammar and one can think correctly without having studied logic, but as was argued by John Stuart Mill, those who consciously use the rules of grammar and consciously apply the rules of logic do have the ability to be more precise and clear than those who lack that knowledge. One can build a house without a knowledge of mechanics, Mill wrote, but there are limits to activities carried on without a theoretical background.

A person may stumble upon a correct interpretation and application of a given law without having made any specific studies in jurisprudence or interpretation. Such fortunate accidents are no argument against the study of the principles of juridical interpretation.

A science of interpretation is necessary, Waskowski wrote, because ignorance is harmful, *ignorantia legis nocet.* In order to know the laws it is not sufficient to learn the legal text by heart. Celsus already remarked that *"scire leges non hoc est verba earum tenere, sed vim ac potestatem."* One should never forget that not only ignorance of the law is inexcusable, but also that a *wrong interpretation is inexcusable as well.*

*

The classic or "traditional" interpretation of law distinguishes three basic phases: a literal and a real interpretation, and a logical exposition.

The literal interpretation tends to explain the law according to the actual meaning of the words.

The real interpretation compares the literal interpretation with the results of all other methods in order to ascertain the real, true, sense of the law.

The logical exposition of the law tends to extract what is there by implication, rather than explicitly.

These three operations are accompanied by what is

called a dogmatic exposition of the legislative material. The dogmatic exposition as Professor Somlo stated, is an indispensible ingredient of the science of law because this science, according to him, is and will forever remain constructive and dogmatic.

In the first or literal phase of interpretation the following rules apply: words should be interpreted as the legislator himself clearly intended them. If such an indication is lacking, then the word in this law should be compared with the text of other laws in which the same word was used. And lastly, when no specific determination of the meaning can be gained from the language of the law, then an etymological study should be conducted. In such a case the legislative history of the given law should be taken into account.

The pertinent elements would be the time and place of the initiation and promulgation of the law, the social group which was to be affected, the syntax of the norm, the logical connection of a given word with other words in the law and norm, and the style of the law including its eloquence, verbosity, or simplicity.

For the second or real phase of interpretation, the following rules apply: the logical connection between a word and the norm must be established, the position of the legal norm within the act should be taken into account, and the *ratio legis* should be ascertained through use of reasoning in a teleological, psychological, and historical vein, and by taking into account relevant external elements not contained in the legal act. Two pre-conditions necessitate and justify employment of external materials in the interpretation of laws. a) The sense of the text remains unclear after all other means of interpretation have been applied and b) the external material is publicly available and trustworthy. The process of real interpretation may show that two norms are found to be contradictory. If this happens, the conclusion of the interpreter should be that there is a *lacuna* or gap in the law and he should proceed according to the rules described below in phase three.

If the means applied through literal and real interpretations do not suffice to remove an ambiguity in a law, then the following rules should be applied: the most just sense should be selected from all possible senses; if they are equally just, the most purposeful one should be chosen; if the most just and purposeful cannot be established, the most probable sense should be chosen. At any rate, the following rules and principles should always be in the mind of the interpreter: When a word has many meanings, the most natural and usual one should be used; no distinction should be made where the legislator fails to make one; that meaning should be chosen which precludes a superfluity of words supplied by the legislator.

The third, and last phase of interpretation, the logical exposition of the norms is necessary only where there is a partial or complete *lacuna* or gap in an existing statute. Most important of course is a definition of what a *lacuna* is. Juridical positivists and representatives of the classical theory of interpretation try to define a gap in the most restrictive way. According to them, a gap can exist only when no norms are contained in the given legislative material and no possibility exists for a logical and legalistic resolution of a given case through the use of the literal and real interpretive methods. A total or partial gap can exist when two norms conflict. Lastly, a gap can exist when a given norm is totally unclear and no possibility for its clarification is found. Where a gap is found, interpretation by analogy, or by contraries should be applied. It is further advisable to employ the following methods of reasoning: the particular should be established through deduction from the general. Furthermore, the existence of the general should be assumed from the existence of the particular.

The following, traditional ways of reasoning which have frequently been used by jurists should be borne in mind: whoever is authorized to act is presumed to be authorized to achieve the end toward which the act points; if a given end is prohibited, it must be assumed that acts tending to achieve it are also prohibited; if the act is prohibited, then the end towards which the act leads is also prohibited unless it can be achieved through alternative means; whoever is authorized to have an end or purpose is equally authorized to employ the means necessary to achieve that end. In the event of a conflict between a probable and a trustworthy conclusion reached in expounding a norm, the trustworthy conclusions should be favored.

In the event of a conflict between two trustworthy or two probable conclusions, the same reasoning as described in the second or real phase of interpretation should be applied. The more just, the more purposeful, etc., should be used in that order.

Waskowski defines the social ends of juridical interpretation in the classic positivistic way.

"In order to strengthen legality and secure equality of the citizens before the law, it is indispensable that all the courts and administrative organs correctly understand and uniformly apply the laws."[10]

Formally, the purpose of interpretation was described by the Eastern scholars as: "discovery of the true sense of the legal norms."[11]

Technically, interpretation can be described as a "system of methods which are used in order to understand the products of the human mind."[12]

The two valuable ends of the law stressed by Waskowski (strengthening legality and equality) can be achieved only by observing the rules established in the theory of juridical interpretation. This is the way to avoid errors arising from accidents or subjectivity. The theory of interpretation is nothing but a "system of various rules, principles, maxims, and provisions which tend to realize the principles of legality in the state."[13]

In the same way, one of the greatest philosophers of law in our century, Leon Petrazhytsky, described the role of interpretation in an editorial in *Vestnik Prava* (1899, No. 1, xxv) The fact that Petrazhytsky, founder of the psychological school in jurisprudence, expressed this positivistic approach in a philosophical editorial in one of the most prestigious juridical journals of the Russian Empire is especially noteworthy.

Petrazhytsky, usually described as a "Russian thinker," was of Polish origin; after the October Revolution he returned to Poland. He was an economic and political liberal, became an active member of the Constitutional Democratic Party (the so-called "Kadets"). Petrazhysky consciously defended the positive concept of legality and the interpretation of law. As a traditional legalist he condemned the pogroms, he wrote articles in defense of Beylis, and he continued to develop and proclaim his western humanistic ideals despite persecution and a short term of imprisonment. He continued to write and lecture in the same spirit in pre-World War II Poland. The Polish rulers did not like either his liberalism or his agnosticism. He was denied the chair of jurisprudence at Warsaw University, and finally he committed suicide in despair.

Perhaps it was only a historical chance that two Polish scholars simultaneously became such influential exponents of the positivist theory of interpretation in Eastern Europe and especially in Russia. But this historical event is a noteworthy example of an accident in which, as Hegel used to write, the spirit of the times is reflected. A genuine Russian could have accomplished the same historical task *tant bien que mal*. But the Poles, who suffered double oppression under the Czarist regime, as citizens and as Poles, were especially predisposed to perform this historical task at a time when Russia, with its gradual assimilation of Western culture, was becoming more "civilized," more "legalistic," more "enlightened," and industrialized.

All methods elaborated by juridical positivists tend to secure certainty, legality, and due process of law, with an almost mathematical precision. There is no doubt that this classic method of interpretation represents a historical achievement in the evolution of jurisprudence and the systems of justice. Objectivity and impartiality are the strongest features of the traditional method of interpretation. At the same time, however, the juridical positivists neglect to take into consideration the social environment and the subjectivity of those who apply the law. These deficiencies have been exploited in the twentieth century by the anti-democratic and totalitarian ideologues.

The achievements and deficiencies of juridical positivism as well as of the traditional theory of interpretation demanded an improvement in jurisprudence: a legal philosophy based on the new theory of argumentation.

VI.
COMMUNIST JURIDICAL POSITIVISM AND POLISH NEO-POSITIVISM

1. The Evolution of Communist Jurisprudence

We can distinguish several phases in the evolution of the theory and practice of communist jurisprudence.

The first period began immediately after the Soviet revolution of October 1917. The new revolutionary government announced that the entire legal system and all laws promulgated by former governments had become null and void. The revolutionary authorities and the citizens of the new state were to act according to new legal norms, as they were enacted and their consciousness of revolutionary legality. This period was relatively short and by the 1920s new legal codes had been issued and the importance of the revolutionary consciousness began to wane as a criterion of what was legal and just.

The security organs, of course, had unlimited powers and suffered no restraint in their fight against everything they considered to be counterrevolutionary. In addition to fighting enemies, as they defined them, the security forces launched a campaign of "red terror" to counter the "white terror." Many laws were published during this time that were so general that they could mean almost anything. For instance, laws were passed establishing special inspectors during the famine to inspect private homes and apartments; and those who were accused of hoarding or speculating with food were "tried" and shot on the spot. Such "laws" should be regarded as examples of "legalized lawlessness."

The second period began during the second half of the 1920s and ended in 1953 with Stalin's death. This was the period during which codes and laws of the new state became entrenched and revolutionary consciousness was offically suppressed. But it was also the period of Stalinization and the growth of bureaucracy and the terroristic police force. During this period the basic outlines of the theory of socialist legality were elaborated by Vyshinsky, the leader of the Soviet "juridical front."

In 1944 and 1945 new socialist states were created in Eastern Europe. During their first four to five years their governments were allowed to preserve selected elements of their pre-war laws. The new regimes added new laws to the old ones and pretended that these additions made coherent systems. In 1949 and 1950 the situation changed dramatically and the process of Stalinization imposed by the Soviet government was extended to these countries. Soviet jurisprudence, the concept of law, and its legal system were adopted unaltered. Any residual differences were unimportant. After 1950, the legal order in these countries became similar to the Soviet model.

After Stalin's death (1953), the long and slow process of destalinization began. It had its reflection in the field of socialist law. New elements emerged in jurisprudence and judicial administration in the Soviet Union and in other socialist countries. The most important elements in the theory of law will be analyzed in this chapter.

The theory of law finally elaborated during the Stalinist period was based on one sentence from the Communist Manifesto: "Law is the will of the ruling class." This short sentence was extolled by Vyshinsky as the wellspring of his "scientific" theory of law.

At the same time, Vyshinsky excluded many other ideas of Marx which had been even more important to legal philosophy. From the beginning, official Soviet legal theory was one-sided; it is oversimplified from every point of view: the traditional western outlook and Marx's viewpoint as well.

Vyshinsky's personal career to a great extent illustrates the most vicious elements of the theory which he advocated. He became famous as Chief Prosecutor in the show trials of the "opposition" during the late thirties. He was the chief accuser of the most eminent Soviet jurists and authors whom he charged with distorting "Marxist-Leninist theory." The victims of his rhetoric were at first dismissed from their posts (Pashukanis, Stuchka, Rejsner), and after their civil death, most of them were killed. After 1956 they were rehabilitated posthumously.

Vyshinsky's theory of law can be described in two sentences: Since every system of law is the expression of the will of the ruling class, it serves the interests and purposes of this class; it is an instrument of the class struggle and there can be no provisions of law which serve all the people or all of mankind. To Vyshinsky, what is legal is determined by the class struggle; law serves the purposes of the ruling classes and was created for the sake of the ruling class.

In the light of Vyshinsky's theory, even the notion of

bourgeois legality, to which Marx-Engels and Lenin had attached so much importance, no longer made sense. The Hegelian-Marxian dialectic disappeared as well. Their dialectic indicates that social and political institutions and the respective legal norms can simultaneously be useful and harmful to the antagonistic social forces and classes. In the systems of law of every social formation, there must be norms which are both progressive and regressive, and the true scholar should analyze them from the viewpoints of motion, evolution, and negation (in short: *Aufhebung*). These subtle distinctions were deliberately excluded from the official Soviet theory of law because they would have thrown a "dialectically critical" light on the western legal systems and the Soviet legal system as well.

This Hegelian-Marxian dialectical approach was understood by Lenin; therefore Stalin-Vyshinsky had to censor him as well. In a memorandum to Soviet legislators Lenin recommended that all western laws be scrutinized to find out which of them might be favorable for the people and those elements for the benefit of the workers should be incorporated into the new Soviet laws. These recommendations were never quoted during Stalin's time nor were they resurrected during the post-Stalin era which was officially termed the "return to Leninism." No Communist jurist ever said any western laws were favorable to the people and therefore worthy of adoption by Communist powers.

In Vyshinsky's definition of socialist legality (the "strict," "undeviating" observance of the provisions of socialist law) what is omitted is more important than what is expressed. The following basic points were omitted:

In all Communist countries, the official theory of law identifies the will of the ruling ("working") class with its interests (whatever those "interests" may be). This childish theory has not yet been abandoned by official Soviet jurisprudence even after destalinization. A ruling group may misunderstand its own interests and, therefore, as thousands of historical examples prove, may pass laws harmful to itself. Such mistakes occur in any social system from ancient slavery to modern western and eastern societies. Neither Stalin nor Vyshinsky wanted to admit that a "ruling group" or "class" could misunderstand its own interests because they wanted to avoid coming to grips with the two problems, can a socialist government make laws harmful to the people and can a bourgeois state make laws favorable to the people?

In order to avoid all these philosophical, ideological, and political complications they preferred to rest upon simplistic, "self-evident" truths: bourgeois law only serves the interests of the bourgeoisie; proletarian law only and always serves the interests of the people.

Another reason for their stand was that Stalin and Vyshinsky wanted to avoid any discussion of "illegal" laws and the relationship between law and the requirements of justice. The problem of legalized lawlessness had even been analyzed by Marx in his famous early essays about Prussian censorship, Louis Bonaparte, and in all three volumes of *Capital*, to name only the most important. It was Marx who observed, for instance, that censorship, like slavery, cannot become lawful even if it were to be promulgated as a law a thousand times. One of Marx's elementary philosophical observations was that there were always objective and subjective contradictions between means and purposes, reality and possibility, interests and will, actuality and perception, the objective trend and subjective intention. All these complicated problems were deliberately eliminated from the Stalinist theory of law and in this way the official communist theory of law becomes very simple, and mystifying. Engels very often used to criticize such intellectual primitivism and in this connection Marx made his famous remark that if historical materialism were reduced to such platitudes, he would prefer not to call himself a "Marxist." The Stalin-Vyshinsky theory of law and legality was rather a "Marxist" than a "Marxian" theory. It was ideological, but in the worst Marxian sense, an inverted, distorted presentation of reality.

The Stalinist theory of law, as presented for instance in Soviet university textbooks, did not even mention such a basic political and philosophical problem which must be analyzed by any serious philosophy of the state and law as the relationship between the common and individual goods. To what extent should the one be sacrificed for the other?

At the beginning of his career Stalin wrote a polemic against anarchism. He wrote that socialism thinks about the masses and not about individuals. This is not the traditional western, or even the Marxian approach, but a typically totalitarian view. This interpretation of socialism, as expressed by the young Stalin, took its toll in later years.

Stalin-Vyshinsky and their successors have ignored the dilemma posed by Jean-Jacques Rousseau in his *Social Contract* about the relationship between the individual will, the will of all, and the general will; about the common good and the individual good. To Stalinists, in the context of the socialist state, to bother with this problem would be an exercise of effete intellectuals. Instead of analyzing this problem, they argued that the unity between the individual and the general interests, between the personal and public purposes amounts to an identity. Whoever does not understand this unity, they insisted, does not understand historical necessity, while the understanding of historical necessity is, as Hegel and Marx wrote, the essence of freedom.

The discussion of legality as proposed by Vyshinsky was indeed a simplistic repetition of the old positive "bourgeois" concept. One of the differences between Vyshinsky and Bergbohm or Ihering is that Vyshinsky added to that definition such words as "strict," and "undeviating," but adjectives do not change anything in the substance of the definition. The warning of Ernest Hemingway against the use of adjectives, even if it were known to the Stalinists, would not have been heeded.

At any rate, the "communist" definition of legality left open such basic philosophical problems as: did feudal legality exist? Does fascist legality exist? Can there be a contradiction, between *volonté generale* and *volonté de tous*? Or any contradiction between the theory of socialist legality and the actual observance of the provisions of law in a socialist country? Some Soviet theorists used to answer that fascist legality could not exist because, according to the official Soviet definition, fascism is based on illegality and does not respect the basic rights of the individuals.

The same could be said about the Soviet law under which Soviet citizens could be arrested, jailed, and sentenced to death by a "troika" (consisting of three high-ranking officers of the NKVD-security police), who passed their sentences on the basis of reports by lower-ranking security officers and confessions signed by defendants. The victims could not present their own case and did not even have the right to address the "troika" court. The sentences of the "troika" were in accordance with the terroristic Soviet law; but who would regard such law as legitimate, to say nothing of just or humane?

The official Stalinist definition of legality never came to grips with "legalized lawlessness," or "partisan law" which is, as Marx once described it, against both justice and decency.

Another important change that Stalin made in the Marxian theory of state and law was in the concept of withering away. This theory had never been elaborated by Marx and Engels; theirs was only a general prediction. In Lenin's pamphlet, *"The State and Revolution,"* all the unclear general predictions became even more unclear. Lenin never came to grips with the question, so timely in November 1917, of when the process of withering away should start, immediately after the seizure of power or after a certain period of transformation of the socialist society into the communist? Should the process of withering away start during the dictatorship of the proletariat? If not, how would the dictatorship of the proletariat end? What would occasion its transformation and into what? And what will happen to laws and the judicial system? All these important theoretical questions remained unanswered by the new communist government instituted in Soviet Russia and its spokesmen.

After the October Revolution the process of expanding the governmental machinery began. There certainly were no immediate signs of withering away; on the contrary, the areas into which the state began to intervene multiplied; the bureaucratic apparatus grew incessantly. When Stalin finally rose to supreme power as the Party's leader he tried to explain this growth in a speech to the eighteenth Party Congress (1939). He argued that the Soviet state should expand incessantly, so that finally every social activity would be governmental activity. Accordingly the number and scope of the legislative prescriptions could also grow. When everything would be in the hands of the State, Stalin wrote, nothing would be governmental because all would be social; that is — according to him — the "dialectic" of the socialist state. Stalin's theory of the socialist state and socialist law was a complete reversal of the idea of the withering away of the state and law; it was an attempt to justify totalitarian administrative interference in every facet of social and individual activity.

After Stalin's death there was a very limited "thaw" soon followed by a new "freeze". Those who proposed even modest decentralization and democratization were once more branded revisionists and right-wing liberals treacherously seeking to overthrow the socialist system.

Lieberman, the Soviet economist, was one of the first to propose a very modest plan for decentralization. He was vehemently denounced by many traditional Communist bureaucrats. But some years later all Communist countries were compelled to introduce reforms, some of them even farther reaching than those proposed by Lieberman. There is a necessary link between economic and political decentralization and the role of the law.

The benefits of the half-hearted democratization

were very limited. Democracy after all is incompatible with a centralized bureaucratic political structure and with total economic centralization. New contradictions and difficulties arose and they have created the basis for two trends: retrogressive towards full re-Stalinization, and progressive towards further more consistent decentralization, political democratization and the rule of law. The revolts in Hungary, Poland, and Czechoslovakia proved that people in those countries had become impatient and politically active. In this atmosphere attempts were made to restore the importance of law and the courts which had been completely degraded in Stalin's time. The infamous special courts of the security police were abolished. Many voices were heard favoring restoration of the parity of the defense and the public prosecutions in criminal cases. It was difficult for Soviet authors to support this elementary requirement of justice because of the official doctrine prevalent at that time, that everyone had a duty to help the state to establish the "truth," and to punish any violator of the law. Anyone who refused to cooperate was regarded as a dishonorable Soviet citizen.

Andrei Vyshinsky was the target of especially sharp theoretical criticism. He was posthumously accused not only of violations of Soviet law, but of being responsible for the "anti-Soviet" statement that the guilt of a defendant need not be proved entirely. A partial proof could be sufficient. He was charged with laying a theoretical basis for convicting innocent people during the purges.

Jurists in all the European countries under Soviet domination favored more reasonable and progressive principles and even tried in various ways to reintroduce West European democratic traditions into their systems.

In some people's democracies, especially in Poland, Czechoslovakia, and Hungary, democratic jurists argued in favor of administrative courts authorized to challenge administrative decisions. Discussions are continuing on these proposals; the authorities are opposed to them, but some forward steps have been taken anyway. In Poland was created a special court: The Administrative Tribunal.

After 1953 the concept of the intensification of the class struggle was officially denounced as inconsistent with socialist theory and humanism. Khrushchev and other Communist leaders denounced the idea as an instrument used by Stalin and his henchmen to arrest and exterminate good citizens.

Janos Kadar in Hungary was the first openly to denounce another Stalinist concept: He who is not for us, is against us. Kadar stated that in socialist countries this maxim should be reversed: he who is not against us, is for us, those not opposed to socialism should be regarded as its friends. This theory helped Kadar's government to transform Hungary after the years of terror into what might be the most liberal Communist regime in Europe in the 1970's.

Actually, the theory of the intensification of the class struggle was not entirely abandoned, only transformed. After almost every important international or internal setback for a Communist regime, the particular Communist party used to stress that at this "new stage of development," the class struggle had been intensified by the bourgeoisie. Since 1956, when this theory had been officially rejected, there had never been a single Communist leader to have declared that his country had entered into a period of relaxation and lessening of class contradictions. On the contrary, statements have regularly been issued warning the people and stating that the enemies of socialism were intensifying the class struggle "at this phase of evolution."

In this way, the old Stalinist theory of the continuous sharpening of the class struggle was replaced by a system of continuous warnings concerning allegedly ever-greater intensification of the class struggle "at this phase".

This policy became especially prominent during the Czechoslovak crisis, in 1968, after the two wars between Israel and the Arab countries (1967 and 1973) supported by the Soviet Union, and the uprisings in Poland in 1956, 1970 and 1980.

One aspect of the theory of intensification of the class struggle remains officially intact. According to official Communist theory during peaceful coexistence and detente, the ideological class struggle will intensify because the imperialists — states the official theory — do not give up their hopes to destroy communism but try to accomplish this end by "ideological diversion." In every Communist country, therefore, artists, scholars, journalists, and writers, are periodically accused of "political blindness," of uncritical acceptance of decadent bourgeois fads, of defaming conditions under their Communist governments. The newly reinterpreted "Socialist realism" in literature once more is used as a club to strike against any intellectual creativity. This is the ideology behind ruthless repressions against the heretics and "cosmopolitans" who are persecuted in defiance not only of justice and democracy, but even of Soviet laws. This ideology and policy is behind the "legal" formulations concerning "counter-revolutionary," "antisocialist" activity, which are terms so vague and elusive that anybody can be accused of criminal behavior.

In these complicated circumstances a new trend started in the jurisprudence of Communist countries. This trend has emerged in defiance of official views.

There are various currents in the opposition. They represent different, more or less democratic, and liberal approaches to law. The ideas of the different groups should indeed be analyzed separately. But there are, of course, common features.

The liberal Communist view* of Socialist legality stresses that there can be no justice without the existence of legal procedures to protect the individual from administrative abuses. The liberals maintain that observance of the law is not by itself sufficient proof of the legality of particular government decisions. They are approaching a rebirth of the idea of "legal law," that is, law that protects the interests, rights, and liberties of the individual, as against law that is "legal," because it has been enacted properly.

This new, or rather rejuvenated, concept of justice, serves as an ideological and political justification for de-

---

*Whenever I use the term "liberal communism," I mean the view of the Polish and Hungarian liberals, especially those from the periods of liberalization in 1955-1957 and the Czechs from the period of the Prague "spring," 1968. I include in this group (to a certain extent only) the Soviet "heretics." There is of course a philosophical link between the Soviet "underground" and the Polish or Czech "liberals," many of whom were exiled or jailed.

mands to institute an independent judiciary with power to override the administrative authorities on issues involving protection of the rights of the individual citizens. The objections to these demands, voiced by neo-Stalinists, simply repeated Stalin's claim that a Socialist state can do no wrong to its citizens. Consequently, no protection against the state's activity is necessary.

The liberals argue that the Universal Declaration of Human Rights and the subsequent covenants, and even the Helsinki Declaration, should be respected in Socialist countries; internal law should be adjusted to the requirements of the new international law.The liberals defend the idea that observance of the Declaration of Human Rights is not a limitation on the sovereignty of the state. One should therefore, re-evaluate the idea of the sovereignty and freedom of the state.*

The liberals criticize the simplistic official concept that law should be interpreted according to the "leading guidelines of the Party." They used to compare this principle with the well known Nazi idea that law should be interpreted according to the "will of the Fuehrer." This comparison was regarded as a slap at the official rule concerning the interpretation of law.

The Polish liberals now criticize the new Polish Constitution, especially the new paragraphs that were appended in February 16, 1976. According to Article 3, the United Polish Workers' Party is the "leading political force" of the nation. According to Article 6,friendship with the Soviet Union remains the basis of Polish policy. Professor Leszek Kolakowski is right in his

---

*These questions are discussed to a greater extent in the following chapters.

assessment of these two articles: they constitute pseudo-legalization of the double non-sovereignty of the nation:
— with regard to the party apparatus which is not elected or supervised by society;
— with regard to the Soviet Union with which the alliance must be perpetuated, notwithstanding any unpredictable and uncontrollable changes which could take place in the internal affairs of this country.

"Despotism and non-sovereignty cannot be legal; laws which allegedly institute them are invalid on their face and no one should feel obliged to respect them . . . Resistance against pseudo-law is a revindication of law in its proper sense."[1]

Let us remember that many of the "liberal" or "underground" critics want to improve the socialist system; they do not want to destroy it; they do not want to supplant it with a western socio-economic system based on private property and free competition. Kolakowski's is indeed a non-capitalist, but not an anti-socialist theory of law which proclaims the right to resist the Communist bureaucratic oppression and despotism in order to promote " . . . true socialism," with a "human face."

There is resemblance between these ideas and the old seventeenth and eighteenth century ideas of natural law and the right to resist oppression.

There is one important point which to my knowledge has never been analyzed in the juridical literature of the West. It is the problem of the specific contribution of Polish jurisprudence to juridical thought. I would call it a renaissance of juridical positivism in socialist Poland. The most important representatives of this trend are: Professors Kazimierz Opalek, Jerzy Wroblewski,

Stanislaw Ehrlich, Sylwester Zawadzki, Alexander Burda, Adam Lopatka, Grzegorz Seidler, Jerzy Jodlowski, and especially the eminent albeit controversial, scholar, Stefan Rozmaryn.

What features are common in the writings of these scholars, apart from the differences among them? They all believe that laws should be interpreted and applied according to genuine rules and maxims of legal interpretation. They all argue that the citizens of socialist countries, especially Poland, have certain so called subjective rights. These subjective rights must not be subject to the vagaries of the arbitrary political decisions usually made by the Party and the security bosses behind the scene, through "private channels" ("advice" transmitted by telephone).

All these writers agree that the rights proclaimed by the Constitution have the force of law. Interpretations or application of the provisions of law on various levels (here we face the "socialist" edition of the *Stufentheorie*) should not be made in defiance of the subjective rights created by higher laws.

Professor Jerzy Wroblewski wrote two unique monographs on the theory of the interpretation of law. In highly complicated terminology he tried to apply traditional juridical ideas concerning the interpretation of law under the situation prevailing in Eastern Europe.

Professors Ehrlich and Zawadzki used to defend the idea of court supervision over bureaucratic governmental machine with great skill; they want judicial supervision over the apparatus which is unable to understand or to protect the rights and privileges of individuals.

Although there were many controversies between them, the late professors Burda and Rozmaryn attempted to preserve a special place for the Constitution within the legal system in order to protect democratic values. Burda went further in this respect and his criticism of the Stalinistic past was outstanding and sharp. It cost him a great deal: he was ousted from his post as Attorney General.

The theory of subjective rights and legality, as developed by Opalek, is also an application of the best European traditions to present Polish conditions.

Polish jurists and professors of law are among the best educated and open minded in the Communist bloc. Their position in the new circumstances can be compared with that of the juridical positivists in the nineteenth century. They laid the foundations of the new positivistic and realistic jurisprudence adjusted to the needs of freedom and personal security under the present Polish social and economic order.

Polish juridical, socialist neo-positivism can have an enormous impact. Socialist jurisprudence can be converted into a useful tool of democracy, of personal security, of social and political order without painful surprises. To this day, socialist jurisprudence has been a kind of servant of an unenlightened state. Polish neo-positivism can help transform neo-Stalinist despotism into an absolutism that is at least enlightened; that would be a tremendous leap forward. Without a new concept of justice even a move into a more enlightened phase of absolutism cannot be imagined.

What can we expect after enlightened absolutism has been reached? One cannot forecast with certainty, but one thing seems clear: prospects are brighter under a more enlightened regime rather than a less enlightened one, even though it be absolutism. Absolutism with a kind of legal order and guarantees, although limited in scope, is more humane than a regime without such guarantees. As Plato observed in his *"Laws"* limited absolutism is no longer absolutism.

These are the reasons why we decided to take a closer look at the new, Polish, "socialist," juridical neo-positivism.

2. The Formation of Polish Juridical Neo-Positivism

Because of various historical circumstances, Poland has originated a new brand of juridical positivism which can be called a socialist juridical neo-positivism. This Polish juridical neo-positivism started to develop almost immediately after the communist seizure of power in 1945-46. There were many social, historical, and traditional reasons for its rise, but especially important, from the juridical viewpoint, were these:

— the new communist regime tried to present itself as a true successor of the democratic March Constitution of 1921. This constitution had been abrogated in 1935 by the prewar Polish regime in such a manner which even many non-communist and non-socialist statesmen and jurists regarded illegal and unconstitutional;

— the new communist regime announced that the pre-war legal system remained in force, that the only laws that would lose force were those formally and legally repealed or suspended;

— the new communist regime preserved important elements of the pre-war administrative and judicial apparatus and started to use the services of lawyers educated before 1939; the professors of law who survived the Nazi occupation returned to their chairs to raise up a new generation of Polish jurists in the spirit of the continental, Roman art of jurisprudence.

The period of stalinization started in Poland relatively late (1949) and the "thaw" (after Stalin's death, March 1953) in Poland immediately became more profound and further reaching than in other "people's democracies." Although the period of Stalinism was relatively short, nevertheless it badly hurt the Polish traditions of legality and due process of law.

The Stalinist anti-legal reaction was met with a proportionate counteraction. The most important demands of the anti-Stalinist movement after 1953 concerned law and the strict observance of the articles of the Constitution which guaranteed democratic liberties and civil rights. In 1955 and 1956 the Association of Polish Jurists petitioned the Party and the government publicly to carry out legal and political reforms to guarantee democratic liberties and constitutional rights. During this political upheaval the Association of Polish Jurists started to publish a periodical, *Law and Life*, which in 1956 and 1957 was, next to *Poprostu*, the most outspoken publication for "liberalization, national independence, legality," and briefly, for all those ideals which afterwards were called communism with a human face.

These years were unique ones in the post-war Polish

evolution. The badly divided rulers were unable to block the course of events; they were compelled to become more democratic and liberal. These were also the years when Poland became an arena for relatively free and universal discussion about political and juridical questions. They could have been narrowed down to the following problems: by whom, how, and why were democracy, observance of law and protection of individual rights "lost" under socialist governments and constitutions? Who was responsible for these crimes? Demoralized individuals? Incompetent leaders? Bad laws? Badly conceived and organized institutions?

Educated and critically minded Poles, even those who preserved their ideological and official affiliations with the Party (the Political Bureau and the Central Committee were divided into various factions, including radical liberals and orthodox Stalinists) were not prepared to accept the oversimplistic official Soviet explanations according to which the evil characters of Stalin-Beria and the "cult of personality" were responsible for all the violations of law, crimes, and genocide. In Polish universities these explanations were either called revived platonism or a communist version of subjective idealism combined with non-dialectic materialism and "economism." In various ways, these critical views found their way into liberal publications.[2]

The results of the general national discussion concerning the "essence" and "forms" of socialist law were brought together into a logical concise theory in the book by Kazimierz Opalek and Witold Zakrzewski, *The Problems of Socialist Legality*. Both were professors of law of Jagiellonian University, in Cracow.

The point of departure of Opalek-Zakrzewski is a critical analysis of the traditional Soviet definition of socialist law imported into Poland. The principles of the definition were laid down — as we already mentioned — by Andrei Y. Vyshinsky, then adopted officially by all communist jurists. The handbook, *The Theory of State and Law,* 1955, gives the following version:

> Socialist legality is one of the basic methods for carrying into effect the dictatorship of the proletariat, which consists of the unconditional and precise realization, by agencies of government, social organizations, governmental employees, and citizens of the juridical norms, as they are defined by the laws and by other acts issued by the socialist state in order to provide true security of the socialist state, the rights and liberties of the citizens.[3]

This definition, according to Opalek-Zakrzewski, is verbose, grandiloquent, and imprecise, it mixes theory with tactics, it is a slogan and aimed at mental laziness.[4] They asserted that one of the idealistic, platonic, elements of the period of the "cult of personality" was a belief that a correct definition of a legal norm could solve a problem. The definition of "socialist legality," even a good one, is no "magic formula" which is able by itself to induce the governments and people to realize it.[5]

The problem of observance of law is not only legal, they wrote, it also has practical moral and political aspects. In socialist countries, however, no one knows very much about the practical side of carrying out socialist legality, because sociological research has been non existent; preaching replaced empirical research.

Sociological research is indispensable to law enforcement. Such research should analyze violations of law, draw general conclusions, address them to the politicians and legislators, and influence the government. Without such information law enforcement would work in the dark.

Opalek-Zakrzewski reject the primitive Stalinist assertion that the legal order in socialist countries is wholly politically and morally good. It is impossible, they argued, to accept as moral, without reservations, the totality of any system of norms, even if we were prepared to approve the government, its constitution, its political, social and legal premises. Therefore one of the principal theses of Opalek-Zakrzewski is that the formal observance of the provisions of law is only relative.

In no country, including of course socialist countries, can the "struggle for legality" be separated from ethical values, from good and justice.

The mere existence of legal norms and their enforcement, argued Opalek-Zakrzewski, is connected with juridical formalism; this is one of the distinctive differences between legal and moral norms. Juridical formalism must therefore represent — according to them — a certain social and moral value in itself. But this value is only relative. The value of juridical formalism increases when the legal norms are connected with democracy, even imperfect, which exists in some countries; this value decreases when the legal norms are instituted for the benefit of absolutism, despotism, autocracy, fascism.[6]

There are many prerequisites for interpreting and applying law correctly. The knowledge of the "four laws of dialectics"* and "ideological skill" are obviously in-

---

*The authors are alluding to Stalin's essay on "Dialectical and historical materialism" proclaimed the theoretical bible of modern communism.

sufficient by themselves. What is necessary is the elaboration of a truly scientific legislative political methodology, as was proposed by Leon Petrazhytsky in his *Die Lehre von Einkommen* (Berlin, 1893-5).[7]

It can happen that even a socialist legislator may violate the principles of law, when he promulgates laws violating Article 8 Part 1 of The Polish Constitution: "Laws of the Polish People's Republic express the interests and the will of the working people."[8]

The authors argued that a strict observance of wrong, harmful, or outright "illegal laws" promulgated by socialist legislators, would be illegal by itself. It was a violation of legality when the Polish Supreme Court issued its directives which instead of clarifying the provisions of law, actually changed them;[9] the word "interpretation" was a pretext, the cover up was a deceitful change in the law.

The theoretical and political concept which Opalek-Zakrzewski were promoting could briefly be described as a "Socialist Rechtsstaat." They argued that this idea in the bourgeois state is utopian, and the analysis of bourgeois jurisprudence shows that the idea that the state could limit itself could be only compared to the "squaring the circle."[10] But in the socialist state the situation is different; this is the first type of state in history where government agencies can really act according to the spirit and letter of the laws.[11] It is in the social and political interest of the people and their true, non-demoralized representatives to observe the principles of legality.[12]

In order to transform the existing socialist state into a truly "Socialist Rechstaat" now — they wrote — additional legal norms should be issued. Special institutions and organs should be created which might effectively oppose any norms, decisions, or activities violating the law and especially, the constitutional rights of citizens.[13] The legal norms issued by the socialist legislator should limit the possibilities for arbitrary acts by the administration, they should limit the subjective authority of any organ or employee.[14]

On the other hand, the legislator should avoid too many and too detailed instructions, which in effect kill initiative.[15]

The Sejm, according to the authors, is also responsible for violations of law, because it failed to pass laws necessary to promote and realize the constitutional requirements. As a drastic example of such ommission they mention the fact that the Sejm did not pass a law to realize the right to recall the members of the Parliament and territorial councils, which had been foreseen by Arts 2 and 86 of the Constitution.[16]

Opalek-Zakrzewski presented their "ideal" socialist state as an antithesis of the Soviet state. They indicated that in the U.S.S.R. the state of emergency became permanent. In order to add weight to their statement, they quote one of the deliberately forgotten thoughts of Lenin:

"Any fool is able to rule with the help of emergency laws."[17]

3. Stefan Rozmaryn — A Classic of the Communist Neo-Positivism

Opalek-Zakrzewski's treatise was juridical, but it included political moralization. They achieved their basic purpose: to present as quickly as possible (the book was finished in 1957) a scholarly and journalistic summary of the principal points made in the process of the great discussion during the period of the Polish thaw, liberalization, illusory victory in October 1956, and post-October *"Sturm und Drang"* period. They were unable to put down their thoughts with the logical consistency which had been so characteristic of the classics of juridical thought.

The author who overcame the deficiencies and inconsistencies of the short phase of liberal romanticism was Stefan Rozmaryn. Two of his monographs[18] represent a unique moment in the history of juridical theory and constitutional law. In the 1950s and 1960s Rozmaryn was possibly the best read scholar in Western and Eastern juridical, philosophical, and political literature. For almost a quarter of a century, till his tragic death around 1969, he combined the functions of the head of the juridical department in the office of the prime minister with the duties of a professor of constitutional law; at the same time he was a prolific author, gifted book reviewer, a conscientious editor, a frequent guest-lecturer in socialist and western countries, and an active participant in innumerable international conferences. He was a sponsor of many doctoral dissertations. He was a master of political compromise, yet he never harmed his friends.

In both monographs he pretended to be a consistent Marxist and supporter of Soviet jurisprudence. Yet he was able to express in "pure" juridical terms, the principal concepts and traditions of Western constitutionalism and due process of law. In his writing juridical positivism was once more denounced as a bourgeois ideology, but in fact, the best achievements of this jurisprudence were adapted, under another label, into a new theory of "socialist constitutionalism and legality." He performed the same kind of miracle which was done by the Unitarian "Polish Brethren" in the XVI-XVII centuries; they proved that it was Jesus Christ who was the Father of modern empiricism, that it was the Savior himself who ordered that true Christians be critical and skeptical. Thomas Hobbes used quotations from the Holy Scripture in order to prove that the secular ruler must be supreme, absolute, independent of the Church, and above it. So did every other writer in his time.

While giving Caesar what was Caesar's and acknowledging the divine rights of the Party, Stefan Rozmaryn juridically proved that according to the Constitution of the Polish People's Republic, the rule of law is above the Party and Government. While resolutely denouncing the *Rechtsstaat* as a product of bourgeois ideology, he elaborated a socialist version of the *Rechtsstaat*. He was consistently positivistic. He even used traditional "juridical logic" and the perennial Roman maxims in order to prove his points under cover of the dialectical method in jurisprudence. If it is true that theology could be used to defend philosophical materialism successfully, then Stefan Rozmaryn became the Roger Bacon of socialist jurisprudence. He proved that consistent juridical positivism was a true Marxist theory of law. Bentham, that "genius of bourgeois stupidity" (Marx), was disguised by Rozmaryn under a proletarian blouse and appointed a troubadour of socialist law during the dictatorship of the proletariat.

Stefan Rozmaryn started his mongraph on *The Con-*

stitution as the basic law of the Polish People's Republic with an explanation of the meaning of the basic law. According to him, the particular features of a basic law are, first, the mere name, no other legal act is called basic or fundamental; second, the specific manner of amending the Constitution; third, a special legal force, higher than that of ordinary laws; fourth, a particular scope, regulating all the fundamental economic, political and social institutions of the country.

The fourth quality is most important. It is worthwhile to observe that Rozmaryn rejected the well known categories of the constitution *"dans le sens formel"* and *"dans le sens matériel."*[19] The importance of the Polish Constitution is that it is a complete "totality," "unity," and "amalgam" of those two senses and of the above enumerated "formal" and "essential" features.

The first part of the Constitution, which is not divided into articles or paragraphs, usually called "an introduction" or "preamble," makes it clear that the Constitution is binding upon everybody, including the Sejm (parliament). This is one of the most important of Rozmaryn's points.[20] The special method by which the Constitution is amended, according to Rozmaryn, implies that no other laws can or should be contradictory to the Constitution.[21] This shows the special place of the Constitution in the juridical scheme. Rozmaryn's next conclusion defines the task of the legislator. He is obliged to issue such laws as are necessary to make the Constitution effective. The legislator is bound by the Constitution to take positive action whenever action is advisable in order to transform the constitutional "law in books" into "law in life."[22]

The great problem of interpretation of every Constitution is, is it really possible at all to find out what the Constitutional legislator wanted? What he wished to express in the general terms which he used? What he regarded as basic or fundamental? Rozmaryn's answer: the mere text is a sure and sufficient answer to these questions and no one should look either for the subjective intentions of the individual legislators or for a "common will" of the Sejm which approved it.

"Our purpose and methods are different: we take as the fundamentals the text of the Constitution, and then we start to look for the premises on which the content of the Constitution is built; we look for the premises which according to the text itself one is authorized to suppose."[23]

This classic positivistic attitude was deliberately expressed by Rozmaryn in a complicated manner. Rozmaryn tried in his own particular way to solve the traditional dispute over interpretation between "subjectivists" (according to them a jurist should look for the intention of the legislator) and "objectivists" (one should look for the objective meaning incorporated in the text, which might differ from the ideas which the legislator wanted to express and promulgate).

According to Rozmaryn, one should look for the premises (neither intention nor will) of the legislator of the Constitution. They can be found through the analysis of the Constitutional text itself.

Rozmaryn's theory means from the practical political viewpoint that nobody has a right to make any special explanations about what the Constitution means. The Constitution must stand on its own. In this subtle way, supported by logic and juridical reasoning, the special role and privileges of the Party, the Sejm, and the Government in the sphere of the constitutional interpretation was denied. His conclusion also reaffirms what he did not write but was supposed to write in a Communist country; Rozmaryn wrote nothing about any special role or privileged position of the Communist Party in interpreting or applying the law.

Rozmaryn's approach to Constitutional interpretation is almost *plus positiviste que le positivisme même*. Its importance and significance lies not only in his positivistic, affirmative recommendations, but also in his negations and exclusions.[24]

Especially significant is Rozmaryn's criticism of the renowned Soviet author, D. Kerimov, who wrote that in the Soviet Union, laws existed which he called "quasi-constitutional," such as the laws on court organization or citizenship. The mere expression, quasi-constitutional, is unconstitutional in itself and must be rejected.[25]

Rozmaryn tried to substantiate his idea that the Constitution as a whole has a normative character, and that every constitutional "principle" is really a rule of law.[26] In this way he rejected the ambiguity which was introduced by Stalin in his speech about the Constitution of the U.S.S.R. (1936) in which he said that the Constitution is a "reflection" or a "register" of socialist achievements, of the existing social, economic, and political system. Rozmaryn does not deny the political character of the socialist constitution, but he tries to reinterpret the official Soviet opinions that socialist constitutions are "political programs" and "political declarations." Even if the Constitution is a "program," it is a program, argued Rozmaryn, expressed *sui generis*, in the form of constitutional legal norms[27] and they should be treated juridically . . . Why does Rozmaryn so stubbornly reject the Stalinist and post-Stalinist concept, from which Soviet scholars cannot get away, that the Constitution is a "register," a "political declaration" and a "political program"? Because Rozmaryn consistently defended his positivistic and normativistic concept of the Constitution and wanted to close the door once and for all upon political "explanation" of the Constitution by professional politicians which might change from season to season. Once all the provisions of the Constitution are pronounced norms with *vis coactiva* (and not only *directiva*!) the role of the jurists becomes essential.

Rozmaryn seemed to suggest that once the politicians promulgated the Constitution, they abdicated part of their power in favor of jurists. In order to avoid any misunderstanding or understatement of his true intention, he proverbially dotted his "i" and stressed that even the Council of the State, empowered by Article 25 of the Constitution to give a binding interpretation of the laws, did not have a right to interpret the Constitution itself in a binding way, because it was the Sejm that was the sole constitutional legislator.[28] Let us remember that the members of the Council of the State are the leaders of the Politburo; the chairman of the Council is usually either first secretary or an important member of the close leadership; only then can we fully realize all the ideological and political implications of Rozmaryn's "objective," dry juridical considerations and conclusions.

But Rozmaryn understood that in order to apply and enforce the Constitutional norms, somebody has to interpret it. Who? Every agency of government, within its own function and authority: it can be done by the Sejm, the Council of the State, the Highest Chamber of Control, the Council of Ministers, the courts, prosecutors, national councils, etc. They interpret the Constitution for practical purposes, therefore their interpretation is inseparable from the process of enforcement.

The understanding of the Constitution by those agencies, stressed Rozmaryn, should not be identified with the correct understanding,[29] "as I implied in my previous works,"* because such a stand would prevent any possibility of a critical assessment of existing practice and interpretation. Rozmaryn argued that there cannot even exist any official interpretation of the Constitution. No interpretation contains this special binding juridical force which characterizes the Constitution itself.[30] Contrary arguments can lead to absurdity:

> Then (when the "official" interpretations were pronounced absolute truth—M.M.) the practice of the highest organs would have constituted the law, whereas indeed the legal norms and their reality were not always compatible one with another. Therefore we think the interpretation of the Constitution in the practice of the highest state-organs tells us only what kind of understanding of the Constitution is reflected in their practice . . . But the practice is not empowered to decide what ought to be the correct understanding of the constitutional provisions, which is their proper sense, i.e. what are the true constitutional norms.[31]

The political and juridical philosophy of Rozmaryn becomes clear now: if every government agency can,

---

*This self-critical remark, "hidden" in the long and complicated text, means that Rozmaryn totally rejected, in his own peculiar manner, the Stalinist identification of the *sein* with the *sollen,* or identifying — if I may use Hegelian terminology — what is real (*wirklich*) with what is reasonable (*vernünftig*).

should, and must interpret the Constitution, if, according to the Constitution itself, they are not infallible, if the various organs can interpret the Constitution in their different ways, if many interpretations are permissible and nobody's interpretation is invested with a special juridical power, then it means in plain English that the Constitution in Rozmaryn's presentation legalizes a pluralistic approach if not a pluralistic society. Rozmaryn would not have dared to use the anathematized pluralistic terminology; he would have been the first to deny such an imputation; but indeed he proved that it was the Constitution which had adopted the ideology of a "hundred schools and a hundred flowers." As in the Middle Ages, skillful theologians compelled theology to prove materialism, thus in the gifted hands of the old bourgeois "specialist," who had served for many years as an uncrowned leader of the Polish "juridical front," the Constitution of the "dictatorship of the proletariat" was presented as a legal basis for a pluralistic society. It would be extremely difficult for the Party or Government to accuse Rozmaryn of heresy; he found these principles in the official Sacred Document, in the Constitution of the Polish People's Republic.

All these considerations concerning the nature of socialist law and the Constitution are especially important when one considers constitutional rights and liberties.

Rozmaryn further analyzed a problem which a century ago became very famous in the West. It is becoming more and more important in the juridical literature of socialist countries. This is the problem of "positivisation" of the general constitutional norms. This problem was widely discussed in the political and juridical literature of the Weimar Republic. Do the general, abstract constitutional norms, conferring rights and liberties on the citizens, need any further "concretizing," any further "positivisation," or are they already sufficiently positive *per se* as to be "applicable," observed, and enforced? Carl Schmitt was one of the most vocal representatives of the anti-democratic, "right wing" critics of the democratic constitutions before and after World War II. In his *"Verfassungsrechtliche Aufsaetze"* (1958) he repeated his old warnings against "automatic thinking" and argued for "positivisation" in order to make the constitution truly applicable.[32]

According to Rozmaryn all the provisions of the constitution are binding and should not be violated even if laws enforcing the given provisions have not been issued. "Generalization" or an alleged "loophole" in the legal system cannot serve as a pretext for undermining or ignoring any of the constitutional provisions. In any case, particular, or rather less general, laws to enforce or "execute" the constitution, even if required by the constitution itself, do not diminish the rights and liberties of the citizens, because constitutional norms carry their own juridical force in themselves.[33] The rights and liberties should be respected by all administrative agencies, prosecutors, courts, and the Highest Chamber of Control because the Constitution is a "natural," "autonomous" force *per se*, which is binding without any specific "elaboration" or "concretizing" by the legislature.

This theory of Rozmaryn could be expressed in the traditional American terminology in the following way: The constitution is a source of rights and duties, whether "expounded" or not, if one were to use the term introduced by Justice John Marshall in the landmark decision, *McCulloch v. Maryland* (1819).

A special law, argued Rozmaryn, is required in order to establish an exception, not a rule.[34]

The final question of Constitutional theory is the "legality" of the laws. Stefan Rozmaryn, of course, could not write in a clear and direct way that where there is a contradiction between the Constitution and the laws then it is the Constitution that prevails. The Constitution does not in so many words give such a power either to the courts or to any other organ. Such a "consistent positivist" as Hans Kelsen answered that where there are contradictions in the legal system, we must accept them because they must have been desired by the legislator and no juridical gimmicks could help. But Rozmaryn is not a Kelsenian "normativist," but a true positivist, although restricted by existing political circumstances. Therefore he wrote that there was not a single example in the decisions of the Supreme Court in which the Court found an "insoluble" contradiction between the Constitution and the laws.[35] This statement has a limited meaning — Rozmaryn-as-politician and Rozmaryn-as-government's jurist gave a passing grade to the legislature but with an implied reservation: it was the Supreme Court that found no "insoluble" contradictions. In the last sentence of his monograph Rozmaryn reserved his role as theoretician and scholar. It might happen very rarely, he wrote, that there could be a contradiction between civil or penal laws and the Constitution, but in any event one should be aware that:

"If such a case arose in the practice of the courts, the

problem should be solved by taking into account the role and meaning of the basic law."[36]

The Stalinist ghost, without being named, was finally exorcised. The unshakeable official dogma that in a Communist country a contradiction between the Constitution and the particular legal will of the people, led by the Party and expressed in the law, is unthinkable — was finally rejected by the mere interpretation of the Constitution.

Independent courts, which are the highlight of Rozmaryn's monographs, have a constitutional right and duty to protect the Constitution and the citizens' rights against any illegal encroachments of any legislative or administrative organs. These constitutional requirements were deduced from the Constitution of a country which officially rejects the division of powers, administrative courts and juridical supervision of the legality of the laws! With Rozmaryn, juridical positivism in defiance of the official ideology and political dogma grew higher than, as Pushkin once wrote, the column of Alexander.

4. Recent Developments in Communist Legal Theory

In his analysis of the development of Soviet legal institutions, Professor Hazard drew attention to a phenomenon which had not previously been properly explored in western juridical literature: how the Soviet political structure slowly evolved from juridical nihilism to a social, political and economic system based on law. "What has taken centuries in Western Europe, and even in old Russia itself, had been repeated in the new

Russia in less than a decade. Men who had expressed their desire to avoid all formalities in the settling of disputes found themselves engaged in creating what they had set out to destroy. Politicians justified this effort as essential to the wellbeing of the state."[37]

Professor Hazard elaborated his ideas regarding how law helped to stabilize and modernize other developing societies in his later works, such as "Unity and Diversity in Socialist Law," and "Modernization and Codification."[38]

The concept of law as a necessary instrument in the transformation of contemporary societies can be applied, *mutatis mutandis,* to the changes which commenced within the Communist bloc after Stalin's death and the 20th Congress of the CPSU (Communist Party of the Soviet Union) in 1956. The changes which followed in those countries could briefly be described as an attempt to modernize the political structure of societies which for many years had been subject to a specific type of absolutism, viz., Stalinism.

Jurists and the juridical sciences contributed greatly to that process of "thaw" and "renaissance." It has almost become a ritualistic device for communist political leaders to criticize juridical scholars for their "backwardness" and inability to keep pace with socialist developments. The analysis of scholarly writings, however, contradicts those allegations. Juridical scholars developed and represented ideas in the Soviet bloc which were more progressive and democratic than the political reality in their countries. The ideas developed various aspects of democracy, the defense of freedom, and legality. There are communist countries in which progress advanced more rapidly than in others.[39] The achievements of Polish jurisprudence still remain unique in their originality and postulates. It would not be a great exaggeration to state that the Poles laid down the direction for further theoretical development; they greatly influenced many of their colleagues in the communist world.

It would require a special study to present the evolution of ideas tending toward liberalization in each communist country. For obvious reasons we shall concentrate on the most recent stage of this process which has been documented in the latest World Congress on Philosophy of Law and Social Philosophy, held in Basel, August 27, 1979-September 1, 1979. This Congress was dedicated to the exploration of contemporary conceptions of law. Legal theorists from communist countries actively participated and presented papers reflecting their current thinking. Once more it should be stressed that there is both unity and diversity among them.

The theoretical presentations demonstrated three characteristic trends:

—Elaboration and institutionalization of the new concept of legality in communist counries;

—Elaboration of the concept of subjective rights (including the concept of human rights);

—Attempts to overcome the dogmatic one-sidedness of the existing definition of law, and new attempts to re-assess the primary concept of law.

It can be said about all these spheres that—according to the communist authors—socialist law is in a process of transformation; these laws are not a mere "reflection" of reality (the communist writers who submitted their essays used the German word *Widerspiegelung*) but are a dialectical reflection of the existing social structure.[40] This means that this reflection is not entirely accurate and there exists, therefore, not only the possiblity, but also the necessity, that some provisions of law may be detrimental to society and not reflect the will of the people. This is perhaps the essence of the dialectical approach which has been proclaimed as the official methodology. (Anyone familiar with the social and political sciences under Stalin, however, knows that "dialectic" was interpreted in the same manner as Hegel's "dialectic" had been under the Prussian empire: what was real was pronounced reasonable and necessary. With the official repudiation of the "cult of personality," a revision in dialectical thinking had to be made.) According to this line of reasoning, all that is real can become unreasonable and unnecessary. New demands of reason can appear and their realization become historically necessary.

The new demands of reason had already been formulated by philosophers and jurists from communist countries: more personal freedom, more democracy, more guarantees of legality, better laws, better application of juridical provisions, more opportunities for creative activity. Sometimes these ideas were formulated within a description of the "evolving reality," sometimes as a constitutional description of the future which is embodied in the present situation, and sometimes these ideas are expressed in various postulates *de lege ferenda*.

Scholars from communist countries stressed their positivistic attitudes. They once more confirmed their approval of the traditional positivistic definition of law, given most clearly by Professor Adam Lopatka: "Socialist law, like the law of any other type, is a set of norms of conduct enacted by the action of the state."[41]

All communist bloc authors of course maintained that socialist law expresses the will and the interest of the working man, and that consequently their definition is not as abstract and formal as that of bourgeois positivists.[42]

On the other hand, they stressed that since socialist law is not a perfect reflection of the interests and will of the people, discrepancies may appear in its effectiveness and realization. In that way they concluded that the phenomenon which American realists call the law-in-books as against the law-in-life existed in communist countries as well.

We see therefore that Socialist positivists have reached a stage similar to that reached by their bourgeois counterparts—positivism was supplemented by realistic considerations.

The development of communist theories of law was accompanied by sharp criticism of bourgeois juridical positivism. As communist scholars absorbed the theses of western positivist jurisprudence, their criticism of that very jurisprudence became sharper. Now that they are approaching bourgeois juridical phenomenology and realism, they pay more and more attention to "unmasking" and "denouncing" the theories of the period of "imperialistic and monopolistic capitalism."

At the end of the 1970s, communist scholars started to discuss the primary definition of law, and its relationship to existing laws and the will of the class or the will of the people.

Indeed, this was the first time that the theorists discussed one of the basic notions of their philosophy of law: law, as the will of the people. No one could have written anything reasonable on this subject during the regime of "the cult of personality" because the "personality's" will was at all times the perfect embodiment and expression of the will and interests of the people; therefore, no problem could arise. With the rejection of "the cult," however, this problem could no longer be shelved.

In order to illustrate how the will of the Soviet people is formed and expressed, Professor D. Kerimov described the public discussion of the draft of the Constitution of 1977. As a result of prolonged national discussion, 110 articles out of the 173 in the draft were changed and some new articles were added. Professor D. Kerimov concluded that in this way, the general will of the people found its reflection in the law.

How can and should the general will of the people be defined? In his opinion the general will should not be regarded as the mechanical combination or amalgam of opinions, indications, or proposals. The general will is not simply the sum of wills. In this way we return to the famous distinction of Jean-Jacques Rousseau who distinguished between the "will of all" and the "general will." Needless to say, this is one of Rousseau's most unclear and controversial concepts. The various interpretations of the general will were one of the pretexts for the ideological and political struggles between the Jacobins and the Girondists. In the name of the general will the Jacobins sent their enemies to the guillotine.

D. Kerimov's explanation of the concept of the general will is as follows: the numerous proposals, ideas, and feelings of the people constitute merely the raw material from which those ideas are selected which meet the demands of progressive social evolution. These latter ideas, in the most exact and thorough manner, reflect the needs and interests of the whole nation. After such a critical selection, the general will of the people will truly be crystallized and expressed. It will then be dialectically tied to juridical means to achieve communist ends. The general will expressed in the process of crystallization and transformation into law thus becomes a new will which is "above" individual wills.

The most important problem not resolved by Jean-Jacques Rousseau is not solved here either. Who does the selecting, and who decides which among the individual wills expressed in a national debate meet the demands of progressive social evolution? What are the real criteria for selection? After all, one may assume that most people will favor progress, freedom, humanism, and democracy, and that they will insist that their desires conform to these ideals. From Professor Kerimov's comments it might appear that all the individual expressions of will were recorded and then someone undertook to establish their essence. But what is this famous Hegelian, Marxian essence? One thing is certain; it is not the will of the majority, because no special vote on the proposals is conducted. Can the mere number of proponents or opponents of a given idea be considered an indication of the true support or non-support of the majority? Or is the majority merely the most vociferous and active segment of the population? It could of course also happen that those who had not spoken were a coherent but "silent majority," as Nixon called them for self-serving reasons. How can the voices of the silent be counted? Are they not a part of the mysterious general will?

One can of course agree with Professor Kerimov that one should not identify the will of a "mechanical" majority with the most essential interests of "the people." Our conclusion then would be that according to the mechanism described by Professor Kerimov there can be no incompatibility between the "essential interests" on the one hand and the "empirical will" of the majority on the other, or at least the empirical perception of those interests as expressed by the voting majority.

Rousseau believed that the general will can be presented simply as a component of the will of all. Hegel thought that the general will never is a simple derivative or component but a complicated essence which, of course, reflects historical necessity, which can and should be comprehended. When this necessity is incorrectly understood, law cannot reflect the essence of historical evolution. Such law will be unreasonable, even unrealistic.

Unfortunately, we do not find these complicated reflections of Hegel and Marx in the writings of contemporary philosophers who nevertheless claim to be Marxists.

According to Professor Kerimov, socialist law during the period of developing socialism represents "the general will of the majority of the working people."[43]

That is a different explanation of the general will. The general will here is presented as the general will of the majority of the working people, not of all the people. One can argue, *a contrario*, that the general will is in essence identified with existing Soviet law, so long as

Soviet law, as Kerimov writes, accords with equality, justice, morality, humanity, and internationalism.[44] It is not clear whether these criteria are part of the law, or are someting apart from the totality of legal acts, or are presumed to be incorporated in them.

It would appear that Kerimov accepts the possibility of incompatibility when he declares that the category of legal material should not be limited to legal acts, because law itself encompasses the evolution from possibility to reality and ultimately, reality itself. Law should not be regarded simply as a norm, according to Kerimov, but as the efficient means of socialist development.

It is obvious that Professor Kerimov decided to depart from the traditional, very dogmatic, Soviet theory of law which reduces legal systems to legal matter. It is unclear however, what his aim is. Possibly he represents a new stage in the evolution of the Soviet theory of law, which has certain elements similar to American juridical realism and western European phenomenology.

It is needless to stress that such an approach would have been unacceptable to 19th century positivists. Nor would it have been acceptable to Stalin, Vyshinsky or their followers. It is meaningful that when Kerimow goes beyond Vyshinsky, he is in fact returning to certain elements of the Soviet philosophy of law of the 1920s.

In this respect, Professor Vladik Nersesjanz took a step further in his article, *"Das Verhaeltnis von Recht und Gesetz: Die Geschichte der Rechtslehren und die Gegenwart"* (The Relationship between Right and Law: The History of the Theories of Law and the Contemporary Period).[45]

Professor Nersesjanz writes that there is a long history of differences between right and law, and that non-Marxist philosophers have been unaware of the main differences between them. One of the errors of juridical positivism, according to him, is the narrowing down of the concept of right *(Recht)* to that of law *(Gesetz)* and the elevation of the importance of law to the detriment of right. Professor Nersesjanz believes that, from the philosophical viewpoint, this procedure represents a mechanical oversimplification. Right, according to him, is a kind of essence, a *spiritus movens,* behind laws, and, therefore, the relationship between those two notions should be elaborated and not nullified. He goes further: he asserts that even right and law together do not represent the whole of legal reality which is someting higher than the positivists realized.

To prove his theses, Nersesjanz quotes from the article by the young Marx on Prussian censorship.[46] He knows that Marx was then a young Hegelian who employed an unclear Hegelian style, terminology, and expressions.

To present the relationship between right and law as a distinction between spirit and matter explains nothing. Why did the Soviet bloc scholars return to old concepts and why did they introduce the old "bourgeois" notion of law in the subjective and objective sense? That is a puzzle. One can only speculate that they found too obvious an analogy between bourgeois positivism and their own and that they tried to overcome it. Fortunately or unfortunately, however, instead of really moving forward, they returned to the old "Young Marx."

One can also speculate that Nersesjanz wanted to propose that there is a significant distinction between the notion of right and narrowly interpreted law. Right is directly connected with the idea of freedom; it is "a unit of measurement of freedom" (*eine Masseinheit der Freiheit*).[47] When he stresses that the explanation of legal phenomena should be connected with real social phenomena, he really goes beyond traditional positivism. He moves toward legal realism. Was the "young Hegelian," Karl Marx, a forerunner of juridical phenomenology and legal realism? *Habent sua fata libelli.*

Professor Vladimir Tumanov took a decisive step in the reinterpretation of the concept of right and its relationship to law *(Gesetz)*. In his essay, *"Naturrecht und Juristischer Positivismus in der Einschaetzung des Marxismus"* ("Natural Right and Juridical Positivism in the Light of Marxism"), he writes that according to Marxism, individual rights or liberties should not be regarded as solely deriving from the state's activity or as representing expressions of the legislator's will. According to him Marxism rejects the view that the state is the sole source of all individual rights. Quite the contrary, Tumanow asserts. It was Marx who introduced the theory that the basic rights and duties of individuals were determined by existing social relations. Marx derived these rights and duties from the social nature of man because man, for him, was totality of social relations. Therefore the accusation that "there is no place in Marxism for natural, inborn, inalienable rights" should be rejected.[48]

The earth-shaking significance of this statement that Tumanov made can be compared to the pronouncement of Pope Leo XIII at the end of the 19th century that the Church has always favored true democracy. The Pope simply disregarded as non-existent the statements which his predecessor had made only two decades earlier which condemned all those who argued that the Church could, and should, come to an agreement with modern democracy, parliamentarism, and general elections. One can find numerous Soviet writings in which the idea that the individual has rights existing independently of law and the state was condemned as idealism, clericalism, and a pure fabrication of anti-proletarian ideology. Tumanov of course is at liberty to claim that Marx and Engels scientifically established the concept of human rights. However, he knows as well as his readers do that in his country until now the writings of Marx have not been interpreted in that way.

Tumanov's reinterpretation of Marxism should be regarded as a new phase in the evolution of the theory of law by historical materialism. It is doubtful whether those who call themselves Marxists will agree with him. It is quite possible that certain "Marxists" will view this theory not as a development but a revision of the teachings of Marx. Whether Tumanov correctly or incorrectly interprets Marx is irrelevant. It is important that Marx's theoretical premises are used by Tumanov to reach political conclusions which one may describe as more progressive and democratic in this respect than Soviet jurisprudence has ever seen before.

It is meaningful when Professor Tumanov stresses that in a socialist society neither the state nor the constitution create what he calls *"praegesetzliche Recht,"* but that they only establish conditions which enable the realization of these rights.[49] Does this mean that Soviet citizens might have certain *praegesetzliche Rechte* (pre-legal rights) which have not been duly considered or promulgated by the state and the legislature? One can easily imagine that there are certain dogmatists in the communist camp who would shudder at such a thought. This idea is nevertheless implicit in the words of Tumanov.

Tumanow observed that the state, the legislature, and society may influence the rights of the individual favorably or unfavorably. Every reasonable philosopher of law must agree with Professor Tumanov here. The effect of government and society on personal rights is indeed one of the basic contemporary problems existing in every state, in every political system, even the most democratic. How is one to realize the generally acknowledged rights of man? That may be the most fundamental and crucial problem of our epoch. The fact that Soviet jurists have begun to be aware of this problem which exists in every type and form of the state is important from both the scholarly and political viewpoints.

There is of course a difference between Tumanov's interpretation of the rights of man and the theories which connect the rights of man with the biological, or anthropological, existence of men. Tumanow correctly observes that Robinson Crusoe had no need for inborn rights because he lived outside society. The rights of man according to Tumanow are determined by the social and economic relations and the historically formed personality and character of man. In this way Tumanov transforms the problem from a biological to a sociological one. At the same time he uses his newly elaborated theory to defend Marxism against accusations of "étatisme" and totalitarianism.[50]

To what extent this defense of Marxism-Leninism is pertinent does not depend on theoretical determinations only, but on practical ones as well.

* * *

Professor Adam Lopatka attempted to classify the so-called fundamental principles of socialist law. He enumerated them as follows: the principle of government by the people, democracy, humanism, justice, equality of rights, the rule of law, the interdependence of rights and duties, combining persuasion with coercion, and finally, the principle of internationalism.[51]

Adam Lopatka was the only communist bloc representative to write: the principle of humanism ". . . recognizes the personality of a man and himself as the supreme good."[52]

Lopatka adds: "It [law] serves more and more to create the conditions for self-realization of individual men. The catalogue of personal goods protected by the law is ever expanding, particularly concerning the intimacy of man's life; there follows an extension of protection of employee's goods, particularly concerning his dignity; the sphere of personal and public liberty of citizens is ever increasing; protection is given to man's personality against any interferences in connection with the development of science and technology."[53]

To what extent these words are an expression of wishful thinking or of reality is irrelevant to our analysis here. One thing is certain: progressive legal thinkers at times present myths as reality and believe that through this means they can exorcise the evil demons and transfer power to the just and the wise. It is a myth, but like "... all myths, it may have influence upon future policy direction."⁵⁴

The mere presentation of the myth or wishful thinking as a reality, however, is a very specific form of criticism of existing social and political reality. Therefore one can ask a fundamental question: are these jurists in opposition to their governments and their Politbureaus? Not at all. They simply have a better and deeper understanding of the interests, needs, and will of their fellow citizens than the professional bureaucrats and aparatchiks. They understand better than the careerists the value of legality and the value, for example, of the presumption of innocence. They know that disorder and the "rule of conscience" lead to the rule of terror. They truly want to develop the new society according to more reasonable and humane patterns. One may write about this new breed of communist scholars, jurists, and professors of law what John N. Hazard observed about their predecessors:

> In opposition to the supreme politicians there stood most of the men of law. In a sense, they were not in opposition, for they were largely, but by no means entirely, members of the communist party, and as such they were pledged to achievement of the same ends as the supreme politicians. Yet within the area revealed in the record they were in opposition. They pushed forward whenever the opportunity was presented to do so without losing their heads to the supreme politicians in a quiet but unending effort to create limitations on arbitrary powers. They sought what they often called "legality." They professed on every occasion that it was a "revolutionary legality" or "socialist legality" they hoped to achieve. By this they tried to indicate their acceptance of goals, their willingness to work for an economic and social structure which would be quite different from that of the tsarist past or contemporary western Europe and the Americas.⁵⁵

Various legal writers have various ideas and intentions in pursuing these goals. Under a dogmatic dictatorship these exercises are always dangerous. One can as easily fall into disgrace as gain favor with the dictator, ever exposed to new privileges and dangers. There are no insurance policies for those who decide to walk the tight-rope. Broken careers and lives—that is the normal price that mankind pays for progress.

VII.
THE NEW THEORY OF ARGUMENTATION AND AMERICAN JURISPRUDENCE

Preliminary Remarks

Classic Western juridical positivism can and should develop in consonance with the European tradition of rhetoric and the American school of jurisprudence, represented by Holmes, Cardozo, and Dewey.

Professor Chaim Perelman revived the rhetorical tradition after WW II, calling it the "New Rhetoric," or the "New Theory of Argumentation."

Within a relatively short time, the New Rhetoric made phenomenal incursions into the field of philosophy, sociology, and jurisprudence.

The New Theory of Argumentation and its broad philosophical notion of pluralism constitutes a methodological basis for juridical positivism which has long been lacking. It provides a basis for the further development of juridical positivism free from the political limitations so characteristic of the doctrine since its founding by Bentham and Austin. These limitations became even more acute at the turn of the present century.

The revival of a doctrine does not in itself explain much. It is the manner in which the revival is brought about that is important. Of special significance are the elements which have been revived and those which have remained in oblivion. The revival of a formerly popular philosophy, political doctrine, literature, or art, will always be a selective process—e.g., only those aspects of the Greek and Roman heritages were rediscovered and developed during the Renaissance which mankind required at that particular stage of its cultural progress.

The New Rhetoric, or the New Theory of Argumentation, is by no means a mere republication of Aristotle's works. The New Rhetoric constitutes the Hegelian *Aufhebung* of Aristotle's rhetoric. It is at once a continuation and a negation of that rhetoric. The novelty of Perelman's theory is chiefly his introduction and elaboration of the notion of "audience." Another new and thoroughly expounded element in it is the elaboration of the rhetorical discourse in close connection with jurisprudence and the philosophy of pluralism. The rhetorical notion of pluralism is a milestone which leads to answers to many of the traditional problems of the philosophy of law, without recourse to fiction or mythology. Bentham's dream of the purification of the theory and practice of law by expunging the then prevalent fictions has at long last been accomplished.

American jurisprudence of the twentieth century has taken a tremendous step forward compared with Europe, which took a long step backward during the interwar period. We do not intend to analyze all or even the most important original elements of the American contribution to Western jurisprudence in this volume. The second volume will be devoted to this problem in its entirety. We here wish to present only those elements which clearly indicate the dissatisfaction of American jurists with the tradition of "dogmatic" adherence to the logic of syllogisms and the American drive for a new, more flexible, a more reasonable methodology which could help to preserve old and valued ideas in modern times.

1. Where Holmes and Dewey Stopped

The purpose of this chapter is to compare American legal philosophy with the new theory of argumentation developed by Chaim Perelman. Oliver Wendell Holmes, Benjamin Cardozo, John Dewey and many other eminent representatives of American philosophy and jurisprudence found that in order to develop their ideals and theories, they had to go beyond the formalistic logic of syllogisms. They started to search for new methods but they never did resolve their problem. The answer that they sought, however, was provided by Chaim Perelman, professor of logic, philosophy, and jurisprudence at the Université Libre of Brussels, founder of the newly elaborated theory of argumentation which he has called, the New Rhetoric, after Aristotle. Here we concentrate chiefly on the problems of jurisprudence and morality in politics.

In the twentieth century the most eminent representatives of American jurisprudence found that formal logic alone is inadequate for the interpretation and application of legal norms, either statutes or the common law. For many social, economic, and political reasons, Americans realized long before their European counterparts that the life of the law cannot rest on the logic of syllogisms. Why Americans grasped this point first is a topic for a special study, which is not pertinent to our theme.

From the very beginning of his practical and theoretical activity, Justice Oliver Wendell Holmes helped to lay down the premises for the new juridical methodology.

In the lectures on *Agency* which were delivered in 1891, Holmes asserted "that the whole outline is the resultant of a conflict at every point between logic and good sense—the one striving to work fiction out to consistent results, the other restraining and at last overcoming that effort when the results become too manifestly unjust."[1]

Could this sentence be interpreted as a condemnation of the use of logic, or of common sense? Is there really an unbridgeable chasm between the two? It would rather appear that Holmes wanted merely to state that an indiscriminate use of formal logic (the logic of syllogisms) could lead to "manifestly unjust" consequences and that therefore we should use tools other than formal logic in the process of interpreting and applying the law. We should not abandon logic, but we should not expect or demand too much from the rigorous use of syllogisms.

Should we, on the other hand, decisively turn to "good sense" as well? "The jurists who believe in natural law seem to me to be in that naive state of mind that accepts what has been familiar and accepted by them and their neighbors as something that must be accepted by all men everywhere."[2]

The conflict between formal "logic" and "good sense" (which usually presents itself under natural reason or natural law), according to Holmes, sometimes becomes a conflict between an alleged consistency of logic (indeed, leading to injustice) and the naivete of familiar convictions. Rules of law cannot be treated like abstract mathematical axioms because law is directly connected with the real conflicts of life:

> But the provisions of the constitution are not mathematical formulas having their essence in their form; they are organic living institutions . . . Their significance is vital not formal; it is to be gathered not simply by taking the words and the dictionary, but by considering their origin and the line of their growth.[3]

What is "vital" should not be treated like a "dead letter," or like a formula for life which is reduced to its "form." Law is the response to our aspirations, to the experience of mankind, and is not reducible to a formula whose meaning has been predetermined. Mere reading of the legal norms is not sufficient; it is equally necessary to consider their whole line of growth as well. One should start at the beginning, but only in order to realize fully that law, as the "witness and external deposit" of our lives, registers the moral development of society.[4] For this reason, an uncritical or dogmatic application of formal logic to the living organisms of the law brings about results which are repellant from the human viewpoint.

And yet, after numerous criticisms of the insufficiency of logic, we find Holmes making the following statement. "The training of lawyers is a training in logic. The process of analogy, discrimination, and deduction are those in which they are most at home. The language of judicial decision is mainly the language of logic."[5]

These words were to become famous in juridical literature to indicate how important logic is in legal training.[6]

Strictly speaking, Holmes' notion of formal logic differs from that usually accepted in our time. Discrimination and analogy are foreign to formal logic. Nevertheless the fact that Holmes treated formal logic more broadly does not alter the tenor of our remarks.

In an address delivered to the Supreme Court of Massachusetts in 1897, Holmes stressed how vain was the conviction of those who looked for certainty in the application of logic to law: "And the logical method and form flatter that longing for certainty and for repose which is in every human mind. But certainty generally is illusion, and repose is not the destiny of man."[7]

This is one of his most significant observations concerning the importance of logic in legal practice: logic creates the illusion of certainty; actually such certainty either does not exist or cannot be attained. Even should it exist to a certain degree, it would not owe its existence to the logic of syllogisms.

The most dangerous illusion, however, is the illusion that legal conclusions are free from subjectivity, that they are completely detached from the individual who harbors them; that they have a life of their own. The contrary is true. As Holmes wrote:

> Behind the logical form lies a judgment as to the relative worth and importance of competing legislative grounds, often an inarticulate and unconscious judgment, it is true, and yet the very root and nerve of the whole proceeding. You can give any conclusion a logical form.[8]

Legal conclusions can always be given in a logical form. It is for this reason that lawyers are trained in logic. This is not to say that they are not to be trained to apply logic to the interpretation of legal norms (this very often becomes impossible when the quantitative measurements are not known). Instead they learn how to present their own subjective conclusions in an objective, impersonal, logical form. Training in logic does not pertain to the essence of professional activity in the field of law, but to the forms of legal presentation: subjectivity must be presented as objectivity.

These considerations do not make a good case for formal logical thought in the sphere of law. And because one is not able to reach an exact logical conclusion in a given case, one's conclusions

> ... can do no more than embody the preference of a given body in a given time and place. We do not realize how large a part of our law is open to reconsideration upon a slight change in the habit of the public mind. No concrete proposition is self-evident, no matter how ready we may be to accept it. ...[9]

Such is the essence of Holmes's view of the role of logic in law. Every judicial decision (not concerned with technical data), apart from its logical form, embodies the preference of a given body rather than a determination drawn from any "iron logic," which supposedly is the one correct, certain, and absolute expression of Justice. On the contrary, a juridical decision is subjective because it reflects the personal preferences of its author, who is subject to the influence of the changing moods and opinions of the public.

"No concrete proposition is self-evident ..." —this indicates that a proposition must seek the adherence of the minds of its hearers. The so-called compelling force of self-evidence, obviousness, rationality, and logical consistency, are not sufficient in themselves. One must use the force of argument to persuade those to whom the arguments are directed. This conclusion was never expressed by Holmes in such a form—but it is implicit in his reasoning. It portends the great leap from the realm of formal logic to the realm of argumentation.

Holmes did not leave one stone on another in destroying illusions about the role of syllogisms in law. But he did not have anything with which to replace formal logic that would assure reasonableness in juridical practice.

The ground for the New Theory of Argumentation was cleared by Holmes. But it was Dewey who added new dimensions to his analysis.

In his essay, "Logical Method and Law," John Dewey analyzed Holmes's ideas about the place of logic in the interpretation of law. Dewey concluded that whenever Holmes used the words, "logic" or "logical," in his legal writings, he meant "formal logic," logic as "formal consistency," the consistency of "concepts . . . irrespective of the consequences of their application to concrete matters-of-fact."[10]

Jurists are inclined to use the ready-made, familiar, concepts of logic, because it is convenient and economical for them to do so, Dewey argued. No further effort is required to devise a new pattern; furthermore, recourse to logic gives rise "to a sense of stability, of a guarantee against sudden and arbitrary changes of the rules."[11] One should be wary of this use of logic and "a sound logic" will guard against it.

Dewey viewed formal logic, or the logic of syllogisms, as a logic which is not "sound" (concerning applications to law, morality, and politics). But what is "a sound logic?" Here, Dewey's explanations are meager. He did, however, make an important comment regarding Holmes' famous expression: "The actual life of law has not been logic: it has been experience."[12]

Dewey understood that here Holmes used the word logic in the traditional, orthodox way, meaning the logic of syllogisms and Dewey stressed that there exists an antithesis between such logic and experience, between such logic and good sense. Consequently, there is a need for "another kind of logic."[13]

This "other" logic would not assert that reason has "fixed forms of its own" anterior to the subject matter, to which "the latter have to be adapted."[14] Orthodox logic is a logic of "rigid demonstration," but not of "search and discovery," Dewey stated. The logic of syllogisms pays no attention to the social consequences of decisions made with its help.

What can be said of the "other" kind of logic which Dewey recommended? It will be a logic which will reduce the influence of habit; it will facilitate the use of good sense; it will take into account the social consequences of legal decisions; it will deal with the *operations* of social thought and not only with its *results*; it will not arrogate to itself the presumption that every possible case which may arise can be resolved simply on the basis of a fixed antecedent rule.

According to formal logic, a logical conclusion "subsumes" a particular under an appropriate general principle; nothing more needs be said.

According to the "other kind of logic," general rules do not mechanically decide concrete cases; nothing necessarily follows automatically from general statements or general legal rules. General rules can only act as "generic ways" which may aid in solving any given question.

Dewey calls this "other logic" an "experimental logic,"[15] a "sound" logic, a "vital" logic,[16] and finally the "logic of inquiry,"[17] because it is "flexible."[18]

The use of the "logic of inquiry" does not reduce "predictability" in the sphere of law. Quite the contrary, theoretical certainty will be replaced by practical certainty.[19] Social needs will be met because the logic of inquiry relates to consequences and not to antecedents.[20]

There is a gap, Dewey wrote, between antecedents and the new requirements of life. Whoever uses antecedents alone must do so in an arbitrary manner.

Those who use the "experimental logic," however, are more *creative*, more oriented toward reality and give more assurance that the law will be applied as regularly as possible. "Gambling" with old rules does not increase "practical certainty," but instead serves the "virtual alliance between the judiciary and entrenched interests."[21]

Such are the social characteristics of the "logic of inquiry," as understood by Dewey. This logic serves to promote progress, it is oriented toward social justice.

Moreover, this "vital logic" takes into account the fact that "the personal element cannot wholly be excluded"[22] from judicial decision. What should be done if one wants to preserve its authority, its aura of objectivity? The answer can only be through the introduction of the element of the audience.

The absence of the latter element is what separates Dewey's "logic of inquiry" from the new theory of argumentation propounded by Perelman, as applied to jurisprudence.

Holmes proved that the logic of syllogisms can lead to unreasonable, inhumane results. Dewey proved that formal logic can strengthen "the bulwarks of reaction."[23] He subsequently elaborated his logic of experience. Perelman has gone even beyond Dewey.

In considering the reasonableness of moral norms Dewey advanced half a step further toward rhetorical logic.

In the "Afterword" (1946) to his book, *The Public and Its Problems* (first published in 1927), Dewey made the following remarks concerning moral norms and their social values:

> ... in order to interest the citizens ... in an actual war, it has been necessary to carry on a campaign to show that *superior* moral claims were on the side of a war policy. The change of attitude is not fundamentally an affair of moral conversion, a change from obdurate immorality to a perception of the claims of righteousness. It results from greatly intensified recognition of the factual consequences of war.[24]

From Dewey's point of view, as expressed in one of his last writings, what is moral or immoral does not depend on any unchangeable, absolute moral category; it depends on public understanding and the perception of what should be regarded as a right (moral, just) way of acting. According to the absolutistic philosophies of morality and truth, when one party supports a war and a second opposes it, only one can represent the requirements of morality and justice, the other must be sunk in "obdurate immorality." Once we admit the public's opinion into the spectrum of our evaluation, the results of our analysis will be broader, deeper, more humane and more flexible, but by this we do not mean more eclectic. Both factions, pro- and anti-war, may represent moral and social values at least for a time. When the dialogue goes on, when new facts about the conduct of the war and the behavior of the aggressors become known (Dewey refers to WW II), when the public becomes more and more persuaded by the old and the new arguments of the pro-war faction—then, more and more people will perceive who represents "*superior* moral claims." From the absolutistic dogmatic viewpoint, when one changes one's moral attitude, one has undergone a "moral conversion." Not so, says Dewey. In this respect his theory coincides with the New Rhetoric. New moral awareness and a change of mind are a normal, non-revolutionary, development resulting from the public dialogue. It also means that opposition to war may become morally untenable at a certain point, although for a while it may have been regarded as morally justifiable. The majority will view their political adversaries as representatives of obdurate immorality. At any rate, the moral, or immoral, has no absolute content.

In this manner Dewey made another turn toward rhetorical tradition.

2. The Origins of the New Rhetoric

During the forty years of his scholarly activity, Chaim Perelman has become one of the most renowned professors and authors in the field of philosophy, jurisprudence, and logic. He is one of the most prolific and original thinkers of the contemporary world.

Perelman's most important contribution to the humanistic concept of the sciences is the elaboration and enlargement of the Aristotelian theory of dialectical reasoning and its conception as a generalized rhetoric or general theory of argumentation. This theory includes not only the theory of the more or less incompetent audience but it now includes audiences of all kinds, even the most specialized.

In the essay, "The New Rhetoric: A Theory of Practical Reasoning," Perelman tells about his own intellectual evolution and throws some light on a part of the way which he has traveled. His first study of justice was published in 1945. One of the principles he has adhered to is that one cannot draw an "ought" from an "is," that there is an insurmountable barrier between judgments of fact and those of value, between *"sein"* and *"sollen."* Hence the conclusion: every normative system is arbitrary and logically indeterminate; it cannot be subjected to any rational criticism, it is incompatible with "formal necessity" and "experiential universality."

"I was deeply dissatisfied with this conclusion," Perelman wrote, "since the philosophical inquiry, carried on within the limits of logical empiricism, could not provide an ideal of practical reason, that is, the establishment of rules and models for reasonable action."[25]

In this frame of mind he asked himself: " . . . is there a logic of value judgments that makes it possible for us to reason about values instead of making them depend solely on irrational choices based on interest, passion, prejudice, and myth? Recent history has shown abundantly the sad excess to which such an attitude can lead."[26]

Perelman was unable to accept the concept that ends themselves could not be subjected to reasonable analysis "unless transformed into instrumental values"; he was not prepared to accept any form of subjectivism, skepticism, absolutism, or intuitionism in the theory of value. Nevertheless, he was deeply convinced that we were not condemned to such a limited choice as for example between A.J. Ayer's view (*Language, Truth and Logic*) or G.E. Moore's (*Principia Ethica*). Furthermore, he wrote, he could not adhere to existentialist subjectivism, although he appreciated the existentialist criticism of positivist empiricism and rationalistic idealism.

He finally found a way to the solution of his dilemma: the method employed by the German logician Gottlob Frege, who decided to analyze the mere reasoning used by the mathematicians.

Perelman asked himself:

> Could we not undertake, in the same way, an extensive inquiry into the manner in which the most diverse authors in all fields do in fact reason about values? By analyzing political discourse, the reasons given by judges, the reasoning of moralists, the daily discussion carried on in deliberating about making a choice or reaching a decision or nominating a person, we might be able to trace the actual logic of value judgments which seems continually to elude the grasp of specialists in the theory of knowledge.[27]

The result of these investigations and the tracing of the actual reasoning to achieve value judgments is documented in the book, *The New Rhetoric*.

Perelman wrote:

> For almost ten years Mme. L. Olbrechts-Tyteca and I conducted such an inquiry and analysis. We obtained results that neither of us had ever expected. Without either knowing or wishing it, we had rediscovered a part of Aristotelian logic that had been long forgotten or, at any rate, ignored and despised. It was the part dealing with dialectical reasoning, as distinguished from demonstrative reasoning—called by Aristotle analytics—which is analyzed at length in the *Rhetoric, Topics,* and on *Sophistical Refutations*. We called this new, or revived, branch of study, devoted to the analysis of informal reasoning, *The New Rhetoric*.[28]

In this way the old classical pre-Socratic, Socratic, and classic rhetorical tradition was revived. But—as we already mentioned—what is reborn always has original elements and operates in a new manner under circumstances very different from those of its genesis.

There is no doubt that the *New Rhetoric* was born as a result of the practical and theoretical needs of the social, political, moral and legal sciences in our century, and, what is equally important, by the evolution of the forms of social life. Traditional empiricism, positivism, neopositivism, pragmatism, rationalism, all their old forms and all their current re-editions, were unable properly to analyze the new problems nor to answer the new questions. On the other hand, the requirements of life were demanding and pressing: people must make decisions and want to make them reasonably.

Another very specific point must be considered when talking about the twentieth century and its series of waves of irrationalism, which have been propagated not only by all kinds of right and left wing totalitarianisms, but have been emerging in various forms in all the well-established western democracies.[29]

Already in 1939, George Orwell observed, not only with regard to fascism and communism, that the West had sunk to such a depth that the simple restatement of the obvious is the first duty of an intelligent man. This situation did not improve in the last four decades. On the contrary. It would be more difficult today than ever to disagree with the British journalist and author when he states that we live in a period when the "western intelligentsia" is rapidly rejecting both reason and the heritage of democratic freedom and that it is more and more important to appeal to reason and to say that reasonable is reasonable.

From the very beginning, *The New Rhetoric* was meant to be a tool for analysis of social and intellectual life which were escaping formal logic, and therefore being abandoned to control by other forces, usually opposed to the conscious application of the light of reason.

The New Rhetoric was created as an instrument critical of all kinds of irrationalism, prejudice, dogma, and *a priori* judgments. It is a philosophical method, but it gained enormous political weight in our "times of contempt."

3. The New Rhetoric and Pluralism

The philosopher and historian of legal and philosophical ideas, Chaim Perelman, was influenced in his understanding of pluralism by his teacher and mentor, the eminent Belgian philosopher, Eugene Dupréel, who sought to create a counterweight to the classical philosophies which he referred to as absolutistic. He did this in his work on the Sophists. Perelman continued the ideas of Dupréel, but went beyond that thinker.

The philosophers, argued Dupréel, seek truth and values which they try to impose on a unique and universally valid order. Whatever these unique truths, values, or orders may be, they have one feature in common: monism.

To the classic concept of necessity Dupréel opposed his own idea of a convention. To the classic idea of monism, he opposed his own concept of pluralism. Perelman like Dupréel, spoke about pluralism from various viewpoints: axiology, sociology, politics, science (including the field of Academia). Perelman continued Dupréel's initiative and criticized classical rationalism for neglecting the social aspects of knowledge which was one of the intellectual reasons why the rationalists had never been able to reach an understanding of the problem of the *diversity and plurality of minds*.

Perelman drew some of his basic philosophical and rhetorical conclusions from Dupréel's assertion that every informal idea or theory is imperfect. Practically speaking, this means that every program, every order, every mind or group of minds can be improved. If they were perfect, if the achievement of perfection were at all possible, then pluralism would be indefensible.

The way the plurality of (imperfect) minds operates is through dialogue. Whatever the form of the dialogue may be, it is indispensable to understand and to be understood. Dialogue is a nourishment, a stimulant for the mind; it generates intellectual progress and is part of the nature of the mind itself. The isolated man must be even more imperfect than a man who is a member of the community of the "plurality of minds." Dialogue, conceived as the interrelation between speaker and audience, was deduced by the New Theory of Argumentation from pluralistic considerations and became a central focus in it.

Perelman developed Dupréel's idea that progress itself creates new problems and hindrances. The progress created by industrial techniques was a source of new disorders and new difficulties, particularly because militarism, imperialism, and the preponderance of economic power produced excesses.

In this connection Dupréel advanced a thesis which was not entirely new to the sociology of the beginning of our century, but he added a new dimension to it: the classical opposition of the individual and society has become more and more obsolete and should be replaced by the idea of the opposition of social groups because they are becoming the source of power, of exchange, and persuasion. Perelman also saw a threat to freedom in the acquisition of all forms of any activity by a single group; various social functions should be divided among many groups. The reduction to one group leads to totalitarianism which is the ultimate trap for freedom.

Let us stress that rhetorical pluralism is consciously and deliberately opposed to all forms of totalitarianism which are, philosophically, the final uniformity, *Gleichschaltung*, dogmatism, a belief in final truth and absolute value, a belief in the notion of a unique order without inherent conflicts. Perelman argued that the central philosophical and political problem is that in life and in reality we encounter conflicts.[30] Here he followed Dupréel, that what is most difficult and essential is "the search for means to moderate these conflicts, temper the antagonisms through a social technique centered on the notion of convention. Convention results from an accord of minds instituting freely a common order; diverse conventions allow for the institution of multiple order."[31]

Pluralism assumes that the "best" life, the incarnation of *Reason* will never be achieved; pluralism always seeks betterment, compromises, accommodations, and synthesis; it is rooted in the methodological significance of the *unclear idea*.[32] All these phenomena should embody one common feature: reasonableness. What is reasonable? What is rational? These problems will be discussed.

Once we conclude that pluralism must seek accommodation and compromise, then we must also conclude that individuals should not push their interests and convictions too far: they should be moderate. People can live reasonably, as individuals, as members of a group, and as citizens of the state, and in all three capacities at the same time, without endangering the foundation of the social edifice. They can live together in equilibrium, symbiotically, each person pursuing a way of life acceptable to all. Every individual can preserve a certain amount of freedom and individuality. Under any unitary, absolutistic order, Perelman wrote, pretending to represent absolute values, freedom consists only in the freedom to conform. Absolutistic orders impose conformity and every imposed conformity is intrinsically opposed to creative initiative and genuine freedom of choice. Freedom can be enjoyed and exercised only in a differentiated, pluralistic society where the individual can enter into a multiplicity of allegiances and at the same time transcend every group of which he is a member.

An original, pre-social liberty of the "noble" savage

or the anguished existentialist never existed. What exists in reality, if the notion of freedom is to have any sense, is "the freedom of the man who liberates himself from purely social imperatives and is capable of elaborating a moral ideal which gives meaning to his life, an assured direction to his action. It is the freedom of conscious man, who is not the toy of external forces." Consequently, it is misleading to say that man is born free. Freedom is not an attribute of man, it emerges in action. "It belongs only to the one who takes in hand the direction of his life and is completely responsible for his acts."[33]

Perelman's struggle against absolutism and monism did not lead him to a utilitarianism devoid of principles. In this connection let us observe that there is one common feature which Dupréel and Perelman share regarding pluralism. It is their opposition to all forms of pragmatism as a philosophy which esteems all values according to their utility. To Dupréel and Perelman, the merit of pragmatism is that it overcame the exclusive patterns of contemplative philosophy. Its shortcoming is the reduction of all values, even the value of knowledge, to their utility.

Dupréel distinguished between the *critical spirit* and the *dogmatic spirit*. This distinction has an immediate connection with Perelman's elaboration of rhetoric as the methodological foundation of pluralism.

The dogmatic spirit is characterized by an inclination to reject any criticism or questioning; it serves the purposes of certain social groups. The critical spirit is a disposition to respect every truth, known or to be discovered; it favors the opinions of minorities, it defends an emerging notion against dogmatic, conservative, well entrenched ideas, usually supported by established social groups. A critical mind is individualistic and liberal, whereas the dogmatic person attaches importance to tradition; a traditionalist must be more of a conformist than anyone else.

And this is the point where Perelman diverged from Dupréel's philosophy. This departure was not, of course, a rejection; it was a new exploration which went further and deeper into the problems, many of which had previously been explored by Dupréel.

He wrote:

> Personally, I would accord more importance to a notion which plays a significant role in Dupréel's thought, to which he refers frequently in his philosophy and sociology. This is the *agreement of minds* tied to the problem of persuasion. . . .
> . . . It is curious to state that Dupréel who gave such importance to persuasion and the agreement of minds, who knew so well Greek philosophy . . . did not perceive the importance of rhetoric for his own philosophy or its importance as a technique seeking to bring about an agreement of values . . . ."[34]

Dupréel's pluralism led to the rhetorical foundations, but Dupréel never arrived at that point himself. At the end of Dupréel's life, Perelman informed him of his own continuation of the pluralistic approach, and wrote that "as soon as our (Perelman's and Olbrechts-Tyteca's—M.M.) undertaking of a reevaluation of rhetoric was known to him, he perceived an immediate interest in it and received it sympathetically."[35]

4. Logic, Rationality and Pluralism

What are the main elements in the New Rhetoric which make it a methodological basis for pluralism and the reinterpretation of juridical positivism? They are three:

— a new solution for the relationship between the reasonable and the rational;
— the problem of the audience;
— the problem of dialogue.

There have always been a number of intellectuals who believed that to be persuasive one must simply present a clear, faultlessly logical argument, because people are spontaneously inclined to accept the truth. If one's case is just, rational, logically proven, then—as the well known reasoning goes—the mere power of the syllogism will be sufficient to sway the minds of anyone who is able to think and follow the reasoning. Those who accept this view may justly ask: why have rhetoric when we have logic? Do we not know the well established principle of non-contradiction, that two contradictory statements cannot at the same time be true? Do we not know the famous advice of Descartes: if two men have contrary judgments about the same thing, at least one must be mistaken and irrational, although it may be that both are in error?

As Descartes wrote: "For if the reasoning of either of them were certain and evident, he would be in a position to propound it to the other in such a wise as to convince him also of its truth."[36]

The first observation from the rhetorical point of view is that there are many spheres of life, there are human, practical, political, and moral problems which cannot be reduced to the antinomy: true or false.

According to the new rhetoric, the claim made by Descartes that any disagreement is an indisputable sign that at least one party is in error and is lacking rationality, is excessive and unreasonable. It may happen that both parties have good, reasonable opinions. They do not have self-evident truths, but they can be reasonable, which lies at the heart of the new rhetoric and pluralism.

Let us start our analysis of the rational and reasonable with an inquiry into the possible social and political consequences of the strict application of formal logic and experience when used as the *only* tools of demonstration and verification. If one restricts the rational as narrowly as the neo-positivists used to do, then nearly all of life concerning action (politics, morality), "is turned over to the irrational," because logical empiricism does not have any technique of justification "except one founded on the theory of probability."[37]

Strict adherence to the method of logical empiricism is unable to answer the simple question of why one should prefer one course of action over another. How can one *rationally* choose between various, often contradictory, ends? If quantitative measures are the only ones to be taken into account, then

> The only reasonable decision would seem to be one that is in conformity with utilitarian calculations. If so, all ends would be reduced to a single one of pleasure or utility, and all conflicts of values would be dismissed as based on futile ideologies.[38]

This reasoning of Perelman constitutes the heart of his argument against the neopositivistic concept of restricting or reducing the rational to formal logic and its syllogisms; that leads either to irrationalism in politics, law, and morality, or to the most vulgar quantitative utilitarian calculations. The reduction of the rational to one principle represents such intellectual impoverishment that it leads either to *irrational pluralism* (pluralism without reason, without any principles, or conviction), or to the *monism* of values. The monism of values is also irrational and unreasonable but it can be instrumental and often has been used for the purposes of authoritarian, totalitarian regimes, especially those which pretend to be based on rationality ("crackpot realism"—see below). The official Soviet theory of morality, for instance, introduces the following axiom as the basic norm of socialist ethics: what is moral is that which conforms to the task of achieving the victory of socialism and communism all over the world.[39] One may be critical that this concept reduces the problems of morality to the requirements of current Soviet political tactics and ideology. Once the given premises are assumed and fixed however, conclusions concerning morality, being syllogistically correct, are rational and therefore not arbitrary or capricious. But are they reasonable? Are they human?

The same manner of reasoning could be applied to the logical conclusions the Nazis drew from their premises, namely that the good of the *pure* German race should be regarded as the highest criterion of action, of politics, law, and morality. How could the "rational" Nazi conclusions be demolished? Are the logical, positivistic, or neopositivistic methods sufficient? The Nazi, Stalinist, or racist ideologies can be proved unreasonable only by the expanding of the framework of reason beyond formal logic, by rejecting the formalistic limitation of the sphere of reason.

> Now if one is not prepared to accept such a limitation to a monism of values in the world of action and would reject such a reduction on the ground that the irreducibility of many values is the basis of our freedom and of our spiritual life; if one considers how justification takes place in the most varied spheres—in politics, morals, law, the social sciences, and, above all, in philosophy—it seems obvious that our intellectual tools cannot be reduced to formal logic, even when that is enlarged by a theory for the control of induction and the choice of the most efficacious techniques.[40]

The conclusion is that the New Rhetoric is the intellectual basis of pluralism in all spheres of social activity, in every field of political, legal, and moral ideas. The New Rhetoric does not eliminate formal logic, but reserves its proper place for it in the totality of human reasoning. The New Rhetoric does not reject the value of syllogisms where deduction and induction are necessary, but presents them in their proper dimensions. The concept of the reasonable is, in its nature, antitotalitarian.

The question of the difference between the "rational" and the "reasonable" is not new. It has been discussed almost since the rise of modern rationalism. The problem has been dealt with in various ways, using multiple terminology, much of which is misleading, but neither the theoretical nor the practical importance of the question has ever been fully understood.

Well-known forms of presenting this problem are the popular sayings "this is logical, but not true;" or "this is logically correct, but not human."

In order to show how complicated this problem truly

is, Perelman stresses that both words, rational, and reasonable, derive from the same substantive, both connote a conformity to reason, but they are rarely interchangeable; one would call a deduction which conforms to the rules of logic, rational, but not necessarily reasonable; a compromise thereof, however, he adds, may be called reasonable. On the other hand: a rational decision may be unreasonable, and vice versa.

One of the most dramatic examples to illustrate this point was the one given by William Godwin on which Perelman comments. Godwin argued that there was no rationality in loving one's own father more than other persons unless it were possible to prove that one's father was a better human being than other men. Godwin's discussion may serve as an example of rational thinking, but one would hardly call it a reasonable or a human one.

This example and many others like it indicate that "the idea of reason can be taken in at least two diametrically opposed ways."[41]

This observation is one of the most important philosophical premises constituting the foundation of political, juridical and moral pluralism: rationalism may lead to monism and to absolutism; reasonableness to pluralism.

The *rational* may be described as that which "corresponds to mathematical reason, for some a reflection of divine reason, which grasps necessary relations."[42] The *rational* imposes itself on all reasoning beings because "it owes nothing to experience or to dialogue, and depends neither on education, nor on the culture of a milieu or an epoch." It is "associated with self-evident truths and compelling reasoning, is valid only in a theoretical domain."[43]

The true importance of this constrained concept of the rational becomes evident when it is applied to practical life, to the analysis of law, attitudes and behavior.

We qualify behavior as rational when it is "in conformity to principles, to the spirit of the system ... which chooses ends through knowledge of cause, makes use of the most efficacious means ... not allowing oneself to be held or led astray by the emotions or passions. According to Bertrand Russell, the rational man would only be an inhuman monster."[44]

The man who tries to be consistently rational, separates reason from his other faculties. He is a one-sided being, functioning like a machine "deprived of humanity and insensible to the reactions of the milieu."[45] Does this not remind you of the officer in Kafka's *Penal Colony*? The reasonable man behaves differently. The reasonable man is the one who often feels and acts contrary to formal logic. His judgment and behavior are "influenced by common sense, i.e., good sense." He endeavors to do what is acceptable by his own milieu, and if possible, by all. Even more, the reasonable man takes changing circumstances into account, the evolution of mankind, its sensitivity, the development of morality, the changing criteria of decency. For, "the reasonable of one age is not the reasonable of another..."[46] This is the essence of the rhetorical and dialectical concept of the reasonable; it is not fixed; it may even have different meanings for different social groups. Without such a broad concept of the reasonable, reason would become a closed fortress, a force and an instrument of ossification, rather than a basis for rejecting what is obsolete. What is reasonable changes with the development of mankind. It is possible and acceptable for a reasonable individual at one time to be affiliated with a variety of groups and institutions, as well as with many ideals and philosophies. Briefly, there is no theoretical or practical reason why a person cannot be persuaded that it is good to live in a pluralistic environment.

The rational can easily lead to an "unacceptable, biased, or socially inadmissible conclusion" even in the framework of acceptable political and legal institutions. When the rational, logical conclusion really leads to the unreasonable, we have to look for a compromise, or for a re-evaluation, and even the reconsideration of the whole system. In law, Perelman wrote, the idea of "the reasonable corresponds to an equitable solution."[47]

In general, what is reasonable opposes the uncritical acceptance of the established reality and always supports transcendence of an obsolete order. The reasonable pertains to pluralistic development; the rational pertains to stability.

There is an amazing similarity between Perelman's concept of the rational and C. Wright Mills' idea of "crackpot realism." Mills, a unique sociologist of our century, used this term in numerous books and essays with reference to eastern and western rulers, pseudo-intellectuals, ideologues, journalists, and scholars.

Mills wrote:

> In the American white-collar hierarchies and in the middle levels of the Soviet 'intelligentsia'—in quite differing ways but with often frightening convergence—there is coming about the rise of the cheerful robot, of the technological idiot, of the crackpot realist. All these types embody a common ethos: rationality without reason. The fate of these types and this ethos, what is done about them and what they do—that is the real, even the ultimate showdown . . . in our time . . . And it is an epochal showdown, separating the contemporary from the modern age.[48]

Mills accused the contemporary realists of both super-bureaucracies of rationalizing their crazy rules-of-the-game which prepare for world catastrophies. They do it in order to cope with the internal or external contradictions; they appeal to logic and to realism. According to their "rationalistic realism," to be a utopian (an unforgivable sin in today's world), means merely to accept values other than those of the power-elites and the upper levels of bureaucracy:

> But in truth, are not those who in the name of realism act like crackpots, are they not the utopians? Are we not now in a situation in which the only practical realistic down-to-earth thinking and acting is just what these crackpot realists call "utopian?"[49]

Here we approach yet another meaning of "reasonableness" or "reasonable realism": it is the defense of what is reasonable, possible, and desirable rather than a capitulation to what is called necessary reality. Rationalists accept every reality as necessary, whereas the truly reasonable man tries to overcome the reality which has become obsolete, unreasonable, and therefore unnecessary. A pure rationalist must view the first roots of the future as utopian, whereas the reasonable man is able to see in them the first signs of a new development of new future forms, of an enriching pluralistic experience for society. Indeed, one could even argue that it would be difficult to be truly rationalistic without being reasonable, without looking forward instead of backward.

A limited rationalism, reduced to formal syllogisms, is used today as the philosophical bulwark of modern, "mindless" conservatism.[50]

> While the intellectuals have been embraced by the new conservative gentility, the silent conservatives have assumed political power .... The silent conservatives of corporations, army and state have benefited by the antics of the petty right ... these men have replaced mind by the platitude, and the dogmas by which they are legitimated are so widely accepted that no counter-balance of mind prevails against them. Such men as these are crackpot realists, who, in the name of realism have constructed a paranoid reality all their own and in the name of practicality have projected a utopian image of capitalism.[51]

Apart from Mills' various sociological and political concepts one can agree that the above sentences describe the political sense of modern pseudo-rationalism, lacking reasonableness, which serves to justify the social and political status quo in the modern world; it justifies all the basic modern forms of conservatism, the mindlessness which is almost *a priori* inimical to any innovation, to true evolution and to democratic pluralism. Modern rationalism tends toward uniformity, toward *Gleichschaltung*, and presents stability as a logical demand of pure reason, whereas the reasonable counteracts uniformity, undermines any form of absolute order and presupposes pluralism in every sphere of life, in the material and spiritual, the economic and political.

The New Rhetoric, as applied to morality, law, and politics, declares that one can and should find a reasonable basis for justifying rules of behavior, especially political rules. The New Rhetoric rejects that attitude so characteristically expressed, for instance, by Professor Leonard G. Miller, that it is meaningless to seek justification in the sphere of moral principles.[52] Many generations of philosophers since Hume have argued that it is impossible to demonstrate the desirability of one set of moral rules over another. The New Rhetoric, on the contrary, holds that it is possible to find a justification for moral norms and to produce reasonable arguments for legal and political decisions. This process of justification, however, cannot be accomplished by formal logic alone.

The domain of the logician's investigations must be enlarged. This enlargement would complete formal logic through the study of what since Socrates has been called *dialectics*. To avoid all misunderstandings concerning the meaning of this term, Perelman prefers to qualify it as argumentation, and contrast it with formal logic conceived as the theory of demonstrative proof.[53]

One formulates moral principles beacuse one has reasons to formulate them. Anyone with reasons can argue whether they should be adopted at all, and if so, how they should be applied to a given situation or controversy.

According to the New Rhetoric, the mere expression, "the justification of norms," is an oversimplification, and an "inexact way"[54] to characterize various modalities of human behavior. Behavior can be described not as "true" or "false," but as right or wrong.

Philosophical positivism is unable to cope with the problems of the irrationality or reasonableness of norms of behavior. Positivists assimilate the justification of norms into the formalistic, logical, demonstration of propositions. For to ask about truth in our behavior (its rules, norms, principles) is senseless because our actions and decisions cannot be "true." They can be described as correct, expedient, reasonable, equitable, thoughtful, conforming to moral principles or legal rules. Our decisions and actions are of course based on information. The information may be true or false, and truthfulness or falsity may influence our decisions and behavior, but "only on the condition that those truths and facts are appreciated as a function of values and norms which transform them into reasons for pragmatically determined decisions and action."[55]

The New Rhetoric is not a theory of pure contemplation, but a theory of argumentation for practical purposes in order to find a way to make the most reasonable, efficient, and just decisions which might gain the maximum support of an audience divided by various controversies.

These considerations have brought us to the sphere of jurisprudence and philosophy of law.

For over a century, whether what traditionally is known as legal logic actually exists has been in dispute. Perelman argued that to the degree that jurists only use schemes such as the syllogism or the *modus ponens*, there is little basis for speaking of legal logic just as there is no reason to speak of "zoological" or "astronomical". logic, for the simple reason that there is only one logic. The real problem is whether logic reduced to formal logic allows one to resolve juridical controversies.

"Certainly not. It is exceptional that the controversies come about from the fact that one of the antagonists commits an error of formal logic. It would suffice to show him the error so that he might retract it, like every normal person who has been shown his mistake in addition."[56]

For basic philosophical reasons the New Rhetoric rejected as inadequate the so-called *formalisme juri-*

dique, the *Begriffsjurisprudenz* and all attempts to make formal logic "the heart of law."

Formal logic can and should be used, but by itself it cannot interpret or apply the law. Whenever legal rules are interpreted, the spirit of the law and all relevant circumstances must be taken into account and not only the letter.

"The opposition between the letter and spirit is the stumbling block of mechanical jurisprudence."[57]

If it were possible to adhere strictly to the letter of the law and only the letter and to forget about the *ratio juris* completely, then the application of "mechanical jurisprudence" based on formal logic only would be possible but still very difficult. It would be difficult even to observe the first precondition for applying formal logic, the demand that the same signs always preserve the same meaning. Without this precondition, the law of identity ceases to be valid, and as a result, for example, a contradiction would no longer be false.

There are situations to which courts or authorities must find solutions, although the law has not foreseen such situations, nor prescribed any solutions for them. What should be done in such cases? Other means must be found which Aristotle specified as dialectical reasoning, and Perelman characterized "as a recourse to argumentation."[58]

A judge, or whoever applies legal rules, is not only a mouthpiece of the law, or a preprogrammed calculator. He is a social, thinking being who confronts various values pertaining to the given legal, and social system, and he must serve these values and understand their hierarchy. Every decision rendered by a judge, even one based upon explicit legal material, remains nevertheless personal.[59] Every case analyzed by him is the result of an elaborate, individual, practical act of reasoning. All legal reasoning bears this personal imprint. It is not a formal demonstration, but always an argument aiming to persuade those whom it addresses.

The underpinning of a judge's reasoning and the decision he renders is essentially legal, yet it is intertwined with other "good" reasons, moral, political, economic, and religious reasons. The point, however, is that the underpinnings considered good at one period and in one milieu will not be the same as in every other. They are socially and morally conditioned as are the convictions of the audience they address and try to convince.

According to the New Rhetoric, the application of law is creative, and every time legal norms are applied some interpretation is required. The famous rule: *interpretatio cessat in claris* (interpretation ceases when the text is clear), does not make much sense, because in order

> to decide that a text is clear we must see if any reasonable interpretation of it that could be given would lead to a similar solution for all other individual cases. But we are never sure that all concrete situations have been examined. A text considered in relation to known cases could pose a problem of interpretation in a new situation.[60]

There are numerous examples of how courts have interpreted even explicit constitutional texts in terms of the accepted state of affairs at the time the texts were interpreted.[61]

The introduction of the theory of argumentation, or rhetoric, into legal reasoning is necessary because mere legal reasoning is charged with tension because of the propensity to conciliate stability with change, continuity with adaptation, security with justice, equity with the common good. The special esteem which legal security enjoys in legal reasoning distinguished it from other practical reasoning. Legal philosophy, and legal practice, therefore, usually try to minimize the role of the personal will, whims, opinions, and accidental perceptions.

> But the personal factor cannot be eliminated from legal reasoning. Like all argumentation, being the function of the people who argue, its value will depend, in the final analysis, upon the integrity and intelligence of the judges who determine its specific nature.[62]

One more aspect should be borne in mind when assessing the role of creativity and argumentation in the process of justice: the judiciary, under any constitutional system of the division of powers, cannot be subordinated to the legislative power entirely. If it were, then the judge's role would be limited to the establishment of facts, subsuming them under a legal text, and drawing appropriate conclusions in the form of a syllogism.[63] Such would constitute not the rule of law, but the rule of the letter of the law (if this were indeed possible) over the spirit of the law.

Since World War II, the judge's power over the interpretation and application of law has steadily been growing in western European countries. More and more, the general principles of law must be taken into consideration by judges. In this way a rapprochement between the Continental and the Anglo-Saxon judicial systems has begun and is still in progress. "The role of the European judge has markedly grown and approaches that of his Anglo-Saxon colleague .... A less formalistic vision of law is arising in legal positivism in its present form."[64]

The methodological basis for the rapprochement between Anglo-Saxon and Continental jurisprudence and the practice of law is the acceptance of the theory of argumentation and its pluralistic attitude: jurists use this methodology and theory, although, like Moliere's hero, Mr. Jourdain, they do not know that they speak prose. The jurists subscribe more and more to the opinion that:

> In a political community or before a court we may have to choose between several equally reasonable eventualities; the criterion for the decision can be recognized by everyone as involving opportune considerations, but this does not in the least imply that the solution that has been put aside is unreasonable.[65]

Once the restriction to formal logic and its demands for achieving a uniform interpretation and application of a given legal norm were overcome, the specifics of dialogue entered upon the scene. Pluralistic solutions openly became admissible. What is reasonable and equitable is freely asking for its due.

5. Dialogue, Rhetorical Arguments, Truth

Dialogue is the form and the soul of the process of argumentation. The first precondition for the existence of dialogue is the interest of both participants in an exchange of ideas. In order to converse, some kind of intellectual communion must exist. The purpose of all dialogue and argumentation is to persuade minds.

The second precondition for the existence of dialogue is freedom for the participants. The interlocutor must feel free, he should not be afraid to raise doubts, to ask questions, to use counter-arguments. If he is afraid, he may agree outwardly, but his mind will remain unchanged. One cannot gain the adherence of the minds of those who fear to express their ideas openly and hesitate actively to participate in the dialogue. It is also true that the repetition of arguments can have an impact; nevertheless the manner of persuasion can hardly be called rational when the audience is not invited to participate actively, but is merely the passive recipient of what they are supposed to believe and accept.

There are certain devotees of science — Perelman called them "rationalistic"[66] — who say that facts speak for themselves. This is an illusion. No facts, theses, theories, even those which seem to be obvious and manifestly truthful, will by themselves win the adherence of human minds. Every speaker (writer) knows his audience more or less, and knows whom he wants to address.

> We consider it preferable to define an audience, for the purposes of rhetoric, as the ensemble of those whom the speaker wishes to influence by his argumentation.[67]

This concept of the audience is a very important element in the New Rhetoric. One must know his audience in order to select suitable arguments, as well as the right form for presenting them in order to reach the listeners (readers) and to persuade them.

At times one tries to persuade one individual. But generally speaking, for socially valid reasons, the point of departure should not be the individual with his specific emotions, prejudices, or idiosyncracies, but the social group which has combined in itself the *essential* common opinions and interests. The speaker should know what distinguishes one social environment from another; he should understand that the most important factors, from the sociological viewpoint, are: "the social functions exercised by its listeners."[68] Either a speaker (writer) will be able to adapt himself to the given audience or he will risk antagonizing them. He can even make an impression on many individuals who may be fond of him as a human being and appreciate him as an impressive personality, but who would nevertheless reject the cause for which he was pleading. According to the theory of argumentation the speaker (writer) should always be aware that the audience is like Heraclitus' river: it is continuously changing, therefore, the truly great orator should know the art of "continuous adaptation."[69] But one should not identify "adaptation" with a lowering of rhetoric to the level of mere "flattery," of telling "lies" and "pleasantries" according to the wishes of the given constituency. The New Rhetoric is not the art of immorality:

> ... it must not be overlooked that the orator is nearly always at liberty to give up persuading an audience when he cannot persuade it effectively except by the use of methods that are repugnant to him. It should not be thought, where argument is concerned, that it is always honorable to succeed in persuasion, or even to have such an intention. The problem of harmonizing the scruples of the man of honor with submission to the audience received special attention from Quintilian. To him rhetoric as *scientia bene dicendi* implies that the accomplished orator not only is good at persuading, but also says what is good.[70]

One of the most important characteristics of the art of true rhetoric is what rhetoric is not. It is not a *scientia male dicendi*. It is not the art of using immoral means for immoral ends. It is not an art which can be used by unscrupulous public relations manipulators who serve dictators, despots, or depraved politicians who are prepared to promise everything not intending to deliver anything. This explains why the New Rhetoric introduced the idea of the universal audience, including the audience of the philosophers that can be convinced only by arguments acceptable to all.

Only perverted forms of the New Rhetoric can be used by despotic, totalitarian rulers. Why? Because the theory of argumentation presupposes a dialogue with the audience and any active audience will sooner or later detect deliberate lies and misrepresentations. One may or may not be persuaded by arguments. When argumentation fails to persuade, that still does not mean that it was completely wrong, unjust, or unfounded. Arguments can be rejected by an audience for various reasons, but lies used in a free exchange of arguments can be brought to light sooner than in any other way. There are no guarantees against deception, but the deception is more difficult to perform and to remain undetected when the interlocutor is free to think, to speak, to collect material, to investigate the case, when he is free and prepared to take part in the process of argumentation.

The New Rhetoric is meant as an art of persuasion, of gaining the adherence of normal people who are not angels, but not scoundrels either.

The New Rhetoric is the art of winning over the minds and adherence of the people who may be mistaken, but at least have the good will to commence thinking about an issue. The New Rhetoric is meant to be a Diogenes' lamp for those who travel along a road which is dimly lit, full of hazardous curves, and traverses unknown domains.

The New Rhetoric does not take anything for granted. And Perelman's fight against all the open or hidden vestiges of the theory of Descartes that truth is what "I see clearly and distinctly" became one of the most important philosophical battles.

Descartes' postulate first to doubt and then to accept for truth "what I see clearly and distinctly" was important and progressive in the seventeenth and eighteenth centuries. The official theological teachings did not project anything which the common mind could see clearly and distinctly. The simplest Cartesian principles of obviousness, of dividing theses into the most simple predicates, of throughly reviewing the results, were in their very nature anti-theological. As was proved especially by Voltaire in his philosophical essays, common sense could act as the sword which cuts the Gordian Knot of theology, feudalism, and absolutism. But in the twentieth century the same common sense ceased to be such an effective weapon against new attacks coming from the Hobbesian Kingdom of Darkness, especially in the industrial democracies and in the communist totalitarian countries. Why? Because the new Kingdom of Darkness has started to present itself as a realm of logic and reason. And in order to win adherents, it uses what passes for reason. Rationality is used against Reason. Reason therefore should be strengthened by the new theory of argumentation and it should also be clearly stated that reasonable solutions can be and must be pluralistic.

Mass propaganda in a mass society, the "selling" of

ideas, of presidents, and even the clergy, tends to channel thoughts into a one-track, one-way flow, alleged obviousness. It is a pseudo "common sense" which, together with blatant irrationalism, has become one of the worst and the most dangerous of enemies of reason in the modern, industrial democracies.

Rhetoric is a way of overcoming the power of appearances,[71] of dogmas, myths, and the "obvious truths" of common sense. The rhetorical flow of arguments, the appeal to the audience and invitation to join in dialogue — these are the tools for criticism of simplistic ideas which remain deeply ingrained in the minds of people who, generally speaking, are rather critical, innovative, and even creative in their professional lives but unable or unwilling to apply the same demanding criteria to a many-sided analysis of social and political issues.

The New Rhetoric takes into consideration that the lack of a critical attitude is widespread, that many people are not very acute and are unschooled in dialectics. Such people take for granted as logical, obvious, and rational, what needs to be proved. They accept old concepts at their face value in new circumstances which invalidate them. In our century, as before, there are many ideas which have mushroomed to the cancerous proportions of myths, which have been accepted and used out of their historical and social context. These doctrines are not interpreted in connection with the evolution of society, its economic and political structure, its constitutional and governing institutions. Those who interpret "democracy," "freedom," "free competition," "forces of the free market," "rule of the majority," "democratic socialism," "socialist humanism," and others as they were understood in the nineteenth century, commit the error of ahistoricism.

In this situation it is traditional logic which can be used to explain, justify, and rationalize every "being," every thing that is. Formal logic does not question the premises, while Rhetoric on the other hand, examines everything. It does not take anything for granted; it rejects all the explicit or implicit assumptions, premises, and propositions, compelling people to cut down into the roots of common-sense itself.

Two notions are especially pertinent to the problem of the relationship between the New Rhetoric and the democratic concept of pluralism: facts, and truths.

No matter what we may discuss or when we may discuss it, be it the problem of opinions or of convictions, or persuasion — we sooner or later revert to the basic question posed by Pontius Pilate: "And what is truth?" This seemingly simple question posed either through curiosity or cynicism, from concern or skepticism (we return to this problem — see below), compels one to examine the classic Aristotelian definitions and descriptions.

> A falsity is a statement of that which is that it is not, of that which is not that it is; and a truth is a statement of that which is that it is, or that which is not that it is not. Hence, he who states of anything that it is, or that it is not, will either speak truly or speak falsely.[72]

Furthermore

> ... *thought* either affirms or denies every object of *thought* or intelligible object; and this is clear from the definition when *thought* thinks truly or falsely. When it connects in one way by asserting or denying, it thinks truly, when in the other way, it thinks falsely.[73]

And again

> For in the case of truth, affirmation is of objects which are combined, and denial of objects which are divided, but in the case of falsity, affirmation is of objects which are divided and denial of objects which are combined."[74]

Man thinks truly if he thinks, that what

> ... is separated is separated and what is united is united, but falsely if his thought is contrary to the way in which things exist. Now it is not because we think truly of your being white that you are white, but it is because you are white that we speak truly in saying that you are white.[75]

Aristotle's definitions are basic, general and, incomplete. They lay down the main lines, but do not solve all problems of the theory of truth and knowledge; they are an excellent beginning.

Two Aristotelian premises are of great importance for any theory of knowledge (epistemology) and for Rhetoric: the world exists independently of our minds and it can be and is perceived more or less accurately by our minds. Our minds are like mirrors, Francis Bacon asserted, "uneven mirrors," but mirrors nevertheless.

The world of things and that of ideas are not two worlds. There is one world of things and their perception by the human mind. People therefore can be persuaded to change their minds either through real changes occurring in the objective world, including the social and political fields, or through appeals to their minds. Those are the two ways in which the ideas and perceptions of people are changed. Various combinations of the two methods are of course possible. Changes in our thoughts can of course happen, even though there are no changes in the existing world, by a change in the understanding only, which, in turn, can be followed by a genuine change in objective social and political situations. According to the classic Aristotelian understanding, truth is finally a subjective reflection of the objective reality in the human mind. How we should deal with the "objectivity" we more or less know; but how should we deal with the exigencies of subjectivity, especially in the field of politics, economics, and morality? In order to answer this question, we have to enter a new realm: rhetorical epistemology.

Remembering these brief reminders of the Aristotelian concept of truth, let us analyze rhetorical epistemology.

From the standpoint of argumentation, "facts" are certain types of data based on objective reality; "facts" designate what has been agreed upon by a given audience as incontrovertible.

> But it follows that no statement can be assured of definitively enjoying this status, because the agreement can always be called in question later, and one of the parties to the debate may refuse to qualify his opponent's affirmation as a fact.[76]

How is it that a fact can cease to be fact? There are two ways in which this can happen — doubts have to be raised within the given audience, or the given audience has been expanded and the new audience questions what was incontestable to the former.[77]

Does this imply that "facts" are completely subjective, that they depend completely on the agreement of the participants in a debate? The problem is that rhetorical debate does not concern the narrow problems of the natural sciences where an experiment can be repeated in order to dispel all doubts. From the standpoint of argumentation it is the power of an argument that has to influence and persuade the audience, to support, for example this or that political party or the continuation or discontinuation of an expensive weapons' system. There is no ultimate criterion which could make something a fact independently of a listener's attitude.

> Nevertheless, we may recognize that there are certain conditions favoring this agreement rendering the fact easily defensible in the face of the opponent's mistrust or ill will. This is the case in particular, when there is an agreement on conditions for verification. . . . Accepted facts may be either observed facts — this is perhaps the case for most premises — or supposed, agreed facts, facts that are possible or probable. There is thus a considerable mass of elements that is compelling to the hearer or which the speaker strives to make compelling.[78]

Facts become facts in the process of argumentation, when they are accepted and agreed upon as facts. But their lives may be brief during argumentation because they may be challenged at any time by other facts and must be defended against them. A fact without the power of reason behind it cannot survive by itself in our competitive world. A fact does not possess its own vitality or power to live autonomously.

A fact in argumentation is nothing more than a subjective reflection of the objective reality so long as it is not undermined by the counterarguments of its adversaries.

All observations concerning facts are applicable to "truths," as well, albeit in a more complex way.

What is the difference between facts and truths? From the standpoint of argumentation the difference is relative. "The term 'facts' is generally used to designate objects of precise, limited agreement, whereas the term 'truth' is preferably applied to more complex systems relating to connections between facts."[79]

Philosophical discussions concerning the relationship between facts, truths, and their theories are too numerous to explore here. Some philosophers believe that the distinctions must always be imprecise and misleading because in the real world nothing is isolated and it would therefore be difficult to make a reasonable statement regarding facts (with the exception of platitudes, such as, Columbus discovered America in 1492) independently of the whole complexity of relationships. Nevertheless, the above distinction is helpful with regard to the theory of argumentation and is legitimized through the purpose intended, its practical application in discourse. "It is also possible to so conceive their relationship that the statement of a fact is truth and that any truth enunciates a fact."[80]

We return to the fundamentals: the link between Aristotelian *Metaphysics* (with its theory of truth), and Aristotle's *Rhetoric* (as the theory of argumentation) which was re-established by the New Rhetoric, namely, that truth is connected with the reflection of "objective reality," with its assessment, the perception of it and ultimately, with the practical activity which dialectically influences reality.

The theory of argumentation with its discursive concept of facts and truths is wholly dialectical: it connotes nothing, nothing established, nothing taken for granted. And yet it is indispensable in the search for truth, progress, beauty, human freedom. *Eternal values* (with their everchanging content) *can be founded only on the rock of doubt and contradiction.*

We have now established the element linking the New Rhetoric with pre-Aristotelian and Aristotelian contributions. The new theory of argumentation goes beyond Aristotle because among other things it was able consciously to absorb the pre-Aristotelian, sophist period of the evolution of our civilization; the teachings of Gorgias and Protagoras were reevaluated by the tradition of Dupréel.

Western culture has generally held that any conclusions reached by *human thought* must be a personal, subjective conviction, that every conclusion must be examined, the result of an investigation, and not merely blind belief.

Such is the concept of rhetorical discourse. Everything that falls into the stream of argumentation changes its meaning and place in the system of thought, invading the substance of the system itself. Rhetorical discourse reshapes the essence; and the reformed essence itself shines through and becomes more general, yet particular, at the same time. It becomes more distant but it embraces more.

Rhetorical argumentation never ceases, it does not know stops, breaks, or pauses. Rhetorical truth is like Heraclitus' river: you cannot step into the same river twice; it flows continually. And truth, although ever-changing, still remains something tangible and applicable, because it is continuously questioned in the endless dialogue of unlimited and various audiences. Heraclitus observed: "Opposition is good ... everything originates in strife ... hidden harmony is better than apparent harmony."[81]

Rhetoric is an instrument for establishing the true,

hidden, harmony which lurks under the surface. Rhetoric always reminds us that "the fairest harmony comes out of differences."[82]

Those who look for truth and harmony in solidarity, peace, and rest, should be reminded of the philosopher's warning: "Every beast is driven to pasture with blows . . . Asses would rather have straw than gold . . . Dogs bark at the man they do not know."[83]

Are we condemned to eternal doubt and unrest? Oh, no! "In changing, it rests . . ." and that "which tends to destruction . . . is called concord and peace."[84] Such are the pre-Socratic wellsprings of the New Rhetoric.

The intrinsic link between the rhetorical methodology and pluralism is that there is nothing perfect; no social group or party can have a monopoly upon absolute wisdom and knowledge.

We return to the previous ideas of this chapter: the New Rhetoric constitutes a philosophical and methodological basis for the democratic concept of pluralism. It is an instrument of analysis and synthesis not conceived abstractly, but regarded as a part of creative social activity.

The idea of pluralism as conceived by the New Rhetoric is diametrically opposed to the philosophy and methodology of scepticism or relativism, as understood by Hans Kelsen, for instance.[85] In his famous, already classical considerations about Pontius Pilate, Kelsen argued that the act of washing hands was a truly and consistently democratic act because there is no valid criterion to distinguish between the value of life of a convicted criminal and a man who identified himself with the messenger of truth. "And what is truth?" Pilate said ironically, as Kelsen indicated.

Hans Kelsen wrote that once we accept the relativistic concept that truth cannot be known, that everything is relative (except relativity), then we must also accept as justifiable the behavior and decision of the cynical Roman governor. It may be that an intellectually consistent, logical, and rationalistic skeptic and relativist could agree with Kelsen's conclusions. But they are not acceptable to the New Rhetoric or to pluralism based on argumentation.

The New Rhetoric does not reject all moral, political, social, legal, and philosophical ideals as senseless or worthless. It only subjects these ideals, their interpretation, and application to endless critical scrutiny. Rhetoric does not tell people to stop having their conflicts because everything is equally bad or good. It only teaches people the old Roman wisdom: *quidquid agis — prudenter agas et respice finem*. Be reasonable — whatever you do; whatever you decide — subject it to dialectical criticism and argumentation. Look beyond the end of your nose.

According to rhetorical methodology solutions may be worse or better, with every development of society; with the advent of new arguments what was worse can become better (or at least seem so), and vice versa. Even more, one may find a better third, fourth, or fifth solution, because we, our lives, our social and political systems are not confined to the apodictic either-or, take it or leave it, love it or hate it.

The method of Rhetoric is against dogmatism; it is for pluralism, for democracy, for unlimited intellectual freedom.

Rhetorical thought and expression is against conservatism, because it finds contradictions everywhere and struggles for new solutions; nothing is faultless or perfect for it. It is also against all types of radicalism, because every radicalism overlooks or disregards the elements of the existing reality and prevailing philosophy which are, or could still be, beneficial to society.

Rhetoric favors reasonable compromises, not to halt the evolution of social relations, legal systems, or political institutions, but to foster this evolution by critically rejecting what has become obsolete and critically defending what is developing or should be given permission to be born and to live.

For the New Rhetoric, compromise is not an unprincipled, cowardly, solution, but on the contrary:

> At the theoretical level, it is the compromise solution to incompatibilities which calls for the greatest effort and is most difficult to justify because it requires a new structuring of reality. On the other hand, once it is established, once the concepts have been dissociated and restructured, compromise tends to appear as the inescapable solution and to react on the aggregate of concepts into which it is inserted.[86]

Compromise is an instrument and a generator of further evolution, because it is a result of the conflict of opposing forces. Compromise does not pretend to resolve all incompatibilities forever; on the contrary, it creates new sources of struggle and motion. Compromise itself is a result of the pluralistic society. Conscious, reasonable, compromises help to promote the development of democratic institutions.

Rhetorical methodology is consistently pluralistic in the evaluation of reality, in the criticism of ideas and ideals, in acceptance and in rejection. In brief, the New Rhetoric is an indispensable methodology for a pluralistic conception of reality. For the first time pluralism has found a consistently elaborated methodology which it previously lacked. It was lacking in the thought of Dupréel and its lack was obvious in American philosophy and jurisprudence.

6. Rhetoric and Politics

Chaim Perelman created his New Rhetoric after WW II. Regarded from the limited viewpoint of the art of rhetoric, it succeeded two contradictory experiences: The liberal-democratic-parliamentary, and the totalitarian.

The liberal-democratic-parliamentary experience began in Western countries with the advent of democratic-parliamentary forms of government. Various countries reached this stage of evolution at different periods, but the most powerful impetus on the road to liberal democracy was the English, French, and American revolutions.

The importance of rhetoric grew immensely in democratic societies. There was a need for discussions, arguments, and speeches in the courts and in the parliaments, in city halls, and in the myriad boards, clubs and associations during election campaigns and at meetings of every description.

A citizen is always playing two roles in democratic public life: that of a speaker (orator, writer) and that of a listener, that of a proponent and that of an audience. Rhetoric under western democracy serves to achieve various goals: the noble and immoral, the progressive and conservative if not reactionary. It is an instrument for ascertaining truth and it can serve as a tool to promote falsehoods and illusions.

After having taken all the pros and cons of rhetoric into account, one must say that in western democratic systems rhetoric plays the same important role it had in the ancient Greek polis: it is an indispensable tool to strengthen democracy, to search for truth, and to promote the ideas of freedom, justice, equality, equal protection under the law, and the defense of reasonable public laws. Rhetoric can often be perverted and corrupted in a democracy, but it cannot lose its humanistic essence in this system, it cannot be deprived of its inseparable connection with reasonable humane feelings.

Rhetoric in modern Western civilization, as it was in ancient Greece, is the effect, cause, and instrument of the growth of culture and freedom of thought.

Mankind has experienced another kind of rhetoric and oratory in the twentieth century: the totalitarian type.

The fascists, and especially the German Nazis, were able to employ and develop the art of rhetoric against rhetoric's own humanistic, democratic, and rationalistic purposes. For the first time in history the art of rhetoric was systematically, skillfully, deliberately, officially, and openly used against the basic norms of decency and morality. With brutal sincerity Adolf Hitler announced in *Mein Kampf* that his appeals would be aimed at those who are unwise and uneducated, at those who are unable to think critically, who are inclined to believe everything they read and are told. This type of rhetoric must be analyzed closely.

There are three categories — one reads in *Mein*

Kampf — of readers and listeners: First, those who believe everything they are told; second, those who have ceased to believe in anything; third, those who examine everything critically.

> Numerically the first group is by far the largest. It consists of the great mass of the people and consequently represents the simplest-minded part of the nation. It cannot be listed in terms of professions, but at most in general degrees of intelligence. To it belong all those who have neither been born nor trained to think independently, and who partly from incapacity and partly from incompetence believe everything that is set before them in black and white ... They are not able or willing themselves to examine what is set before them, and as a result their whole attitude toward all the problems of the day can be reduced almost exclusively to the outside influence of the others.[87]

Having decided that the great majority of the people are unable or unwilling to think critically and independently, Hitler drew his own conclusions which can be narrowed down to three principles:

1. The state must exercise strict control over the press and its output; it must censor broadcasts, speeches, and all other possible forms of expression and the transmission of ideas and emotions. All that is not in accord with Nazi ideology must be prohibited and eradicated with "ruthless determination,"[88] the state "must not let itself be confused by drivel about so-called 'freedom of the press' and let itself be talked into neglecting its duty."[89]

The first recommendation then is that all forms of information and propaganda not approved by the State and the ruling party, be eliminated; the scene of action must be cleared, *"Macht die Strassen frei"*; only the functionaries and licensees of the government are permitted to move here.

2. Furthermore, Hitler continued, all necessary conclusions must be drawn from the factual findings, namely, that the majority of the people are simple-minded and uncritical; the means of influence and persuasion through propaganda are to be adjusted to the mediocre, low level of the public's intellect.

> All propaganda must be popular and its intellectual level must be adjusted to the most limited intelligence among those to whom it is addressed. Consequently, the greater the mass it is intended to reach, the lower its purely intellectual level will have to be . . . we must avoid excessive intellectual demands on our public. . . . It is a mistake to make propaganda many-sided, like scientific instruction. . . . The receptivity of the great masses is very limited, their intelligence is small, but their power of forgetting is enormous.[90]

In order to grasp fully the substance of fascist rhetoric, it is important to keep in mind that according to them, simple-minded and uncritically thinking people are not only those who lack formal education and schooling, but also those who have earned university degrees and are not "critically-minded." These educated people could still be childishly naive in their political thinking. Representatives of political naivete can be met everywhere, in every profession and even among eminent professors of philosophy like Heidegger or Carl Schmitt, to name two, and in every social stratum. The fascists depended on this group and deliberately lowered the intellectual level of their appeals.[91]

3. Since this propaganda rhetoric is not to be intellectual training and is not to be aimed at those who strive for knowledge or education, it must aim at the emotions:

"The more modest its intellectual ballast, the more exclusively it takes into consideration the emotions of the masses, the more effective it will be . . .

The art of propaganda lies in understanding the emotional ideas of great masses and finding, through a psychologically correct form, the way to the attention and thence to the heart of the broad masses."[92]

Therein lies the clue to the totalitarian type of propaganda conceived as one-sided rhetoric: every issue is to be reduced to a banality which can be expressed in a slogan. This slogan is to be worded and disseminated to appeal to the emotions, to strengthen, or even to create them if need be. The simplistic "truth" which propaganda rhetoric wants to convey must be repeated constantly and everywhere. The carefully selected propaganda slogans must be repeated "until the last member of the public understands what you want him to understand by your slogan."[93] Propaganda rhetoric "must confine itself to a few points and be repeated over and over."[94] Persistence is "the first and most important requirement for success."[95] Every novelty, every change is "the mortal enemy of any effective political propaganda."[96] If any changes are to be made in slogans they should alter the form, but "in the end they must always say the same thing."[97]

The masses move slowly, Hitler said. They require a certain time before they are ready to notice anything. Therefore:

". . . only after the simplest ideas are repeated thousands of times will the masses finally remember them. . . .

All advertising, whether in the field of business or politics, achieves success through continuity and sustained uniformity of its application."[98]

These prescriptions constitute a thoughtful, deliberate attempt to degrade rhetoric, to lower and corrupt it into a tool of deception and misinformation. Totalitarian rhetoric everywhere and always instigates fears, prejudices, hatred, unfounded optimism, the feeling of mysterious dangers, the perception of alienation, and

mystical ties. From an instrument dedicated to the promotion of thought it was perverted into a deadly weapon to kill all culture.

* * *

There are certain important similarities between the times when Aristotle wrote his *Rhetoric* and the period when Chaim Perelman revived the old methodology and created his *New Rhetoric*.

The true art of rhetoric was born out of Greek democracy in the fifth century, B.C. The art of persuasion and argumentation can flourish only in an *open society* (this is the expression used by Pericles in his funeral speech quoted by Thucydides), when its people are not afraid to express their thoughts. Even more, it is their social duty to speak out and say what is on their minds. Free speech, discussion, and exchange of ideas are the prerequisites for normal, open society and social relations. On the other hand, they are necessary for a democratic public life. Democracy and its continuous struggles, which to the inexperienced seem futile, noisy, full of rivalry and selfishness in enhancing an individual's image while distorting and ridiculing those of political rivals, all these ordinary, democratic activities, demand from the people an ability to express their thoughts, project their programs, and describe their true or feigned feelings. The people who participate in the daily business of living must possess the indispensable art of influencing and persuading their fellow countrymen. Democracy without rhetoric cannot exist. And vice versa: rhetoric as the true art of appealing simultaneously to the intellect and feeling[99] can develop and flourish only in a democracy, in a society in which a multiplicity of groups exists — social, political, ideological, and philosophical. Rhetoric at the same time nourishes democratic processes and promotes liberties, creates and dissolves groups. Rhetoric is one of the necessary instruments of developing and strengthening democracy and its pluralistic values.

In his analysis of the contribution which the Sophists made in philosophy, morality, and oratory, Hegel stressed the interdependence of ancient democracy and the foundation of rhetoric:

> Thus the Sophists were more especially the teachers of oratory, and that is the aspect in which the individual could make himself esteemed amongst the people as well as carry out what was best for the people; this certainly characterizes a democratic constitution, in which the citizens have the ultimate decision. Because, in this way, oratory was one of the first requirements for the rule of a people, or for making something clear for them through their ordinary ideas, the Sophists trained the men for common Greek life, for citizenship and for statesmen, without appearing to prepare State officials for an examination in specific subjects.[100]

Aristotle wrote his *Rhetoric* in the decline of Greek democracy and independence. He wrote in a period when the art of rhetoric had been abused, rather than properly used. Aristotle assembled all the known theoretical and empirical elements into one coherent entity. True, he did so, as Hegel would say . . . at dusk.

The owl of Minerva spread her wings at sunset. This observation written by Hegel might be applied to Aristotle's *Rhetoric*. In his hands it became a new branch of scholarly research because it represented the accumulated and organized wisdom of two centuries.

Although the Greek art of rhetoric was shaped by Aristotle at the decline of his epoch, the book itself nevertheless became an immediate and indispensable accessory for any ambitious orator.

The *New Rhetoric* was created during the period of the maturity of western democracy and liberty, when the parliamentary system had accumulated approximately two hundred years of vast, intercontinental experience.

But it is also a period when the western type of democracy is in danger, being threatened from without and from within by various forms of right and left wing totalitariansim and radical extremism. Therefore the New Rhetoric as an instrument and methological basis for democratic pluralism cannot expect a triumphant acceptance all over the world. It will share in the general fate of our democracy, legality, and our pluralistic experience. It will be criticized or ignored by all the adversaries of reason. The future of The New Rhetoric is connected with the future of humanistic progress, with the endurance of liberties; it is inextricably interwoven with the pluralistic society and the rule of law.

VIII.
HUMAN RIGHTS: PHILOSOPHICAL AND JURIDICAL PROBLEMS

1. A Most Controversial and Fashionable Topic

Conventions, declarations, and rhetoric concerning human rights have proliferated enormously. Whether anyone's rights are actually respected more in the various states of our world is of course uncertain. Possibly the important fact is that nowadays everybody at least feels obliged to endorse these principles verbally. Even if this seeming adherence is a deliberate deception, such hypocrisy has to be taken into account because, as La Rochefoucauld observed, "hypocrisy is the tribute that vice pays to virtue."

The juridical and philosophical problem of rights is one of the most complicated and controversial in municipal and international law. "Rights" is an expression freely used by jurists and politicians alike, often in the same speech, but with contradictory meanings. Therefore some effort is needed to define the various meanings given to it.

The terminology of politics and law is as changeable as women's fashions, but the changes in politics are less arbitrary and capricious than a superficial observer might suppose.

Serious scholarly discussions about the nature or essence of juridical rights *(droit subjectif; das subjektive Recht; subiektivnoje pravo*—in Russian; *prawo podmiotowe*—in Polish*)* began with the development of juridical positivism and especially with the revival of the new theories of natural law on the European continent and in America at the turn of the century. It was during this period that the basic theories of "subjective rights" were elaborated by European philosophers of law (Saleiles, Geny, Ihering, Windscheid). A few years later, Wesley Newcomb Hohfeld wrote his subtle analysis, *Fundamental Legal Conceptions as Applied to Judicial Reasoning* (Yale University Press, 1919). The presentation of the conception of rights by Justice Oliver Wendell Holmes, Jr., and several of his contemporaries also belongs to this period.

After WWI, the orderly evolution of the scholarly literature on this subject was ruffled in the Western world, if not interrupted, by the pure theory of law propounded by Hans Kelsen on the one hand, and by several American functionalists on the other. At the same time, the concept of rights came under attack by various fascist and communist ideologues. The total negation of the concept of rights (including narrowly interpreted juridical rights and the broadly conceived rights *"de l'homme et du citoyen"*) by all totalitarian factions was a part of their general attack against democracy, freedom, and humanism.

Interest in the problem of rights in the juridical, political, and broadly philosophical sense revived after the defeat of the fascist governments in 1945 and the establishment of a new breed of totalitarian and despotic regimes. The reaction against inhumane political regimes that had been responsible for the death of millions in the labor and concentration camps was so powerful that a search was undertaken to discover the causes for such tragedies with a view to guaranteeing that such inexpressible cruelties would not be repeated. Included in these endeavors was a return to the concept of legal and political rights. Legal and constitutional guarantees were sought which could protect mankind against a repetition of the inhumane experience. The ideas of juridical and human rights again became politically important, socially popular, and juridically topical.

The euphoria which followed the victory of the allies in 1945 soon was dimmed by the awareness in Western countries of the fact that one of their number, the Soviet Union, had not changed its dictatorial political structure either during the war or after victory. The antidemocratic, inhumane Stalinist regime was going through its most bloody convulsions just before the dictator's death in 1953. "Rights" began to be used as an ideology against Stalinism. The Stalinist regime was considered especially dangerous because it claimed to be truly democratic and humanistic. Criticism of Communist totalitarianism in the 1950's came to be connected with theories of rights, their juridical and political foundations.

The third reason for the renewed interest in human rights was the struggle of colonial peoples against colonial governments. Colonial peoples claimed that they were fighting for the basic rights taken from them by the colonial powers, the highly developed European industrial democracies. Unfortunately, the post-colonial regimes in Africa and Asia usually were unable to realize the principles of democracy and legality; most of the political systems of the Third World are authoritarian, often cruel and oppressive, at times even genocidal. The problems of political and juridical rights became highly topical in those countries because of internal and external conditions.

And, finally, the problem of rights also became important in the Western democracies. Many constitutional and legal norms concerning justice, equality, equity, non-discrimination, fair trials, the rights of defendants, the rights of employees and of consumers were found wanting. Those rights often appeared to be mere declarations, the typical rights-in-books, not rights-in-life. With the development of political, social, and juridical awareness in the Western democracies, the people, as represented by various democratic organizations, parties, and parliamentary factions demanded not only expansion of their rights, but more important, they demanded guarantees and the means to transform the existing laws on the books into laws in practice. The development of Western style democracy will depend on the expansion of individual rights and on making them more and more concrete.

From this short survey we see that there are basic social, political, and philosophical reasons why the problem of subjective rights has become so timely and important, why political phraseology based on that terminology has become the fashionable political jargon, and why the word "rights" is one of the most frequently used and abused in the second half of the twentieth century.

The causes of the popularity of "rights" are still operating and will not lose their validity for decades to come. Quite the contrary, it may be that in social, political conflicts, both internal, and international, every party will appeal more and more to the ideals of human rights and endeavor to justify every act of aggression as a vindication of the requirements of these "rights."

These are the reasons, scholarly and political, why the idea of rights and its connection with juridical positivism should be thoroughly examined.

The concepts of subjective rights are today even more differentiated than the concept of law itself. One can distinguish several theories of rights and every general theory of law produces at least one theory of rights. Most of the definitions of subjective rights are akin to the *kariatydes*, as Somlo observed; they appear to be supporting their own house but they are mere ornaments without any useful function.[1]

This critical remark of the great German jurist is only partially true. He was highly disappointed by the fact that the philosophies of law, rights, and justice were falling apart. On the other hand, however, that development did help to clarify issues, shook the dogmas, and at last pointed out how complicated and internally differentiated the problems are.

2. Human Rights and Sovereignty

There are many international documents dealing with the subject of human rights in one way or another. The Universal Declaration of Human Rights of 1948 and the two implementing Covenants of 1966 are the most famous and may be the most important, but they are by no means the only ones. There are also conventions prohibiting torture and genocide, and the use of bacteriological and chemical weapons. There is a European Convention on Human Rights with five protocols, one of which even established the first international procedure for protecting individual rights. There is an international bill of rights proclaimed by the States of the American Hemisphere.

There is also the Helsinki Agreement, with special reference to the problems of elementary rights and freedom of information.

The more diverse human rights issues become, the more complicated and controversial their philosophical and juridical treatment becomes.

One of the basic problems of human rights in the philosophy of law and state is the relationship between the Universal Declaration, the Covenants, and other similar documents, and the principle of sovereignty. In modern history the notion of sovereignty was introduced and elaborated at the time of the rise of national states and the bankruptcy of the universalistic tendencies of the Middle Ages, both secular and religious. Modern international law, whose foundations were laid down in the seventeeth and eighteenth centuries, set forth the principle of the absolute sovereignty of the State, explicitly insisting that it is not the individual human being but the State which is the sole subject of international law and of international relations. There is no doubt that international law as a whole, although it has contained many controversial principles, has aided much in the development of our civilization, but one should remember that this development considered individuals to be mere objects of international law. States are the subjects. If alienation characterizes social processes in all countries of the world today, no doubt the development of international law was connected with this reification (in the Hegelian sense) of the individual and his position in society.

The first major change in the place of the individual in international law occurred with the adoption of the Hague conventions at the end of the 19th and the beginning of the 20th centuries. All the provisions of international law concerning more humanitarian methods of war introduced the concept of a moral responsibility on the part of governments for the humane treatment of individuals. Although the First World War, like all previous wars, was a clear defiance and contradiction of these prinicples, nevertheless they had been solemnly proclaimed, referred to, and reaffirmed during the hostilities and in the treaties that followed. It was also significant from the philosophical and historical viewpoints that the purpose of the military intervention was described by President Woodrow Wilson in broad nonmilitary terms: "to make the world safe for democracy."

The world, as we know, became neither safer nor more democratic after the First World War, but the foundation of the League of Nations and the description of its aims and tasks marked a new stage in the development of international responsibilities on the part of states. Internalization of many duties, especially the protection of minorities, labor relations, the fight against slavery, and women's humiliation constituted a great preparatory step toward the legal and ideological accomplishments that followed the Second World War. The purpose of the Second World War, as officially declared by the Allies, was the triumph of the four freedoms, as Franklin Delano Roosevelt declared, and "the enthronement of human rights," as Winston Churchill put it.

The notion of human rights was introduced into the

most important documents of international law in 1945, The Charter of the United Nations and the Statute of the International Court of Justice. The principles of national sovereignty, although once more expressly reiterated, found themselves cheek-by-jowl with the proclamation of human rights; these two concepts were obliged somehow to coexist peacefully and compete at the same time, which, as we know, can be fruitful for both sides. New avenues for their development have in fact been opened.

It is almost universally accepted by Western thinkers that promotion of internationally proclaimed human rights must be accompanied by a reevaluation of the concept of sovereignty. Given that acceptance there is no need to quote the long list of names of the most distinguished authors defending this view in the Western world, unlike the situation that obtains in the Eastern bloc, even though the principle is hedged about with many qualifications. The Soviet Union still regards the concept of sovereignty, interpreted in the broadest absolutistic way, as the foundation of international law and international relations—with the exceptions of relations among "socialist states," (particularly the "friendly" ones) and the right to give aid to the liberation movements of oppressed peoples.

The qualifications concerning sovereignty can be narrowed down to the principal question, should acceptance of the obligation to respect certain human rights be regarded as a limitation upon sovereignty?

Discussions of this issue are usually fruitless from the viewpoint of juridical formalism. A broader philosophical outlook is required. After all, one can argue that every contract between individuals or independent states limits their freedom, choice, or movement. If, as Thomas Hobbes argued, freedom consists in lack of hindrances, then every contract is a restraint upon freedom. Of course, lack of obstacles is one aspect of freedom, but the reduction of the notion of freedom to this aspect alone would be more than an oversimplification—it would be an outright error.

It is a fact that at the very basis of social life and international relations must be the principle, *pacta sunt servanda;* any social and international order depends on the presumption that duly negotiated and accepted contracts and the fulfillment of their concomitant obligations are binding. Should we argue that the prohibition against robbery, murder, and rape, is a limitation upon individual freedom? Is it not true, on the contrary, that this prohibition is one of the preconditions for the realization of individual freedom? Is not such a prohibition one of the necessary preconditions for the bare existence of civil liberties and even of life itself?

We should give up the mechanistic, Hobbesian concept of freedom in favor of the Renaissance idea, expanded later by Hegel and Dewey, in accordance with which freedom should be interpreted as the possibility of creative activity, of realizing one's potential and ambitions. Hegel and Dewey introduced a limitation into this doctrine: one must understand the necessities and existing limitations while setting one's goals, because one aspect of freedom is that it is comprehended necessity. In light of such a philosophy of freedom, which should and can be applied *mutatis mutandis* to the concept of sovereignty, the prohibition against murder, torture, and enslavement, will not be regarded as a hindrance upon, but a prerequisite for, true freedom.

From the standpoint of this philosophy, the Universal Declaration of Human Rights and the succeeding covenants, agreements, unilateral declarations, should not be viewed as limitations imposed on sovereignty. The obligation voluntarily accepted by sovereign states to respect and guarantee the elementary liberties and rights of their citizens is not a "greater" restriction upon sovereignty and independence than the similar restriction imposed on individuals prohibiting them from committing murder, selling slaves, or violating traffic regulations. Why should a prohibition against piracy not be regarded as a limitation on sovereignty and *habeas corpus,* guaranteed by the international community, be regarded as such a limitation?

The Declaration of Human Rights and its sequels express the evolution of our culture and civilization. That is a fact that cannot be taken away even by universal violation of the Universal Declaration.

By means of the internationalization of human rights mankind is returning to the primary sources of Western culture. We are returning to the Stoic concept that mankind, *humanitas,* is indivisible, and that individual freedom should be regarded as a natural condition of the existence and preservation of mankind.

It is from this point of view that one should assess the speech delivered by A.J. Vyshinsky during the discussion in the United Nations concerning the Universal Declaration. The Soviet representative insisted that it should be proclaimed the duty of every state and government to put these rights into effect. The United Nations later returned to the problem raised by the Soviet Union. The idea of the Declaration was to enumerate the basic standards, ideas, and achievements of mankind apart from the opinions of any particular sovereign government. It has been a deficiency of the Declaration that there is no formally binding juridical force built into it, but there is also an advantage in having an official statement, embodying the consensus of the world's thinkers. It was natural that following the proclamation of principles, the next step would be the formulation of the covenants, and their transformation (too slowly) into binding and enforcible legal norms.

3. The Notion of Human Rights: Historical Approach

Let us return to the basic classification of legal theories, natural law and juridical positivism.

According to natural law theories, a genuine, universal, natural law exists *per se*; it has its origin either in nature (as variously interpreted, including the concepts of the nature of man or the nature of society) or—according to the theological philosophies—in God himself. The feature common to the secular and theological theories of the natural law is their recognition that the norms of natural law exist independently of the state or government and that the juridical, moral, and eventually political binding force of natural law is above laws of states or governments. Those norms of natural law impose duties and bestow rights based on their own autonomous force and authority. Those laws can be supported by states, although that support only helps to carry these norms and the respective duties and rights into effect. The help of the state does not and cannot add anything substantial to the authority and force of the natural law. The provisions of natural law, according to all these theories, are the source of universal human rights and liberties and therefore they are, as Rousseau called them, inalienable. Such rights—in today's terminology, human rights—are directly derived from the natural law. In some theories they coexist with natural law, they are inseparable from it and bind every rational human being.

According to the traditional interpretation of juridical positivism, it is the positive law, which is the only source of the individual's "subjective" rights. The only real, legal, existing rights are those which have been derived from positive laws enacted by governments. What was not created or granted by governments does not exist as a feature of the legal system; consequently, no one may claim any privileges, immunities, or rights under them. In the 20th century, juridical positivism has been criticized from various points of view. Many of these criticisms are based on political and ideological premises, usually tending in the West to identify this philosophy of law with the concept of the omnipotence and the irresponsibility of the state. The speech of Pope Pius XII to the Italian jurists, in which the crimes of fascism were described as the immediate result of juridical positivism and its disregard for "natural rights," was most significant. If eternal law were considered an absolutely sovereign norm, the Pope argued, if natural rights were regarded as being superior to human law, then people would not have dared to commit the terrifying crimes of totalitarianism.

This general evaluation of juridical positivism has never and nowhere been correct, but its erroneousness has become even more evident in the light of recent history, which has witnessed the "positivisation" of human rights.

How should human rights be interpreted as expressed in various United Nations documents in connection with these two basic philosophies of law?

International law is under permanent pressure caused by the evolution of international relations, by new requirements, by new needs, and by political conflicts which tend to manifest themselves either in the new interpretation and application of existing norms of international law or in the mere application of that law to solve new problems. International law is never static, its content and form are always changing.

One of the most important conflicts in the world today is the antagonism between a group of parliamentary, democratic states and the anti-democratic, despotic, often totalitarian, states which exist on every continent and represent a majority of all governments.

One of the manifestations of this conflict is the attitude toward human rights. The democratic parliamentary states have no consistent, fully elaborated policy on violations of human rights. Nevertheless the issue of human rights is one of the most important political and philosophical problems dividing and uniting various forces, tendencies, alliances, sometimes aggravating and sometimes soothing antagonisms.

Human rights is a problem of international law which has a direct impact on the internal situation of many countries. It is a question which can be used, at any time, more or less forcefully, by the political adversaries of every regime.

This social and political background must be remembered in analyzing human rights.

Human rights have become a part of positive international law, and therefore recourse to natural law and "inalienable" or "self-evident" rights, has become unnecessary. Every jurist, except for the supporters of Kelsen's pure theory of law, who has a minimum respect for the positive sources of law, should agree that legal systems all over the world now have a new means of determining the content of positive law. One may even argue that the new international documents on human rights constructed a bridge between the juridical positivists and the natural law theorists. The gap which existed for many years has been narrowed—at least theoretically, since, as usual, practice lags behind doctrine.

The proponents of natural rights theories today are propagating their lists of individual rights, which are more abstract and general than those of any of the United Nations' conventions or declarations concerning human rights, the rights of workers, prisoners, women, children, the mentally retarded, etc.

On the other hand, the juridical positivists favoring democracy and the securing of individual liberties are on solid ground, firmer by far than that of the supporters of natural law.

Therefore, the Western criticism of legal positivism as a source of inhuman abuses of power is obsolete. Let us also remember that every reasonable juridical positivist regards constitutions and other high ranking legal acts as a direct source of subjective rights. Human rights are not exclusively derived from laws below the constitutional level, because then the constitution would be reduced to an object of veneration, without any practical force or effect. If one interprets the legal system, including the constitution, as a source of subjective rights—and this is the usual practice at least in the Western world (see also Chapter VI on the Polish theories of law and the constitution)—then again it appears that the contradiction between natural law theories and juridical positivism is now far from absolute, and there is no need to return to Locke, Rousseau, or Paine to explain the nature of human rights.

But on the other hand it is necessary to realize that the old concepts of natural rights (popularly known as *"the rights of man"*) is one of the philosophical and historical sources of the contemporary concept of human rights.

The differences between natural and positive philosophies of law are still substantial. The ideas of natural rights are anti-historical; their formulations, according to their supporters, are given once and for all, like the institutions of the proverbial Kingdom of Reason so extolled by the philosophers of the Enlightenment.[2]

The positivist theory of human rights, as it is developing today, is historical, is based on the present social and political realities, is topical, and answers the urgent questions posed by the actual state of mankind.[3]

Apart from legal formulas and norms, the sources of the modern notions of human rights are political, social, economic, philosophical, and ideological (including religious).

Human rights interpreted from the historical, evolutionary viewpoints, should be seen as a result of the intellectual, moral, and social evolution of mankind. They are the result of the development of the modern juridical conscience and consciousness. Innumerable legal acts all over the world directly or indirectly refer to these new degrees or phases in the development of the juridical consciousness and undoubtedly emanate from it.

This historical and philosophical interpretation of

the nature of human rights, of their roots and actual current content, goes beyond traditional idealism and mechanical materialism. It is an application of the principles of philosophy laid down by both Bacon and Descartes, by empirical and rational philosophies enriched by the renewed Aristoletian heritage of the theory of argumentation.

4. The Notion of Human rights: Philosophical Background

If all philosophies of law could be separated into two basic groups, namely, legal positivism and natural law theories, then the problem of human rights would be simple to resolve as well. Legal positivism has been able to enunciate precisely the basic differences between itself and other theories, but unfortunately traditional juridical positivism can supply only a "basic" "fundamental" explanation, far from complete or exhaustive; it is only the beginning of a endless process of refinement and clarification. But we need this basic explantion in order to have a realistic viewpoint, a point of departure for creative jurisprudence which could play the role defined briefly but conclusively by Jerome Hall: ". . . the principal function of jurisprudence is to express and increase the knowledge of law."[4]

One of the greatest advantages of this observation is its generality, which should not be equated with vagueness. There are many ways, none of them complete, which "increase" our knowledge of law: investigation of the historical background, analysis of the purport of norms, comparative studies, determination of general notions, and generalization of particular ones. Jurisprudence understood as a general theory, as a philosophy of law, is one of the most important and even indispensable tools to "increase the knowledge of law." How should we proceed in order to create this philosophy?

Immanuel Kant jibed at the jurists of his day for their inability effectively to answer the most basic questions concerning the science of law: What is law? What is its essence? What is the nature of rights? Kant indicated that it would be impossible to ascertain the nature of law from an analysis of legal norms only. One must go deeper and further into the problem. The jurist who strives for theoretical results only by studying the codes and decrees of a government should be reminded of the old myth of Phaedrus whose head was beautiful, but wooden and empty. The essence of law is not to be found in the legal norms themselves, any more than ideas could be found in the head of Phaedrus.

How should one set about establishing the essence, the nature of law? Although Kant's reply to this question can no longer be accepted today, his basic observation still is valuable: philosophy, in a very broad sense, including sociology and political science, is as important a source of the theory of law as are the texts of the statutes.

If the most eminent jurists of the past had been asked what is law, right, legality, human rights, and so on, most of them probably would have answered the way Baumgarten did when he quoted the famous words of St. Augustine, albeit to suit a different situation: *Si rogas nescio, si non rogas scio* (when you ask me, I do not know. When you do not ask me, I know).[5]

Should legal philosophy decline and be neglected in

a democratic society? Can we afford to be indifferent to the philosophy of law when the very nature of western democracy is being challenged?

Some would answer that it is not a precondition for the practical mastery of a subject to know its theory; there are millions of good drivers who know nothing of the foundations of mechanics. They continue to achieve their ends without endangering public safety. One could further argue that in our societies there are many gifted lawyers and judges who could answer, what is law, what is right, or what is legality in a very simple fashion only, yet every day these same persons are able to analyze and resolve complicated juridical problems and render well founded judgments.

The Kantian assertion that the theory of law cannot be deduced from legal norms themselves should be extended to the interpretation and application of law, which cannot and should not simply be based on legal norms either. It is necessary to resort to other fields and ideas in order to interpret and apply legal norms correctly. The answer to the Kantian question: what is law? is relevant to the next problem that inevitably follows, namely, how should legal norms be expounded, interpreted, and applied?

Quite obviously, formal logic should be employed in interpreting them. But if one limits oneself to formal logical rules in interpreting and applying the law, one would be like a worker repairing a computer with an ax. The interpretation and application of law should not violate the rules of logic, but conformity with logic is not by itself enough to achieve a desirable result.

In daily practice it is not necessary to resort to the philosophical foundations of law in order to resolve typical, relatively simple juridical problems. It often happens, however, that the "usual" and "typical" case contains some unusual, atypical, specific, feature which changes the entire picture, and one finds that after all it is necessary to study the case and the pertinent juridical norms and precedents from their very beginning, and take social relations and philosophical ideas into account.

New problems emerge in every society, even in well established societies with long traditions. And these unforeseen problems cannot and should not be solved in a simplistic or routine way. Such new phenomena must be analyzed from a broader, more philosophical viewpoint. Let us examine a few examples. In the beginning of the 1970s, jurists faced problems which required a fresh and thorough theoretical analysis of various spheres of life in order to be able to make reasonable juridical decisions. One of these problems is the right to die with dignity without the artificial prolongation of a vegetative, unconscious manner of existence. This problem provoked discussions in which various moral, philosophical, and theological arguments were used. Can a jurist dissociate himself from these theories, viewpoints, and attitudes? When does the act of killing commence? When does the natural process of living come to an end?

Again, within the sphere of political and constitutional law, American jurists had to decide where the limit was upon "executive privilege." The Constitution and practical experience gave little indication of what answer would be sufficient in this age of new technology, new tensions, and new antagonisms. In order to resolve the problem, not only precedents from previous epochs had to be taken into account, but also the philosophical foundations of democratic theory which deal with the relationship between a citizen and his government, individual freedom and the *raison d'état,* the right of the people to know and government secrecy.

New problems also arose in the sphere of international law, such as the meanings of aggression and the right of self-defense. When Israeli planes, on the night of July 3-4, 1976, landed in Uganda and rescued more than a hundred hostages of various nationalities from the hijackers, several new legal problems arose: Is the act of kidnapping citizens of a foreign country and jailing them with the help of a host country an act of aggression, and if so, on whose part? If it is aggression, can it lawfully be countered with the use of all available means of defense, including the invading of the host country? Should such a rescue as a Entebbe Airport be called an act of aggression, albeit justifiable?

The answer obviously will depend on one's phillosophy and values: are human lives more important or the inviolability of foreign territory ruled by a sovereign despot, as was Amin's Uganda? Even if the law had been on the side of President Amin (which it was not), what would be more important for the international community, for all of mankind: the "formal" (if such a thing exists) interpretation of law, or regard for the highest human values, the human rights of the hostages, the preservation of life? Of course, if the provisions of international law had been correctly and humanely interpreted, the controversey between international law and morality (on the grounds of the value of human life) would easily have been resolved. A genuine, insurmountable incompatibility between the provisions of international law covering the territorial sovereignty of a state and the protection of human life does not exist. But in order to substantiate this thesis one must turn to philosophical interpretations and not merely "formalistic" ones.

Let us repeat once more: the ways of understanding what law is and the methods of interpretation are not and should not be chosen arbitrarily. They depend on general legal philosophy, including the present-day understanding of human rights. It can happen, of course, that there is a difference between the personal philosophy of a jurist and the immediate results of his activity. Such a difference will be strictly personal, such as the contradiction between one's religious beliefs and one's sins.

The conflict and contradiction between the definitive, concrete, unchangeable norms of natural law and a reality which is in permanent flux, in constant and endless transformation, has throughout the ages been so striking and obvious that the adherents of natural law are forced to defend themselves. Rudolf Stammler's resolution of this dilemma was his concept of *Naturrecht mit wechselndem Inhalt* (natural law with changing content).

If one re-examines the writings of the proponents of the natural law doctrine, one will be amazed to find that Rudolf Stammler explicated what others had expressed in a more veiled form; he brought to the surface what others had sought to suppress. Stammler's concept even influenced many Thomists, who also started to stress the changing elements in the "eternal" rules of law and morality.

Professor Czeslaw Martyniak, professor at the KUL

(Catholic University of Lublin) interprets the legal doctrine of St. Thomas as if the Angelic Doctor himself believed in the changing content of natural law.[6]

The upshot of these considerations is that the concepts of human rights, codified or not codified in various legal documents, are still developing. They are determined by the totality of human relations and perceptions, by current moral sensitivities, by philosophy and the prevailing human, individual and social values.

The above historical and philosophical considerations indicate that the notion of human rights can have the following meanings:

A. Human rights as expressed in the basic international documents, especially in the Charter of the United Nations, the Universal Declaration of Human Rights, and the U.N. Conventions on Human Rights.

B. Human rights as expressed in the aforementioned international documents and incorporated in various ways into the legal provisions of various nations, especially their constitutions and legal codes.

C. Human rights as proclaimed, understood, and interpreted by philosophers, jurists, statesmen, and scholars; their concepts sometimes represent wishful thinking but usually they are connected with the existing juridical (international and national) notions, norms, and political realities.

Progressive thinkers usually reach further because of their philosophical beliefs, which push them toward more extensive interpretation or toward developing new ideas representing future, further advanced stages of spiritual and political evolution. Scholars and philosophers (including theologians) can and should repre-

Human Rights: Philosophical & Juridical Problems

sent the most advanced conscience and consciousness of mankind. In this way they can set standards for the future, even if that future be very distant. In various epochs "philosophers" were a progressive, evolutionary (and sometimes revolutionary) force; they were the proverbial "standard bearers" and "pacesetters." Thinkers have always been a "leaven" and always will be. The future is always ingrained in the present. Therefore, today, in the proclaimed or existing notions of human rights, one can detect the seeds of the future, and every correct progressive, humanistic, political, or juridical interpretation of human rights is at the same time a reaffirmation either of actual practice or of the spiritual climate, or both—and at the same time transcends them. As Hegel suggests, ever we have reached the limit, we have already transcended it.

These three meanings of human rights are not in separate, closed compartments. Indeed, non-jurists very often use them interchangeably, because in the present complex political and social situation it has become common to mix up the spheres of *"sein"* and *"sollen,"* of "is" and "ought," of reality and hopes. Such a mixture can be viewed with horror by faithful Cartesians, who would argue that any lack of clarity in drawing distinctions must harm mankind. But on the other hand, as was proved by Dupréel and Perelman, what is "entirely clear" (if this term has any meaning) bars further investigation and progress; only ideas and ideals which need further clarification, determination, and refinement are the true generators of progress.

The concepts of human rights are today by no means finally shaped. They are becoming more and more acknowledged and more and more controversial, more ambiguous and more clear. Every clarification, definition, resolves certain doubts but creates new problems.

5. Law and Right

What is the relationship between law and right? Roman lawyers, the founders of Western jurisprudence, described it as follows:

> "Positive law either contains," as Mackelday writes in his monograph, *Roman Law,* "general principles embodied in the rules of law ... or for special reasons they establish something that differs from the general principles. In the first case they contain a common law *(jus commune),* in the second a special law *(jus singulare s. exorbitans).* The latter is either favorable or unfavorable ... according as it enlarges or restricts, in opposition to the common rule, the right of those for whom it is established. The favorable special law *(jus singulare)* as also the right created by it ... in the Roman law is termed benefit of the law *(beneficium juris)* or privilege *(privilegium).*
> "Law creates rights; this is the essence of the theory of rights in Roman jurisprudence. This theory was inherited by many European philosophies and—what is even more important—was introduced into the practice of law in Western countries."[7]

The existence of rights is connected with the existence of historically evolved general juridical principles, and the latter are embodied in the norms of positive law. Rights, as far as positive law is concerned, are an expression and a reflection of its general principles and particular norms. If a "favorable" special positive law comes into being, it immediately creates a new right, which is termed either a privilege or benefit of the law *(privilegium aut beneficium juris).*

According to the traditions of Roman jurisprudence, alive in the West, one can reach the following conclusion: right follows naturally from principles embodied in legal norms, but certain benefits can either be deviations or extensions, or both at the same time, of existing rights.

The word, privilege, connotes, at least in all major European languages, special advantages conferred by law. Although these privileges are legal, there is no assurance that public opinion will consider them just. Public opinion regards with a jaundiced eye special privileges or benefits conferred upon individuals or a group (class), as contrasted with rights enjoyed by all. Special privileges have an abrasive effect on a sensitive public because the public remembers the long struggle for justice against those very privileges. Wesley N. Hohfeld writes: "... more than this, the dominant specific connotation of the term [privilege] as used in popular speech seems to be mere negation of duty."[8]

This remark by Wesley N. Hohfeld leads us to another observation: in the opinion of the people, rights should be connected with duties; otherwise they are regarded as unjust, unearned privileges.

In American legal literature it was Justice Oliver Wendell Holmes who adopted the conception of legal rights in the Roman, continental spirit. In his book, *The Common Law,* he makes the following philosophical remarks:

> A legal right is nothing but a permission to exercise certain natural powers, and upon certain conditions to obtain protection, restitution, or compensation by the aid of the public force. Just so far as the aid of the public force is given a man, he has a legal right, and this right is the same whether his claim is founded in righteousness or iniquity. Just so far as possession is protected, it is as much a source of legal rights as ownership is when it secures the same protection.[9]

The juridical definition of right, as presented by Justice Holmes is much narrower than his philosophical interpretation. He repeats almost a historically typical formalistic interpretation of right:

> Every right is a consequence attached by the law to one or more facts which the law defines, and wherever the law gives anyone special rights not shared by the body of the people, it does so on the ground that certain special facts, not true of the rest of the world, are true of him.[10]

There is of course a philosophical link between Holmes' juridical and his philosophical interpretation of the concept of right. The common connotation in comparison with the philosophical one consists in the restrictive interpretation of rights: they are something which is enjoyed in certain circumstances by a limited number of people. They are not, and they cannot be, by definition, something to which everyone is entitled at any time and under any conditions. Let us make it clear at the outset that while Holmes's point of departure does not represent the philosophy of the Universal Declaration of Human Rights, or the clarifying Covenants adopted by the United Nations, it does not contradict it. Indeed, Holmes's philopophy of rights precedes the present phase and was instrumental in creating it.

Whatever one's concept of "legal rights" might be, one should at least agree with Justice Holmes that a legal right gives one a permission, if nothing more, to exercise one's "natural powers." The question arises whether the rights proclaimed by the Universal Declaration and in the UN Covenants grant permissions of any kind to exercise "certain natural powers." Of course, a mere proclamation does not allow a "subjugated" nation to exercise any real, material, tangible "natural powers" such as the "right to self-determination" (International Covenant on Economic, Social and Cultural Rights, Art. 1), but it creates certain promises and "privileges" which must be taken into account by others.

That Covenant also proclaims "equal rights of men and women" (Art. 3). Once more the same question arises: Does this right allow any individual to exercise "certain natural powers?" Maybe it does not, but it substantially encourages people to use the "entitlement" given to them and thus helps to create a new "reality." Although Human Rights, as proclaimed by the UN, differ from the traditional notion of "subjective rights," they have and they form a juridical basis.

The Roman jurists already recognized that the problem of right cannot and should not be reduced to negations, to limitations and separations of spheres of influence or activity. They realized that an important, if not the most important, aspect of rights is the positive faculty of being able to exercise one's powers. Following the wisdom of the Roman jurists, several philosophers of the eighteenth century (Grotius and Puffendorf, among others), defined right as the *facultas moralis*. The word "facultas" in this instance means the power and ability to perform; the word *"moralis"* as used by Grotius means vital, animating, and it is this meaning of the term which is important in the futher elaboration of his ideas.

In the eighteenth century, the eminent Polish thinker, Hugo Kollataj applied two terms to the meaning of right: freedom and ability. The Polish word used by Kollataj is *"sposobnosc,"* which means the *ability* combined with the capacity necessary to achieve a purpose.

Kollataj was more precise and perspicacious than the majority of his contemporaries. Right is inseparable from the notion of free activity, "freedom of movement" and "free initiative." Such freedom is essential to the existence of rights; it is a *conditio sine qua non*. This condition is necessary, but not sufficient.

Of course, Kollataj was neither the first nor the last to connect the concept of right with "real," "substantial" abilities, possibilities, and liberties. These rights must be supplemented or complemented by the real power of an individual, by his *"forces propres"* and his social standing which, together, can transform the given theoretical, abstract possibility into a reality. Right without the actual possibility of transformation into reality, without tangible, substantial, almost measurable conditions of "materialization," is defective, is a mere empty declaration—is, juridically speaking, an imperfect entitlement. Philosophically, such an "empty," "abstract" right would be like a sermon, a morality play, or a recommendation which cannot be implemented by those who are addressed.

The term right is sometimes even identified with liberty, and especially with liberty recognized by law.

In the case, *Quinn v. Leathan,* (1901, A.C. 495, 534) Lord Lindley wrote:

> The plaintiff had the ordinary *rights* of the British subject. He was *at liberty* to earn his living in his own way, provided he did not violate some special law prohibiting him from so doing, and provided he did not infringe on the rights of other people. This *liberty* involved *the liberty* to deal with other persons who were willing to deal with him. This *liberty* is *a right* recognized by law; its *correlative* is the general *duty* of every one not to prevent the free exercise of this *liberty* except so far as his own liberty of action may justify him in so doing.

But a person's *liberty* or *right* to deal with others is nugatory unless they are at liberty to deal with him if they choose to do so. Any interference with their liberty to deal with him affects him.[11] (Italics by W.N. Hohfeld).

In the first part of the excerpt, liberty is identified with right; whoever is endowed with a right, is at *liberty;* whoever enjoys *liberty* is endowed with rights recognized by law and has the right and liberty to deal with other persons. The rights, or liberty, discussed in the opinion, are *erga omnes,* including organs of the Government, meaning that from the juridical viewpoint their correlative is the general duty of every one not to prevent the free exercise of such liberty. Such reasoning coincides with Wesley Newcomb Hohfeld's classification. According to him the juridical opposite of right is "no right," whereas the juridical correlative of right is "duty."

Immanuel Kant was perhaps the first philosopher, as already mentioned, who clearly defined legal freedom as freedom reaching to the boundaries of another person's freedom. His critics used to deride him, remarking that according to Kant a man is enclosed in a cage of his own liberties and has the duty not to impinge upon the freedom cages of his neighbors. The first philosopher to have expressed such a philosophical and juridical concept would be difficult to trace. One must consider that since Greek and Roman times jurists came very close to that conception of law and freedom. This idea has now become so widespread that there are jurists who agree with and quote this idea without referring to Kant. Let us compare Kant's theory with the theoretical juridical opinion formulated by Justice Cave in *Allen v. Food* (1898, A.C., 1, 29):

> Thus it was said that a man has a perfect right to fire off a gun, when all that was meant, apparently, was that a man has a *freedom* or *liberty* to fire off a gun, so long as he does not violate or infringe any one's right in doing so, which is a very different thing from a right, the violation or disturbance of which can be remedied or prevented by legal process.[12]

Justice Cave does not identify freedom (or liberty) with right. Violation of right can be remedied by legal process, whereas freedom or liberty is not necessarily guaranteed by legal process. It seems as though Justice Cave regarded right as a guaranteed freedom, whereas liberty or freedom, not transformed into a right, would constitute either an imperfect right only or an "ideal," "spiritual" seed of an eventual future right.

In his monograph *Fundamental Legal Conceptions as Applied to Judicial Reasoning*, Wesley Newcomb Hohfeld quotes the opinions of three justices, Strong, Jackson, and Sneed, who defined the term rights. Justice Strong, in *People v. Dikeman,* (1852, 7 How. Pr., 124, 130) gives a dictionary definition according to which right means, among other things: property, interest, power, prerogative, immunity and privilege. In law, according to Justice Strong, right is used to designate power, prerogative, privilege; in a restricted sense right is most frequently applied to property.[13]

According to Justice Jackson, in *US v. Patrick,* (1893, 54 Fed. Rep., 338, 348) there are many meanings of the words "right" or "privilege," including: that which one has a legal claim to do; legal power; authority; immunity granted by authority; "the investiture with special or peculiar rights."[14]

Justice Sneed in *Lonas v. State,* (1871, 3 Heisk., Tenn., 287, 306-307) warns against using the words:

rights, privileges, and immunities, as if they were synonymous. "The word *rights* is generic, common, embracing whatever may be lawfully claimed."[15]

Justice Sneed's opinion will be the point of departure for our futher considerations concerning the philosophical and juridical meaning of the conception of "rights."

The traditional notion of the term, right *(jus subjectivum)*, in theory in European and later in American juridical literature and practice has the most general and embracing meaning; it can be used in the special connections or contexts identified with liberty, prerogative, immunity, privilege, power, claim, authority, and so on. But the term *right* in its truly general sense is broader than all those terms taken separately and together. All the meanings given for the word right are also general, but their generality is of a lower degree. Let us take one example. Wesley N. Hohfeld points out that the term, "license," is used at times as if it were synonymous with "privilege." This usage is not correct according to Hohfeld, because license is a "generic term to indicate a group of operative facts required to create a particular privilege."[16]

License in this particular context, one reads in one of the court's opinions, connotes special permission to act in a specific way without which an act "would amount to a trespass."[17] (Justice Adams in *Clifford v. O'Neill,* 12 App. Div., 17; 42 N.Y. Sup., 607, 609).

The difference between license as a privilege and as a permission is that a privilege is by nature continuous whereas license is limited in time, space, and person.

Within the context of a general theory of rights, privileges and licenses should be interpreted as "single," "specific," or "accidental," but not as essential *(wesentlich)* "forms" of right. They are a particular "deduction" from the "general," "essential" notion. But on the other hand, the most "general" and "generic" notion, right, would remain empty without particular specifications and determinations. The so called "Scandinavian Realists" tried to prove that the old juridical concepts of rights and duties (and of course of command and sovereignty) should be excluded from the theory of law because they do not have any real meaning. Alf Ross writes that "the concept of rights is a tool in the technique of presentation."[18]

When quoting the above, Friedmann emphasized that this concept was "convincingly shown" and continued: "In other words, it serves as a convenient 'shorthand,' a simplification of a multitude of conditioning facts and conditioned consequences, e.g., in the description of 'ownership'."[19]

The point is that "rights" are not appearances or illusions which contribute one more example of the famous neo-Kantian, positivistic and empiriocritical *"Scheinprobleme."* Indeed they are and should be one of the signs on the road to defining the social position and situation of the individual in a society and in the state, in the so called civil and political body, as the philosophers of two hundred years ago used to say.

The point of discussion should not be whether "rights" exist in a more or less democratic society with a legal order. If the concept of "rights" were an illusion or a mere "shorthand," then its use as a tool in politics could be either very limited or even non-existent. And it could not have played the truly useful, progressive, social role it has throughout the centuries, but only an "ideological" or propagandistic one.

The concept of rights is a useful "tool in the technique of presentation" and it is a "convenenient shorthand," because it is a correct presentation of the powers, possibilities, and freedom of choice and activity of an individual under a democratic legal order.

Professor Kazimierz Opalek, in his monograph *The Subjective Right*—the only monograph written in a socialist country on this theme—tries to interpret the notion of right in a very narrow sense, as the Scandinavians used to do.[20]

But, *si duo faciunt idem non est idem,* if two persons perform the same action, it is not the same action, the old Roman sages tell us.

Opalek's ultimate conclusion and recommendation is that one should divest oneself of the ambiguous, controversial term, right. This term should be deleted from the vocabulary of jurists and replaced by the term *"uprawnienie,"* which might be translated, "authorization," "claim," or "entitlement" based on the provisions of law.

The *American Heritage Dictionary of the English Language* defines the phrase "to authorize" as meaning: a) to grant authority or power, b) to sanction, and c) to justify. *Webster's Dictionary* adds among others the following meanings: to empower; to give legality or effective power.

These meanings correctly reflect the interpretation given by Professor Opalek. But, the shift in terminology advocated by him does not solve the underlying problem; it is not possible.

In this way he expresses his conviction that the provisions of law should not be mere declarations or a facade covering an empty structure, but should be norms representing life. The objective political result of Opalek's considerations is the following: let us forget oratorical exercises on constitutional rights, which, according to Stalin, were real only in Socialist countries, but instead, let us keep our feet on the ground and analyze the real rights, namely, those derived from specific legal norms; let us forget about ideological illusions and let us return to reality, to the legal system based not only on a constitution but on specific laws as well.

This realism could be called a "limited realism," but it is realism just the same. Its virtue is that it denounces deceptive ideological constructions.

The hidden aspects of this interpretation (the author himself did not return to these ideas in his later writings, to the best of my knowledge) became evident several years later. Dissidents in the Soviet Union and in other socialist countries started to refer to basic human and constitutional rights more and more frequently when fighting against government oppression, denial of basic liberties, and the persecution of individuals who dared to think and express their convictions. Anyway, Opalek's monograph, *The Subjective Right*, should be regarded as a milestone on the road to converting official communist theory of law into jurisprudence with a human face.

The UN Covenants constitute a right which jurisprudence might call a positive right. Do they constitute a right *against* a specific government or any other body or group, requiring them to perform any "positive act?"

On the basis of our analysis, the answer should be affirmative.

An exploration of the relationship between subjective rights, as a juridical expression of human rights, and the concept of freedom, will provide further arguments supporting our view. For the time being let us conclude: the notion of human rights is the broadest juridical and philosophical term; its nature is at once juridical and philosophical, political and moral.

This term is so broad and general that it cannot easily be perverted by despots. And it is sufficiently concrete, precise, specific, and determined to serve as an instrument in the struggle for freedom, privacy, and the preservation of human dignity.

6. Human Rights and Freedom

Juridical positivism was always connected with the ideas of "privacy" and "freedom" the spheres free from "interference by state authorities."

The problem of the connection between rights and freedom is very broad. The question of individual freedom can be viewed differently by the various branches of the humanistic sciences. The broadest and the most controversial notions of freedom are the philosophical ones. We will concentrate on selected albeit basic philosophical questions which have an immediate bearing on our topic.

Kant, Hegel, Marx, and Dewey are four authors whose philosophies represent four contributions to the evolution of the idea of freedom. Within little more than a hundred years, these four sophisticated theories of freedom were elaborated. They are qualitatively different

A. Kant's Philosophy of Autonomous Freedom.

An analysis of Kant's concept of freedom should start with his distinction that man is a *phenomenon* and a *noumenon* at the same time.

The phenomenal human being is part of the physical world and is subject to the laws of nature. He is part of the chain of cause and effect. As a physical being man cannot rightly be regarded as free.

But man is also a "thing-in-itself." He is a noumenon and as such he has freedom of choice. This freedom is the most important feature of his humanity and is connected with the exsistence of reason. Kant went so far as to say that freedom is man's only birthright. All other rights are acquired.[21]

For a human being freedom means that he is not dependent upon the will of any other human being.

Because man is born free, it follows that there exists an "innate equality belonging to every man," and "he ought to be his own master by right (sui juris)."[22]

Man also has "the natural quality of justness," he is presumed innocent, has freedom of contract, and "he may do towards others what does not infringe upon their rights".[23]

On the other hand, Kant wrote, human freedom should also be limited because it is subject to reason. As controlled by reason, freedom cannot be identified with licence or unbridled desire. According to Kant, freedom can be conceived only as *rational* freedom, that is, subject to the "laws," and "requirements," of reason.[24]

Freedom also is the foundation and source of moral and legal responsibility. Without freedom neither the categorical nor the practical imperatives, neither legal obligations nor rights would make any sense.

A reasonable man knows what he *should* do and once he knows it, he *can* do it.

If, however, one is ordered by a legitimate superior to do an act contrary to one's consciousness of duty, one should reject such an order and act according to one's true duty instead. He who acts according to his duty (based on the categorical imperative) is free, even if he is persecuted by the author of immoral orders.

Kant's freedom, as something which belongs to the world of the noumena, is truly abstract. Kant regarded freedom as a potential existing in every individual rather than as a reality in social relations.

According to the tradition of ancient philosophy, rejuvenated during the Renaissance and the Enlightenment, an individual is free when he can act according to his desires, will, and talents. True human freedom must be expressed in social activity and not limited to the process of thinking. This is the basic deficiency of Kant's philosophy of freedom: He did not bind freedom to free human activity. His concept is theoretical, whereas the chief problem of freedom is practical. Nevertheless, Kant tried to draw political conclusions from his philosophy.

According to Kant, the idea of freedom must be placed at the foundation of every constitution and of every law. The ideal should be: "A constitution allowing *the greatest possible human freedom* in accordance with laws by which *the freedom of each is made to be consistent with that of all others.*[25]

Kant understood that this ideal would not be reached without obstacles. These obstacles do not necessarily arise out of human nature but rather out of prevous legislation and experience. If there has been bad experience, then, Kant argued, we should be even more energetic in our endeavors to harmonize legislation and government with the ideal.

Kant wrote that he would be prepared to accept Plato's ideal as our own: a society in which punishment is unnecessary and therefore non-existent. No one after all can say how wide the chasm should be between the ideal and reality. No one can say where the development of human nature and its perfectibility will stop. Because of these unknowns, we should agree "that it is in the power of freedom to pass beyond any and every specified limit."[26]

It is obvious that Kant distinguished between an ideal of political freedom and the reality of political freedom. He dististinguished various levels of perfection of actual freedom. The ideal of freedom is unchangeable; the reality of freedom however is always in a state of transformation. In this way, Kant prepared the ground for the Hegelian dialectics of freedom. Kant's *a priori* idea of freedom was easily transformed into the absolute idea; the rest depends on logic and profound studies of historical realities.

Even more important is Kant's contribution to the theory of law. He connected the general idea of freedom with human rights as an instrument of the limitation and realization of freedom. Kant is perhaps the first philosopher who elaborated the idea that the philosophical notion of freedom is inseparable from the juridical and political concepts of the rights of man.

B. *Hegel's Dialectic of Freedom*

There are fervent adversaries of Hegel's philosophy in the Western as well as in the Eastern world. Even now, a hundred and fifty years after his death, Hegel is still attacked as a living antagonist by liberals and conservatives, by Stalinists, fascists, and Bertrand Russell.

Hegel wrote that the most frequently repeated concept of freedom identifies it with the ability to do what we please. One who thinks in this way, Hegel argues, reveals "an utter immaturity of thought."[27] Those people disregard the nature of social life, of morality, and of law. Freedom must be connected with understanding, responsibility, and an awareness of moral obligations.

In this way Hegel approached one of his most important statements; freedom is necessity understood. Hence there are two elements in freedom: the subjective and the objective. Man can be free not from the laws of nature, but thanks to them. The more he understands, the less he is subject to the caprices of the external world and the more he can control them.

The history of mankind is the history of the acquisition of knowledge. Hegel therefore described the history of the world as the " progress of the consciousness of freedom."[28] He continues: "The idea of freedom . . . is the absolute goal of history."[29]

Whenever Hegel wrote about history, he meant the history of the people who struggle for survival, have their own interests, passions, and ambitions. Every individual tries to attain his own goals, but what he achieves usually is contrary to his intentions, particularly in political and social life. The idea of freedom is a product of battles in the social jungles, where freedom was hardly a welcome guest—this is the dialectic of progress.

The essence of any dialectic, including the Hegelian and Marxian dialectic, is the concept of the struggle of antagonistic forces. A thesis exists in unison with its antithesis. The forces are antagonistic, but the one cannot exist without the other.

If the history of mankind is the history of the development of the idea of freedom, then one can say with the same justification that the history of mankind is the history of various kinds of slavery, of unfreedom. In every successive epoch forms of slavery, of unfreedom, have become more sophisticated and refined. The highly acclaimed individual freedom is not a static state enjoyed by individuals, societies, and nations. Freedom is always a process of fighting for freedom, of the struggle for its own expansion in the face of forces which, consciously or unconsciously, oppose it vigorously. Freedom is a way of life and of struggle; it is the expansion of human possibilities and powers. It is a way of operating in order to make maximum use of an individual's talents and skills.

This is one of the most important contributions of Hegel's philosophy of freedom: freedom is *essentially positive,* its blessings consist of affirmative activity not in isolation from society. Freedom does not consist of erecting walls around spheres of influence separating one person's sphere from that of his neighbor, as is argued in the Kantian philosophy of freedom. This is the basic difference between Kant and Hegel.

The extent of freedom, at any stage of the historical development of society, is determined by the totality of the objective and subjective conditions, by the totality of economic and social relations, and by the consciousness of the people, their understanding, beliefs, and prejudices. There exists an intrinsic interdependence between every stage of human civilization and the forms of freedom, law, and the state. Legal forms are necessary for the assurance and realization of freedom. They may not, however, be capriciously or arbitrarily imposed on society. When juridical norms are either too conservative or too "progressive," too far ahead in any given stage of evolution, when the law is incompatible with prevailing social conceptions, then these laws will simply be "unreal", they will be "appearances," empty pronouncements in books, but they will not be "laws in life." Hegel's dialectic is one of those philosophies which led to the famous American distinction between "law in books," and "law in life."

Hegel's concept of the development of the idea of freedom as transcending more and more its boundaries and localisms, his concept that the new content of freedom must sooner or later be accompanied by appropriate legal norms and political institutions—all these concepts lead to notions of "freedom" and "rights" more universal than before. These ideas were premature some hundred and fifty years ago, although they could have played a progressive part in the political struggles of that time. In the new epoch, with its new universalistic developments—the new concepts of freedom expressed in various documents, constitutions, and declarations on human rights—these general notions of rights and liberties are in accordance with the "spirit of history," they reflect the wishes of the newly enlightened people, they are instruments which undermine the old nationalistic barriers and despotisms as well as the "unreasonable" interpretations of state sovereignty.

This new application of the Hegelian dialectic to the new concept of human rights is a dialectical negation of the traditional concept of natural rights, albeit in accordance with the spirit of the dialectical method.

The fact that Hegel's dialectical philosophy of freedom, law, and politics can lead toward the concept of universal human rights, as understood at the end of this century, is proof that in this century "all roads lead to Rome," and "Rome" in our century is the historically determined notion of human rights.

C. *Marx's Dialectic of Liberation*

What Marx wrote about freedom might be termed an *Aufhebung* of Hegel's philosophy. Marx was particularly impressed by Hegel's view that freedom has a concrete content and form at every stage of history. According to him, however, the stages in human development were not, as Hegel implied, different stages in the development of the idea of freedom, because Marx absolutely rejected absolute ideas. For Marx the ideas of freedom developed according to the evolution of civilization, of the economic bases and political institutions which constitute the superstructures of all societies.

All this notwithstanding, Marx and Engels still wrote that it was Hegel who made the greatest contribution to the philosophy of freedom because he had established that freedom was necessity understood.

It is significant that the first signed article published by Marx concerned the problem of censorship. He never disowned the points he raised in it. They cannot be regarded as products of youthful romanticism as Stalinists and neo-Stalinists usually declare, for they were many times repeated by the "adult" Marx.

According to Marx, no government should ever impose restrictions on freedom of thought and publication. Every restriction, every censorship, is the cry of a "dirty conscience," according to Marx. Needless to say, these words have never been quoted in Communist countries and several attempts to remind people of them in the Communist bloc were requited with reprisals against such rash "heretics."

In a speech in his own defense, when he was tried for publishing articles in the *Neue Rheinische Zeitung,* Marx said: "It is the function of the press to be the public watchdog, the tireless denouncer of the rulers, the omnipresent eye, the ominipresent mouth of the spirit of the people that jealously guards its freedom."[30]

Could Marx have foreseen that freedom of the press would be so drastically curtailed after the socialist revolution? Whatever Marx's vision of the dictatorship of the proletariat might have been, one thing seems certain: He never anticipated that such a system would be accompanied by the triumph of censorship and the abolition of the civil liberties enjoyed under parliamentary democracies. There is nothing to indicate that Marx and Engels believed that the future state would be a centralized, despotic bureaucracy. On the contrary, in analyzing the Paris Commune of 1871, Marx stressed that under that system every official had been freely elected by the people and could have been recalled at any time.

Marx wrote that the Commune had to protect itself against its own servants.[31]

Unfortunately, the two devices which Marx and Engels regarded as "infallible" were of doubtful value. Neither has ever been employed in any Communist country for long. Although we have no direct evidence to judge their efficacy, we have every reason to believe that had these devices ever been consistently tried in Communist countries, they would not have effectively protected the people against the cancer of a centralized bureaucracy.

Marx and Engels believed that the ideal of individual freedom would only be attained in a society without a state and without a government, without private property, and without wars. Such is the Marxian vision of the kingdom of freedom, described by his adversaries as utopian, and by Marx himself as a scientific prediction of the future.

> Men's own social organization which has hitherto stood in opposition to them ... will then become the voluntary act of men themselves. The objective, external forces which have hitherto dominated history, will then pass under the control of men themselves. It is only from this point that men, with full consciousness, will fashion their own history.... It is humanity's leap from the realm of necessity into the realm of freedom.[32]

As we see, for Hegel and Marx freedom is not static. A free man is not passive; he is a social being continually overcoming objective and subjective difficulties along the path of his development. Man is not born free; he may become free. Man can realize and extend his power over external circumstances only in cooperation with other free people. Freedom is not a subjective feeling. Man cannot be liberated by a mechanical transfer from the country of bondage to the kingdom of freedom. Mere institutional, social, and economic changes by themselves cannot truly liberate people. Prior to and during liberation the minds of the people must be reformed and adjusted to the new circumstances.

The man of the future, the free man, will be educated, civilized, and disciplined. He will voluntarily observe the moral norms and accepted rules of social behavior. He will not regard them as a burden, they will be self evident for him. In this society man will be able to develop all his natural talents and reasonable inclinations. Not everyone will have the talent of a Raphael or a Leonardo da Vinci, Marx observed, but everyone possessing such a genius will be given an opportunity to develop it for his own and public's benefit.

The gist of Marx's considerations on freedom is:

> In Communist society, where no one has any exclusive sphere of activity, but each can be accomplished in any branch he wishes, production as a whole is regulated by society, thus making it possible for me to do one thing today and another tomorrow, to hunt in the morning, fish in the afternoon, rear cattle in the evening, criticize after dinner, in accordance with my inclination, without ever becoming hunter, fisherman, shepherd or critic.[33]

Marx's prediction that division of labor will disappear in the future society is one of the weakest elements of his theory; it is an obvious utopian wish.

On the other hand, one aspect of this theory should not be overlooked: In order to develop his personality a free human being should be given more opportunities to use fully *all* his latent talents and dormant interests. Marx interpreted social freedom as a liberation of the individual.

An individual in the future Communist society will on the one hand be disciplined; on the other however he will resemble an "anarchistic" intellectual. His way of life will constantly change, together with his profession and his artistic tastes.—According to Marx there were two basic philosophies of freedom in every society based on exploitation: that of the oppressed exploited masses and that of the exploiters. In the future communist society, lacking class antagonisms and political oppression, when the state and law will wither away, the freedom of each individual will be compatible with the freedom of all—and this Kantian, "powerless" (Engels), ideal will be finally realized. There will be no law, Marx continues, meaning that there will be no external restrictions or commands; they will be replaced by the conscious discipline of highly educated, enlightened, self-disciplined, and unselfish members of the communist society. These members will govern themselves, ultimately expressing the Kantian ideal of self-legislation. And human rights will become non-juridical ideals flourishing in a stateless society.

Kant doubted that his optimum state of self-legislation could be attained. Marx and Engels had no doubts. For them such a future was the inevitable stage which society must reach in accordance with the "iron" laws of its development. Marx and Engels were more Kantian than Kant himself.

D. *Dewey's Great Synthesis*

In his essay, "Philosophies of Freedom," Dewey criticized the notion of freedom which, he thought, prevailed in the West.

According to this simplistic theory, Dewey wrote, freedom consists of freedom of choice, although it is only the beginning of the problem.

Without freedom of choice there would be no basis for praise or blame, no responsibility or liability.

A man nevertheless, Dewey argued—and here appears a fundamental link with Hegel's philosophy—is always a human being in the concrete and his so-called free will is not an unmotivated force. On the contrary. The will is an amalgam of habits, desires, and purposes determined by society and by historical development.

The intrinsic connection, Dewey wrote, which exists between freedom of choice and freedom of action, depends on an *intelligent* choice. It must be a choice which is able to generate actions and powers which are desired by us, which affect or create the causes of expected and desired effects.

Hegel wrote that freedom is "comprehended necessity"; Dewey wrote that freedom depends on intelligent choice.

Hegel wrote that history, being the evolution of the idea of freedom, develops as a spiral; Dewey asserted the same: an intelligent choice enlarges our sphere of action, and then the new greater experience opens wider possibilities of an even more intelligent choice and therewith the *spiral* of freedom widens.

Freedom is in something which "comes to be"; it is "in consequences, rather than in antecedents"; we are free not in a static but in a dynamic sense; we are free "as far as we are becoming different from what we have been."[34] Freedom is interpreted as a process by both Hegel and Dewey. History for Hegel is the evolution of the idea of freedom; for Dewey it is "human progress in freedom." For both philosophers freedom takes on various forms; it embraces multiple contents; it must overcome endless obstructions that arise.

Intelligent choice, Dewey wrote, on the part of an individual reflects his forecast of the consequences of acting upon the various competing preferences; it reflects the anticipation of the results of acting one way or another.

Once Dewey connected the problem of choice with the question of future activity and participation, he shifted his attention from thought to practicality, from subjectivity to objectivity, from ideas to effects, from thinking to acting.

He wrote: "Freedom is the power to act in accordance with choice. It is actual ability to carry desire and purpose into operation, to execute choices when they are made."[35]

Institutions and laws, Dewey argued, can constitute obstructions preventing the free execution of one's choices. These obstacles are called oppression. The struggles for freedom, the endless battles for it, have never been battles for freedom of choice, but for freedom of *operation* and *execution* of choice. A freedom which is worth fighting for can be attained by the abolition of impediments which traditionally were the oppressive measures of government, its laws.

The process of the abolition of oppression is a process of liberation, of achieving "rights" and removing obstacles.

In the eighteenth and nineteenth centuries the concept of freedom, as initiated by John Locke, blended in the ideas of liberalism, Dewey wrote. According to the economic and political ideas of *laissez-faire,* every positive action of the government must be oppressive; "hands off," therefore was the main slogan of the liberals. Freedom, by its very existence, they believed, would solve all economic and social problems. The situation changed in the twentieth century.

In 1929, John Dewey wrote in his *Individualism, Old and New:* "We may then say that the United States has steadily moved from earlier pioneer individualism to a condition of dominant corporateness ... Associations tightly or loosely organized more and more define the opportunities, the choices and the actions of individuals ... It was stated at a recent convention of bankers that eighty percent of the capitalization of all the banks of the country is now in the hands of twelve financial concerns."[36]

The remedy against this specific threat to freedom according to him is an active government. Provisions of law alone are not sufficient because the movement toward mergers is too vast, complex, and powerful. The Sherman Anti-Trust Act, Dewey wrote, is no barrier against trusts: "Aside from direct evasions of laws, there are many legal methods of carrying the movement forward."[37]

What is required to change this situation? "The political control of the future to be effective must take a positive instead of a negative form,"[38] Dewey wrote.

This is Dewey's main concept in the sphere of the theory of law and the state: laws are necessary but insufficient to save and to foster freedom; they should not only "protect", but also actively promote desired results.

Hegel wanted to use the centralized state power against feudal stratification, which he regarded the main impediment to freedom. In this way he reached his famous conclusion that the state is a "kingdom of freedom," a conclusion which has often been misinterpreted. Marx radically rejected any defense of the state, writing that states exist in order to restrict freedom. State power, therefore, should be limited and diminished to the point of eliminating it altogether. This sounds like a paradox; in fact, however, Marx moved from Hegel towards liberalism. Dewey, in contrast, accepted Hegel's idea that the state should combat all impediments on the road to freedom. Such obstacles in the twentieth century are created by the powerful business corporations. The paradox here is that Dewey was more Hegelian and more anti-liberal than Marx. The state is a realm of freedom for Hegel, but for Dewey it is an instrument to gain freedom.

Dewey stressed that it was the government that should take the initiative to remove all kinds of obstacles, especially economic, where self-expression "of a few may impede, although manifested in strict accordance with law, the self-expression of others."[39] Therefore, in the 20th century, inactivity of the state is harmful for freedom. What we need is a positive, affirmative action by the government to create the necessary social conditions in which an individual can operate according to his free choice.

Law, according to Dewey, can serve as a means to an end. That end should be freedom. As political, economic and social conditions change, laws must also change. Our civilization, culture, and mutual interdependence are becoming more and more universal. That is one of Dewey's most important observations, originally made in the 1920's and reaffirmed many times. It is therefore necessary that reasonable laws and rights also must become more and more universal and more humane in order to achieve the ends which more and more become universal, embracing all humanity. The democratic rights of individuals and of republican systems all over the world are the necessary although ponderous and difficult means which promote progress on the road to humanism. Progress must take place on the national and on the international scale.

E. *Freedom and Privacy*

The questions of democracy, freedom and privacy are inseparable. It is significant that in the most comprehensive description of ancient democracy put forth by Pericles at the beginning of the Peloponnesian War, the concept of privacy was as classically defined as democracy itself:

> And, just as our political life is free and open, so is our day-to-day life in our relations with each other. We do not get into a state with our next-door neighbour if he enjoys himself in his own way, nor do we give him the kind of black looks which, though they do no real harm, still do hurt people's feelings. We are free and tolerant in our private lives: but in public affairs we keep to the law.[40]

In the same paragraph we find the famous definition of democracy:

> Our constitution is called a democracy because power is in the hands not of a minority, but of the whole people . . .[41]

In this way three important ideas were combined in one single declaration: democracy, legality, and privacy.

In order to enjoy all three, the citizens must be "free and tolerant in their private lives." Privacy, according to Pericles, means that there are spheres which are not subject to political, public, or legal regulation, spheres in the life of every person which are exclusively his own, with the right to "enjoy himself in his own way."

The concept of privacy was judicially defined in the United States at the turn of the century.

In an article which is considered a classic, Samuel D. Warren and Louis D. Brandeis wrote:

> The makers of our Constitution ... sought to protect Americans in their beliefs, their thoughts, their emotions and their sensations. They conferred, as against the Government, the *right to be let alone—the most comprehensive of rights and the right most valued by civilized men.*[42]

The most comprehensive recent explanation of the concept of privacy was made by Thomas I. Emerson in the following way:

> Generally speaking, the concept of a right to privacy attempts to draw a line between the individual and the collective, between self and society. The right of privacy, in short, establishes an area excluded from the collective life, not governed by the rules of collective living. It is based upon premises of individualism, that the society exists to promote the worth and the dignity of the individual. It is contrary to theories of total commitment to the state, to society, or to any part thereof.[43]
>
> Legal protection for the right of privacy has progressed at two levels. At one level is the body of law dealing with interference by government with the right to privacy ...
>
> At the other level the law of privacy is directed not against government interference with privacy but against invasion of privacy by private individuals and groups.[44]

The right of privacy should not be confused with freedom itself. We have argued that according to the classic ideals, freedom should be interpreted in a positive, creative, sense, as a "power" of an individual. The right to privacy assures only one element of this power. This right could be likened to a wall surrounding the structure of a power plant. The walls and other protective devices do not create new values, the real process of creation is the most essential feature of freedom.

Every individual must have the right and the opportunity to "shut out the community,"[45] to go into "seclusion" in order to restore his spiritual and physical forces. But the real problem is not so much the right to seclusion, but to have the opportunity and genuine authority to act, to create.

Privacy cannot exist today without laws protecting the individual against intrusion and infringement upon personal activity. These laws accord persons a power and a liberty to act in accordance with their own personal feelings, selfish interest, private convictions, resentments, prejudices, and inclinations. The rights of others however, may not be invaded.

The problem that should be explored in this connection is the relationship between the right of privacy, and *other* human and constitutional rights, and democracy—which is after all a political system in which the will of the majority (if not the "will of all") prevails. To what extent can the "general will" interfere with the rights described as "constitutional," or "human"?

Jean-Jacques Rousseau presents the concept of "general will" as if it were the simplest mathematical equation: one should just cancel out all "pluses" and "minuses," all the "extremes" and "exigencies" from the total sum of all wills, and the result will be what is "generally" desired and approved—the "general will."

Unfortunately, in the process of cancelling out, so many political antagonisms and passions arise that—as shown by Lion Feuchtwanger in his classic *It Is Folly To Be Wise*—they can not be peacefully resolved.

Let us suppose that we were able to distill from the "will of all" the mystical "general will" and act according to it. Would it really be possible to attain the kingdom of freedom in which everybody is free by virtue of being subject to his own will alone through the medium of the "general will"?

Human activities are diversified and can by no means be limited to political and economic activity. Even if one could be "free" in the narrow sphere of public life regulated by the "general will," there would be still many other areas of life in which the beneficent influence of the general will would not be felt.

Of course it is also possible that the general will could regulate all of life. The result would be the total regulation of an individual's life. According to this philosophy more regulation would mean more freedom. Absolute regulation by the general will would mean absolute freedom; but in actuality it would be the total subjugation resembling total slavery a great deal more than anything most people would describe as freedom. If there is any sense in the old Roman saying *"summum ius, summa iniuria,"** *"absolute freedom"* in Rousseau's Orwellian counter-Utopia would mean *absolute slavery.*

The same analysis could be used *mutatis mutandis* for the problems of freedom under the rule of the majority.

In sum, it is important to create, protect, and develop safeguards to protect the freedom of the minority, because without such safeguards no majority can long succeed. These qualifications are necessary to avoid the trap which could come from an oversimplistic interpretation of the "general will" or the "will of the majority" as the source of political freedom. In legal and political terms it means that there are certain areas of life, called "privacy" and "rights," which should not be subject to the arbitrary and capricious will of any government, even one that represents the "general will."

---

*The highest law is the highest injustice.

Analyses of the documents adopted by the United Nations indicate that the concept of privacy, as elaborated and developed since the time of Pericles through the Renaissance and the era of Brandeis, down to the latest achievements of American jurisprudence, has become "internationalized." Although the Declaration and Conventions reflect a confluence of various philosophies, social theories, and political programs, they all tend to increase individual power to engage in real action and every person's right sometimes to "be let alone."

IX.
JURIDICAL POSITIVISM RECONSIDERED AND UPDATED

1. A New Phase in the Evolution of Juridical Positivism

Juridical positivism is a theory which matured during the rise of national states when—as Austin's commentator, Robert Campbell, observed—the principle that "the command of the State largely pervades the relations and transactions of its individual members—a principle inherited from Roman institutions, and which is the backbone of modern civilization, became prevalent."[1]

Exactly when the command of the State started largely to pervade the "relations and transactions" of its citizens cannot be determined with mathematical precision. The period was not brief. Even the concept of "pervading" is not very clear. Nevertheless Campbell's comments on Austin, in substance, are correct: juridical positivism is a philosophy which developed in modern societies (or those becoming modernized) with modern industries, commerce, private property, means of communication, bureaucracy, and courts. It is a stage in which the division of labor is reflected in some form of division of governmental powers.

There were periods when the distinction between

state-enforced laws and other social norms was not so clearly defined; there were periods when it was difficult to distinguish a command as the essential feature of legal norms as contrasted with recommendations or advice. All these facts from the past, even if truly presented and assessed, should not be construed as a denial of the possibility of the existence of a general theory of law, but rather as an indication that in modern times one should have a modern theory of law which "implies a State and an organized ruling power within it."[2]

There have been periods in the history of humankind when the norms that were observed did not have a legal character, although they were respected and enforced in various ways. The definition of modern law cannot, and should not, encompass this "prelegal" phase of human history.[3]

We will consider the modern form of juridical positivism and its latest phase. In government, this is the phase of highly advanced "étatisme", bureaucratization, and the enormous proliferation of statutes and norms.

As was mentioned in the Introduction, it has become fashionable to criticize juridical positivism for being obsolete, antihumanistic, and amoral, a theory by which even unrepresentative governments gain respectability and the badly needed appearance of legitimacy.

Is there any cure for these asserted evils of juridical positivism? The accusers reply: let us return to the eternal source of wisdom, equity, and justice, to the natural law.

Indeed, after a thorough and objective examination of the real philosophical and social meaning of juridical positivism, one is driven to conclude that it was and has remained the best scientific approach to an explanation of the nature of law, which, like every scientific theory, must be elaborated and adjusted to modern times, to new experience and modern requirements of life. In the philosophy of juridical positivism one can find elements of timeless values and truths combined, as usual, with elements representing past values and ideals.

We have already shown that it is not true that juridical positivism has any specific qualities attractive to tyrants. It is true, however, that any philosophy, including any philosophy of law, can be abused and misconstrued for antihumanistic and despotic ends. The theories of natural law connected with the American and French Revolutions were not exempt from this fate either; on the contrary, the concepts of natural law were more frequently and for longer periods used for antidemocratic purposes. The historical experience of the fight against despotism and tyranny does not support the claims of the natural law theorists any more than it does those of juridical positivism.[4]

The philosophy of law known as juridical positivism, if scientifically and correctly interpreted and construed, presents one of the most precise instruments society has for defending democratic liberties and human rights and for securing economic, social, and political progress. If juridical positivists today are in retreat or on the defensive, if they prefer to hide or just call themselves by some other name, that is the result of a mixture of terminological misunderstanding, ignorance of history, social hypocrisy, and political mythology.

If the history of mankind can, by a deliberate simplification, be presented as a history of social and political struggles, if the history of philosophy can be regarded as a history of the struggles between rational and irrational ideas, then the history of the philosophy of law can be presented, although with considerable but still admissible oversimplification, as a history of the struggle between natural law theories and juridical positivism, between the law of Creon and the right of Antigone. But one qualification is necessary: the values of these theories and laws in the course of historical evolution were interchangeable; at times it was Creon and at times Antigone who represented the "truth," humanity, the spirit of the epoch, and the cause of progress.

In the last decades of the twentieth century we have definitely entered into a period when juridical positivism, if defined and interpreted according to its progressive historical tradition and not as a "pure theory" in support of accidental despots, can serve as a shield for freedom, progress, tolerance, humanism, and human rights. Because of the evolution of international law and national legal systems, because of governmental legislative acts, constitutions, and declarations (whether sincerely intended or not, since in any case these are positive facts), a sufficient number of positive legal norms now are in existence to defend noble ideas, ideals, and attitudes. Antigone today would not have to appeal to a "higher," "divine," or "natural" law in order to defend her cause. She, or her lawyer, would know all the appropriate provisions of international, constitutional, administrative, penal, and civil law in order to fight the illegal edicts of Creon, their interpretation and application, and his sophisms which violated the basic provisions of law, morality, and subjective rights. Creon's statement that he alone represented the *raison d'etat*, as well as "law and order," should, and could, have been challenged successfully in an independent court. A modern Antigone would fare better by appealing to the pertinent provisions of the internal and international law than to divine laws. We know that courts are not independent in a despotic system, and therefore under such systems, judgment would have gone against Antigone. But, what difference would it have made for her if she were to appeal to the "higher," or "divine" laws instead of quoting the constitution, the Declaration of Human Rights, the Helsinki Accord, or the appropriate articles of the penal code? Certainly, she would not have fared better. On the contrary, appeals to "higher law" are appeals to "law" that the Court does not recognize.

We live at a time when declarations of freedom, human rights, and tolerance have been transformed into rules of positive law. Today at least three-fourths of the existing governments and regimes regard these humanistic and liberal norms as a burden and try to treat them as if they were meaningless. Those governments avail themselves of every conceivable perverted argument, irrational philosophy, and obsolete ideology to nullify them. But arguments resting on the constitution do not let those governments and their ideologues get away too easily with their bad conscience, phraseology, misinterpretations, and common lies.

Even hypocrisy and lies have their logic and their often undesired consequences in politics. Once governments undertake to respect human rights and liberties, they can be hounded and pursued by the vindicators of the law as Macbeth was tormented and harassed by the ghosts of Duncan and Banquo. The philosophy of juridical positivism today constitutes one of the best elaborated, even if not yet very efficient, instruments with which to achieve the goals of freedom, democracy, and peaceful cooperation among nations.

2. Juridical Mythology and Demythification of Juridical Positivism

Juridical positivism prepared an ideological basis for juridical dogmatism, for what its adversaries call juridical "idiocy." This does not mean that juridical positivism should be held responsible for the absurdities of its followers. Is there any social philosophy or political theory which cannot be perverted? Even the best theory of interpretation based on the philosophy of positive law can easily be perverted for purposes alien to law and justice. The traditional theory of interpretation is not dogmatic in the sense of complete detachment from individual human affairs and indifference toward equity. Indeed, legal norms are incorporated in the legal systems of every modern country which can and should be used to avoid the extremes, not to say the cruelty, of a literal and strict application of laws.

These norms include such doctrines as those prohibiting unjust enrichment, or allowing the defense of insanity or irresistible impulse.

Application of these juridical doctrines to particular cases, can immediately annihilate any possibility of dogmatism. But even if one takes these notions into consideration, it would still be possible to present any case in dogmatic form.

Every case has its own peculiarities which must be taken into consideration by jurists; and from these peculiarities the "essence," must be deduced which fits the description provided by a legal norm. Every legal norm is general although degrees of "generality" are different and represent various "steps" (*"Stufen"*—as the Austrian positivist, *Adolf Merkel,* used to argue) of the juridical ladder. Oliver Wendell Holmes in *Schenck v. U.S.* (1910) observed:

"We admit that in many places and in ordinary times the defendants in saying all that was said in the circular would have been within their constitutional rights. But the character of every act depends upon the circumstances in which it is done."[5]

What is a "circumstance?" Everything which exists in nature and society can become a "circumstance" in a given case. Factors irrelevant in one case can become essential in another apparently similar one. But what is essential or non-essential will be determined in the rhetorical "give and take" of discourse in which, as was argued previously, the rules of formal logic and syllogism must be observed, but cannot replace reason.

Referring to the same case *(Schenck v. U.S.)* Justice Holmes analyzes the problem of "the substantive evils which the Congress has a right to prevent," and adds the following clarification: "It is a question of proximity and of degree."[6]

Are there any fixed rules to measure "proximity or degree?" Of course not, but that does not mean that the distinction between degrees is completely arbitrary and undefinable in a democratic society in which all the freedoms including a free judiciary exist. Holmes's famous criterion of "a clear and present danger," is not a fixed rule with an absolute, eternally established, content, but it is a convenient instrument whose applicability and validity also depend on the "circumstances" and on "proximity" and "degree."

The ability to use any legal rule or norm, juridical maxim or criterion, depends on many factors. One of these may be most general and vague, but it is nevertheless indispensable: creative imagination. This necessary feature of the juridical mind was stressed by the positivist H.L.A. Hart when he defended the positivist school and the positivist Holmes: He wrote: ". . . I wish first to say why I think that Holmes, whatever the vicissitudes of his American reputation may be, will always remain for Englishmen a heroic figure in jurisprudence. This will be so because he magically combined two qualities: one of them is imaginative power, which English legal thinking has often lacked; the other is clarity, which English legal thinking usually possesses."[7]

Imagination is a quality of mind which can be developed by study and experience, art and science. It is a quality indispensable to every act of intellectual creation. To what degree depends on the branch of science or art concerned and on many other factors. But there is no doubt that the requirements of the "imaginative power" are more demanding for a true positive jurist than for a representative of mechanistic jurisprudence who tries to remain within the self-imposed limits of "a rigid scheme of deductions"[8]

Legal positivism and especially its realistic 20th century form must combine strictness of observation and interpretation of legal norms (statutes and precedents) with sociological imagination. The correct interpretation of law depends, among other things, on the imaginative power of the jurist; legality (or due process of law) depends on the correct interpretation and application of law. Legality and imagination are not contradictory; they are really inseparable.

The level of imagination nevertheless remains in direct proportion to the general culture of society, its education, scholarly level, artistic inclinations, and moral sensitivity. Law, ethics, aesthetics, art, personal culture mixed with juridical culture are mutually interdependent and they meet in the great hall of imagination. They constitute the only effective antidote against mythology, whose role in jurisprudence cannot be overestimated.

Mythology, together with all its panoply of symbols and images, pervades the interpretation and application of the provisions of law. One can apply to law the remark made by Walter Lippman with regard to politics: "There ... [has] been passed down from generation to generation a collection of concepts which are so hallowed and so dense that their only use is to excite emotions and to obscure insight.

"How many of us really know what we are talking about when we use the words the state, sovereignty, independence, democracy, representative government, national honor, liberty, and loyalty? Very few of us, I think, could define any of these terms under cross-examination, though we are prepared to shed blood, or at least ink, in their behalf."⁹

Mythology matters much in a democracy, especially during elections, disappointments, defeats, and political reaction. But myths are especially significant and ominous in every totalitarian regime.

The people of Germany were fed with the myths of the omniscient Fuhrer, of the "purity" and "superiority" of German blood, of "the Versailles *Diktat* and robbery," of the "encirclement" by the "Jewish superpowers." In the Soviet Union there was created a myth of the "dictatorship of the proletariat," which was endangered by omnipresent "enemies of the people" using every natural and supernatural means to undermine the "people's power." On this sick ground the crime of slandering of the Soviet Union was invented.

Let us call to mind the decision of the Supreme Court in the case of *Minersville School District* v. *Gobitis* and the famous tirade of Justice Frankfurter in favor of patriotism.[10] Almost every word which Walter Lippman or Ernst Cassirer[11] would regard as mythical was used there.

The power of myths, including juridical and political ones, rests on the fact that to a certain extent they reflect social reality. They partially reflect various social and political relations and they form perverted images—but there are elements of truth even in the most perverted image. Therefore the distortion can appeal to the human imagination. Myths reflect the desires, fears, wishes, prejudices, and illusions of people. They are so powerful that it is doubtful whether mankind can ever overcome them. History was and will be the history of various myths. Jurisprudence cannot completely be cleansed of myth, one can only get rid of the most obsolete and malignant forms.

These considerations lead to one of the most important problems and its mythical expression: the rule of law. To what extent can this famous ideal become a reality and to what extent must it remain a social myth?

What is the real sense, apart from ideology and philosophical phraseology, of the expression, the rule of law? Is there any justification for Paine's famous pronouncement:

"But where, say some, is the king of America? I'll tell you, friend, he reigns above, and does not make havoc of mankind like the royal brute of Britain. Yet that we may not appear to be defective even in earthly honors, let ... a crown be placed thereon, by which the world might know that, so far as we approve of monarchy, in America *the law is king*. For as in absolute governments the king is law, so in free countries the law *ought* to be king; and there ought to be no other."[12]

The first and most important conceivable meaning of the expression, "the law is king," is juridico-positivistic: when provisions of law are duly promulgated, they become relatively independent of their creators and the creators are bound by their own rules and restrictions, and by the rights granted to others. Paine's concept of law combines the revolutionary ideology of natural law with the concept of established "law and order." "King" to Paine is a symbol of the paternal stability and security. The king is positive. He can solve problems and he is a safe shelter for those who need one. Unfortunatley these beliefs represent a new mythology arising in the new society, still rural but with strong urban industrial strata governed by parliamentary institutions.

Unfortunately stability and certainty do not depend on law alone. Law as a ruler can be as capricious as any living ruler.

The mere existence of law is already an open admission that there are conflicts, controversies, and contradictions in society which cannot be solved without legal instruments in the hands of the government. Law is one of the methods of solving problems (at least temporarily), or of controlling antagonisms, at least so that they do not get out of hand. Law is not and cannot be a panacea for all social diseases. Other remedies are needed as well and it should be no wonder that there are also contradictions among the possible and applicable remedies. This is characteristic of all norms: the mere existence of moral norms proves that there are situations, activities, and ways of behavior which certain people regard as improper, immoral, or unjust. Similarly, the existence of aesthetic norms indicates that there are situations or ways of behavior which various people assess as beautiful or ugly. Legal norms exist because our earth is not a paradise but is full of vices and passions. In these human conditions moral and legal norms must coexist, fight each other, support and defeat each other. There must be an endless interplay, cooperation, and struggle between law and morality, and these conflicts can either be resolved by dialogue, arguments, or compromise or, in the absence of amicable settlements, there will be violence; then it will be force that will decide what is "just" or "unjust."

It is a dream, becoming more and more obviously unreasonable, to think that by subjecting law to morality or to "hypothetical" natural law, social, moral, or political dilemmas will be solved. They will remain alive persistently and stubbornly; their forms and substance will be changed, and with the lapse of time they will be formulated in another way. The disputes will continue. It is quite possible that the forms of the arguments will change, without changing their meritorious contents.

By its very nature, law and tradition exercise a

powerful influence on the conscience of every individual. But the ideas and feelings of charity and equity, especially in the countries where Judeo-Christian systems of religion and ethics prevail, also influence minds, characters, and the behavior of people. Does that mean that positive law, as understood by juridical positivism, is incompatible with charity or equity? Conflicts are unavoidable but law does not prohibit the exercise of one's rights with an eye on the traditional virtues.

Legal norms seem more solid, clear, and stable than any other social norms; they are better codified and expressed. Therefore, they can create an illusion, which was developed into a myth, that they can assure stability and an orderly system of change and reform. Almost everybody, sooner or later, becomes a victim of this myth. One could also counterargue: if almost everybody is a victim of such a malaise, then perhaps this mental discomfort is the normal state of mankind, necessary for its normal functioning? If we can rule over nature by being its minister, as Bacon observed, than it is quite possible that we can overcome certain myths, by at least a partial subjection to others.

Oliver Wendell Holmes observed that he, as a justice, could not solve the problems which the politicians were unable to solve. Law is inseparable from politics; political conflicts are reflected in the system of law, in its theory and practical administration.

The content of politics is the complex of relations between:
—various social and economic classes, and groups;
—social strata and state power;
—social groups and political parties;
—individuals and the social classes, parties, state power;

—individuals and social classes on the one hand and the nation (nationalities) on the other;
—individuals, their social groups, the nation and state on the one hand and the world community (mankind) on the other.

The driving forces of politics and morality are the antagonisms, the inevitably staggering differences among the actors. Among all these antagonisms, the most important and persistent are the economic ones. Sometimes they do not seem to be the most emotional issues because they are overshadowed by problems which at any given moment are more sensitive and visible, but nevertheless they raise the question of economic advantages or disadvantages which are behind the majority of existing antagonisms.

All observations pertaining to the content of politics can be applied to any legal system, its theory and practice.

One of the most destructive myths in existence is that government and law can resolve the problems and antagonisms inherent in a given economic and social structure of society. Governments and legislators can smooth over, or exacerbate, many basic antagonisms, but they cannot achieve what can only be accomplished through far reaching changes in the social and economic structure.

The mythology surrounding the state and law is so enormous that it is second only to the mythology surrounding gods and the origins of nature. Therefore we have to return once more to our previous question:

How do myths come into being? Is a myth ultimately derived from fantasy, from the play of subjective ideas? Is it a result of persuasion by others, or does it rest in the last resort upon a reflection of reality? Is mythological thinking a primitive form of knowledge, or can it be connected with the higher, more civilized forms of thinking and knowledge?

There is no such thing as an "absolutely pure," "absolutely independent" fantasy. Fantasies in the final analysis are also the reflection of the external world in the human mind. Even the most daring results of creative fantasy can always be traced to reality and to sensual perceptions. A myth is born, let us repeat once more, out of perceptions of reality. But these perceptions are distorted, one sided, mutilated and exaggerated. When the aggregate of these exaggerated perceptions becomes a "solid" subtance in human mind, something "steady" and "indissoluble" over a period of time, then the myth is born. Once the myth has been created in and by the "heat oppressed mind" *(Macbeth)* it does not behave passively; it does not remain any longer one of the relatively innocent elements of human consciousness. On the contrary: a myth becomes a filter and poison at the same time. A myth is an intellectual cancer. Whatever enters the mind and is even remotely related to the body which we call myth, can immediately fall victim to the censorship performed by it; the new idea is filtered and reshaped according to the demands of the absolute ruler in the mind, the myth.

Kalif Omar, when ordering the burning of the Alexandrian library, gave a classic example of mythological thinking combined with the activities instigated by mythological passions. He explained: "Whatever is in accordance with the Koran is unnecessary, whatever is against the Koran is harmful and should not exist." Myths are not only destructive of the mind, but they also liberate and instigate a passion for destruction. Mythical thought by its very nature is intolerant. It is a way of reflecting that is not based on reason, thereby making the products of reason suspect and usually repudiating them. In the sphere of mythical thinking, even the law of contradiction, not to mention other laws of rational thought, is invalidated. When a reasonable, civilized man is convinced that his reasoning containes a logical error, he becomes persuaded. A mind damaged by myth (ideology, religion, myth of race, myth of equality, myth of revenge, etc.) would reject all the principles of Aristolelian logic, rather than give up the myth.

One of the most popular current political and juridical myths is the thesis that law can be a ruler (or a king). It is one of the most popular and appealing illusions produced by Western civilization in the last two hundred years, but it is still only an illusion. It is a myth fostered by wishful thinking. People long for stability, justice, freedom; they want to feel secure; they want to be free from fear, hunger, and arbitrariness. They have lost faith in God as the promoter of these unfulfilled dreams; they have become sufficiently experienced and critical to have lost confidence in the good will of secular rulers; they no longer trust kings, presidents, governments, parliaments, party secretaries, politburos and even, last but not least, the courts. They live in political societies, in states under governments and they know that they cannot escape their fate. They must be the subjects of political power. They trust no one, however, because experience has shown that every part of government, every branch of the state, of the Leviathan, has deceived them, persecuted them, deprived them of their rights, their property, their decency. To whom should they look to rescue them? What can represent stability and hope in such a social jungle? It seems that after the gods and kings have been dethroned, only the law remains as a last resort. Legal mythology has replaced theology and magic. One could easily and justifiably expand Thomas Paine's assertion to say that "the law is king and God at the same time." Law becomes Providence.

Gods were created by fear, Epicurus and Lucretius observed a long time ago. The same could be said of the belief in legalistic divinity, about the law being king, providence, protector of justice, and the hope of a hopelessly divided world.

Legal and political fictions are "useful" only in unusual circumstances, such as those described by Bentham himself: "As well might the father of a family make it a rule never to let his children have their breakfast till they have uttered, each of them, a certain number of lies, curses, and profane oaths; and then exclaim: 'You see, my dear children, how necessary lying, cursing, and swearing are to human sustenance.'"[13] Repeated a thousand times, this procedure will create a myth: lying and cursing is useful.

Legal norms by themselves produce nothing positive and substantial. They are helpful, however, when they reflect both social reality and social needs. They are useful when those who interpret and apply them want to use them for good ends; they can be harmful when manipulated by social outcasts. Law cannot be king; it cannot replace a good government, but it is an indispensable help and instrument of a good political system.

The effectiveness of every declaration on individual or human rights, the effectiveness of every constitution or statute, even the most democratic, elaborated with all possible legal and institutional guarantees—does not depend on law alone. Law is always and everywhere only a part of the social and political system, only one of many institutions existing in society. In the life of every society are ups and downs, periods of growth and decline, periods of growing moral sensitivity and phases of moral numbness. Good constitutions and laws can help to overcome difficulties, tame passions, and increase the accountability of rulers. But even the best laws cannot create what the society, or at least its active part, does not want to accomplish; laws cannot prevent disasters if disasters are demanded by those who are in control of public opinion and the centers of power.

In his volume, *The Growth of American Constitutional Law*, Professor Benjamin F. Wright observed:

"The history of judicial review does not furnish the evidence to indicate that the Supreme Court will, in periods of intense feelings or hysteria, afford a sanctuary to those whose views run counter to the popular will."[14] Charles A. Beard commented that this sad prediction meant that the Supreme Court would not afford a sanctuary " in the very periods when courage is most needed."[15]

The sense of these observations is very significant from the sociological and political viewpoints: the judicial branch, even its highest level, furnished with the most effective and far reaching guarantees of independence and personal security, is influenced by the political moods and atmosphere of the country and finds in the allegedly petrified legal formulas the concepts that prevailing opinion wants them to see. And they make decisions which they themselves would have found strange in a period devoid of "intense feelings and hysteria."

Nevertheless, in these periods of degradation we need good constitutions, good laws, and good juridical precedents because they can serve as an ideal which is not utopian and can be helpful in the progressive shaping of reality.

3. Interpretation of Law and Modern Values

"Analytical positivism," Wolfgang Friedmann writes, "by its emphasis on logic and obedience to written law, tends to regard stability and certainty as the paramount objects of legal interpretation."[16]

Friedmann expresses two ideas here:

a) Analytical positivism regards "stability and certainty" as the chief purposes of law;

b) These purposes can be deduced from the fact that emphasis is put on "logic and obedience to written law." The attitude described in point "b" is, for Professor Friedmann, one of the proofs of the correctness of the idea stated in point "a."

One can agree with the assertion under "a" without qualification, but not necessarily with the reasoning of "b."

The use of formal logic to interpret the law cannot by itself assure stability and certainty. What the provisions of law are and what are their relations to social reality are also important. If a law is the result of legislative doubletalk, then nothing logicians can do will clarify where clarity was never intended. In such a situation logic can be used, or rather abused, to produce more uncertainty.

Sometimes laws are obsolete and are regarded as antisocial by much of society. When that is true, a strict logical interpretation and application can be disruptive and cause disorder and uncertainty rather than create stability. The institution of *lettres de cachet* in pre-revolutionary France, "strictly" and "logically" applied could have had but one effect: indignation, fear, and revolution—indeed it is absurd to apply "logic" to "laws" concerning *lettres de cachet*. According to Stalinist law the verdict of a secret tribunal consisting of three officers of the security police was final; the tribunals acted on the basis of a record produced by lower security officers. Neither the defendant nor his lawyer (lawyers were almost unheard of) had any right to appear before this tribunal; defendants could not offer evidence or explanations of any kind. Death sentences under that law were executed almost immediately.

In such a "juridical situation," what good is it to emphasize "logic and obedience to written law"? In inhuman circumstances formal logic and "obedience to written law" aggravate the cruelty and add insult to injury.

There are many good reasons to argue that the decision in the case of Dred Scott was logically faultless. But it was inhumane. One could argue that the decision of the court was discordant with the Constitution of the United States. In hindsight, that is true. But for three quarters of a century the existence of slavery and the Constitution were considered to be compatible; in fact, there would have been no Constitution and no United States if they had not been compatible.

It was not formal logic applied to the interpretation of the Constitution which changed this abominable situation. One must use more "subtle" or more "crude" instruments to interpret the law in order to prove the incompatibility of slavery with the Constitution. Formal logic is useful to assure "stability and certainty" but is not sufficient. We already discussed other aspects of this problem in the chapter on the rhetorical interpretation of law. Here we return to one such aspect: Roguin's *(La Science Juridique Pure, 1923)* assertion that the interpretation and application of law should be regarded as beyond logical science.

Roguin considered himself a pure legal scientist and a consistent positivist. His "pure theory" was far removed from Kelsen's, however, Roguin believed that juridical norms only should be taken into consideration in juridical practice and juridical science, and not their application.[17]

Such a concept represents a basic misunderstanding of the role of legal norms, of the importance of legal science, and of positivism itself. Roguin narrows positivism down to the knowledge that legal norms exist and he does not want to go beyond this trivial understanding, leaving the rest to anyone who might be concerned with it. Indeed, the science of law, and especially of juridical positivism, defines what law is, not for the sake of a definition *in* and *for* itself, but—first all all—to define a point of departure for the legal sciences, particularly that of interpreting and applying the law in connection with the social sciences and with social situations.

But Roguin's oversimplification leads to a basic problem: does the philosophy of law have any practical meaning and influence? A general philosophy which one accepts more or less consciously, can determine the attitudes of the people, their behavior, choices, decisions, biases, prejudices, and inclinations, to a certain degree only. A philosophy of law is more down to earth than a general philosophy, being at the same time an integral part of a general philosophy; it is a part of the general *Weltanschauung*. As such it also flies high and is one of the sources of general moral and philosophical precepts. On the other hand, being at once general and particular, a philosophy of law can influence the general attitudes and ways of thinking of a people and can influence the interpretation and application of law generally. As a matter of fact, in every important decision (not merely technical, such as terms, fees, prescriptions, signs, etc.), made by jurists, and especially that reached by the courts, the philosophical, ideological, *"Weltanschauliche"* attitude is influential.

One of the tasks of a modern philosophy of law is to convert an unconscious dependence on philosophy and morality into a conscious one in the process of selecting values while interpreting and applying the law.

A narrow view of juridical interpretation is one of the products of a narrow understanding of legal positivism, but it is not legal positivism itself that should be held responsible for that. In his famous dissertation, published in 1906, Paul Van der Eycken defines that juridical interpretation tends to find solution of a given case with the help of the written provisions of law.

Chaim Perelman characterized the above definition as *"plus positiviste que le droit positif."*[18]

One of the reasons for Perelman's assertion is that

Paul Van der Eycken excludes from his method of interpretation not only natural law, but the notion of the general principles of law as well.

What are these general principles? Is it possible to forget them or neglect them? Is it possible not to find them in the legal material? This important problem was raised by Dworkin but not solved by him (see para 5). Anyway, there is no need to depart from positive law in order to resolve this dilemma.

The controversy between consistent legal positivists and those who reject positivism to support natural law is colorfully reflected in the famous comparison made by Saleilles. He described his own approach as *"Au-dela du code civil, mais par le code civil."* Geny's approach is characterized as: *"Par le code civil, mais au-dela du code civil."*[19]

If one agrees that Saleilles' approach is feasible, then we have no need to resort to the concept of natural law in order to improve or fill the gaps in the system of law of a modern civilized country with a contemporary constitution. Saleilles' symbolic cliche ought simply to be transformed into a broader, more general formula: *"Au-dela du droit positif, mais par le droit positif."* (Beyond the positive law, but by means of that law).

Saleilles' approach is more legalistic and positive than that of Geny. One should apply the general principles of law, and combine them with justice, equity, and common sense to achieve reasonable and justifiable results without violating the provisions of the law in force and at the same time fill the gaps.

In order to achieve this result, we must consider the legal provisions *in toto*, all parts of the law, not only selected portions. Lord Coke, therefore, "considers the preamble as a key to open the understanding of the Statute."[20]

A preamble can be helpful in ascertaining the true meaning of a juridical act. To be specific, the preamble can be resorted to "in restraint of the generality of the enacting clause, when it would be inconvenient if not restrained." (Kent, Commentaries, I)[21]

The second reason why a preamble may be useful is to explain "the enacting clause, if it be doubtful."[22]

Let us briefly remark that it is possible to be a juridical positivist and consider that the sources of law are not only normative, but also normal "prose," the prose of Mr. Jourdain, when used in preambles or in introductions explaining the intentions of the legislator.

Kent distinguishes between the real and the literal sense of statutes. He writes:

> The true meaning of the statute is generally and properly to be sought from the body of the act itself... It is an established rule in the exposition of statutes, that the intention of the lawgiver is to be deduced from a view of the whole and of every part of a statute, taken and compared together. The real intention, when accurately ascertained, will always prevail over the literal sense of the terms.[23]

Is incompatibility between the "real" or "true" meaning of a statute and the "literal sense" unavoidable? Must such a problem emerge?

Our approach to the interpretation of law throws a special light on the problem of the "authentic" interpretation of law, that is, the interpretation made by the legislator himself. According to the old maxim: *eius est interpretari legem, cuius est condere*. If an authentic interpretation has power as binding as law itself, then the term "interpretation" is misleading, for indeed the legislator has issued a new law calling it an interpretation.

Considering the contents of the interpreted norm, there are three possibilities:

1. The behavior prescribed by the "authentic interpretation" is exactly the same as that prescribed by the norm; or

2. The interpretation changes the behavior prescribed by the norm; or

3. The norm is so unclear that one cannot determine its meaning, and consequently a practical application of its is impossible without the interpretation.

If the "authentic" interpretation completely coincides with the norm, there is no need for it. But as far as jurists are concerned, any "official" interpretation is the source of additional trouble. If they believe in a dynamic theory of interpretation and feel that the legal provisions have objectively started to exist independently of their creator, should they then dig into the text of the law only, or should they also search for the "deep" meaning of the norms in official interpretations?[24]

If the interpretation changes the ascertained meaning of the norm in an obvious way, then the legislator has changed the law, but not in the usual way, not in good faith, and perhaps in a manner contrary to the constitution.

If the change in a law is not apparent, so that specialists are needed to detect the change, then one must conclude that the legislator was afraid to disclose his real intentions, that he was attempting to deceive his constituents. Laws in books usually survive their creators. Should successors be obliged to follow a false interpretation which was rendered *in male fide*? Should they not return to the original text of the law and put the interpretation aside?

The legislator's decision to issue his own "authentic" interpretation which is contrary to the law is always a political decision, inviting a political counteraction against an allegedly juridical pronouncement. The result must be a debasement of law.

In such a case an additional interpretation is advisable, not to say necessary. Without this interpretation jurists would have to interpret norms through the use of the rules of interpretation. If in the process of interpreting an unclear norm the intention of the legislator is distorted, then only the legislator himself is to blame, but what about applying the maxim: *nullum crimen sine lege*?

Our conclusions concerning authentic interpretations do not in any way contradict one of our fundamental theses, that the meaning of legal norms by their nature is at the same time both determined and limitless, because every new set of circumstances gives us a new opportunity to refine and ascertain the meaning of a norm.

The legislator usually knows what he wants to express and he also knows what he does not want to say. But his influence on the objective meaning of the norm is limited because once he promulgates the norm it becomes someting independent of him; its independent life commences. The legislator is bound by the meaning of the words he used to the same degree as any other citizen in the country.

When the norm becomes "independent," then the

legislator himself, when he invokes it, must interpret it. He also faces the problem of what is clear and what is obscure in the process of applying this norm to the given case.

Is it necessary to interpret every juridical text on every occasion in order to apply it?

According to the Cartesian way of thinking the answer should be: I must interpret every text so long as it is necessary in order to understand it clearly and distinctly. When I reach this level of understanding, I can stop interpreting and start applying the clearly and distinctly understood provisions of law to the various situations, to the facts.

The Cartesian approach gives rise to a perennial problem: is it possible to reach such a stage of clarity? Is clarity an objective state, or a subjective conviction? If it is subjective, then I am the person who decides when to stop interpreting and start applying a text. If it is an objective state, then, once again, a new question arises: how do we know when we have reached it? Such criteria, as we know, have not been found and unanimously accepted by all mankind. In fact, they can never be found, but one can argue, according to the principles of rhetoric, *for* or *against* the criteria used in any given case. Whenever we face a new set of facts which need to be legally evaluated, we start by interpreting the relevant legal norms because in new circumstances no norms are clear or obvious.

One can generally argue that every juridical norm must be interpreted before it can be applied. Every legal norm is an abstraction and needs to be "brought down" to earth; it must be reduced to more simple elements in order to be able to come to grips with the facts of a particular case. Every application of law is connected with some kind of interpretion, although not every interpretation must be applied in practice. As Ch.B. Nutting observes: "While students of semantics may explore the problem of 'meaning' at their leisure, courts must decide cases."[25]

Students of law, especially philosophers of law, can engage in endless disputes concerning the real meaning of a norm, but jurists—attorneys and judges—must decide the case before them, even in the midst of the most heated public controversy.

Philosophers and theologians, for instance, can engage in endless discussion about the origin of life, whether a fetus is a person, or whether life stops with the death of the brain or the beat of the heart, but the courts must decide such questions quickly, from a practical point of view, because it is their duty to do so and their failure to do so promptly affects the legitimate rights, liberties, and duties of others.

The courts cannot wait for the end of a discussion among scientists, moralists, and politicians; they must make their decisions according to their best knowledge and understanding at a given time, and in this way they contribute to the process of making the law objective.

The meaning they achieve is never absolute but only rhetorical; it is not static, but dynamic; it is not metaphysical, but dialectical; it is not established once and for all time, but is always a stage, a phase in an endless quest for clarity.

Therefore the maxim: *"interpretatio cessat in claris"* (interpretation stops when norms are clear) is itself unclear. "But when can one say—writes Perelman—that a text is clear? When the sense which was given to the text by the legislator is clear? Who created the norms? When is the sense, actually given in the text, found clear by a judge? When do these two senses coincide? Indeed, such a coincidence is insufficient because the legal norm necessarily must be interpreted within the context of the juridical system, and it can oblige one to resort to the reading of the text, the general clauses, which, while supporting the structure as a whole, are not quite clear."[26]

Perelman's reasoning represents a crucial argument against the simplistic application of the maxim on *"interpretatio cessat in claris."* If every legal rule must be interpreted in connection with the "spirit of the laws," the emergence of new doubts is unavoidable. After we start to reinterpret "clear" norms, those which are understood "clearly and distinctly," it will inevitably occur that the norm deemed clear is indeed more abstruse, has more than one meaning, and indicates more than one possible pattern of behavior. The mere act of subsuming facts to norms and vice versa, is conditioned by a set of juridical and social factors, including the general principles of law, the juridical culture of the society, the skill and traditions of the given legal community and the legal profession in general and the "sociological imagination" so highly appreciated by C. Wright Mills.

Traditionally, interpretation used to be classified either as subjective or objective. Followers of subjective interpretation defined the purpose of an interpretation as the determination of the will of the legislator.

The "objectivists" insisted that once it has been duly promulgated a statute started its own life independently of the original legislator and had its own objective sense. This "objective" sense was to be ascertained through the process of interpretation. We will return to the problems of the "subjectivists" and "objectivists."

According to the more modern, but far from exhaustive or generally accepted classification, the two types of interpretation are static and dynamic. This classification, to a certain extent, is related to the division between "subjective" and "objective" interpretation, but it has other, more far reaching consequences.

> "Static interpretation endeavors to determine the will of the legislator who produced the law."[27]

Perelman's description of a dynamic interpretation, however, is not merely the simple antithesis to the subjective; it is much broader and more specific: "The dynamic interpretation consists in interpreting the text as a function of the common good or equity. In the static concept it should not be the judge but rather a historian of law who should prevail . . . The contrary occurs with the dynamic concept, this way of interpretation risks replacing the will of the legislator by the will of the judge. There is a danger that the difference will be erased between the norm which was promulgated and the norm which the judge would like to institute. The interpretation *de lege lata* will be substituted by the ideas *de lege ferenda*, which will not take into account the will manifested by the legislator."[28]

Perelman is right to point out the dangers inherent in the dynamic interpretation. But is there any method of interpretation which is safe? Is it not true that non-interpretation, if such were possible, contains even more dangers? Today, who believes in Montesquieu's utopian recommendation that a judge should restrict himself to acting as *"la bouche des lois"*?

Anyway, the dynamic interpretation of law puts aside the traditional dispute between "objectivists" and "subjectivists." Whatever the point of departure, "objective" or "subjective," the results of the dynamic interpretation of law should be the same. The traditional quarrel between "objectivists" and "subjectivists" is becoming more and more obsolete, although the problem requires a thorough, and critical reevaluation.

The first premise of any theory of the interpretation of law is acceptance that legal norms have certain contents, certain meaning. From the viewpoint of positivistic jurisprudence, a norm can be defined "as an *abstract imperative for human conduct*".[29] The notion of imperative presupposes a double will: "it passes from a *person* to a *person*";[30] it also presupposes *"two* opposing wills—a stronger and a weaker."[31]

Nature herself does not know imperatives, they are an entirely human phenomenon.

The fact that the Supreme Court (and, indeed, any other court) can completely reverse itself, as in the case discussed by Benjamin N. Cardozo, can lead to the conclusion that legal norms do not have any sense at all, that they are empty jars into which one can pour anyting which will easily take the shape of its container just as any fluid would. This is one of Kelsen's famous assertions, and by the way, it illustrates one of the basic differences between the pure and the positivistic theories of law. Of course, one could produce a whole battery of logical arguments that the provisions of such a document as the Constitution are indeed meaningless, because it is illogical to assume that A can be A at one time and at another time A can be not A. But once we apply to the interpretation of law the theory of argumentation and introduce the rhetorical principle of the audience—then the different interpretative operations and the different outcomes become reasonable and acceptable. Let us return to Cardozo's example: in the year 1915 the court thought that it would be more reasonable (one can also say moral, practical, just, equitable, etc.) to find one solution within the existing law, but eight to ten years later the audience and the circumstances changed (a new generation, new experience and moral sensitivity, better arguments, greater appeal of the authors of the decision), and therefore what was previously regarded as less reasonable became more reasonable.

Whoever feels that there can be only one rational interpretation and application of any given norm falls into the dogmatist's trap. The dogmatists and absolutists are consistent and logical, but they are neither humane nor reasonable. *Errare humanum est!* The errors which result from discussion and arguments are not entirely unreasonable. But the errors which result from dogmatism, from "absolute" consistency and logical, rationalistic deductions may be entirely unreasonable, and even more: they can be devastatingly antihuman. What is reasonable can be false, but will always be more or less humane. What is absolutely logical can be a "crackpot" realism, can be inhuman and lead to deeds morally outrageous, if not outright criminal.

The basic philosophical directive in the contemporary interpretation and application of law can be expressed in the following way: all legal norms should be interpreted in such a way that human, democratic rights are not violated but on the contrary, preserved and expanded.

The old Roman maxim: *in dubio pro reo*, should be changed: *in dubio pro iuribus homini* (in case of doubt — decide in favor of human rights).

This concept is philosophical, juridical, moral, and political at the same time.

The use by the police of informers or undercover agents, had not been challenged legally in the United States, say, on the basis of the Fourth Amendment prohibiting unreasonable searches and seizures. The problem arose in the United States first in 1978 in connection with the following developments:

1. The Freedom of Information Act
2. Increased social, political, and moral sensitivity in the post-Watergate era.
3. The extensive interpretation of the notion of "searches and seizures" which started with the dissenting opinions of Justices Holmes and Brandeis in *Olmsted v. United States* (277 US 438, 1928).

It did not take too long for the dissenting minority to become the majority. On the juridical bases of the decisions of the Supreme Court in cases like *Berger v. NY* (388 US 41, 1967; *Katz v. US,* 389 US 347, 1967) the ACLU could have argued that the indiscriminate use of informers, acting without due judicial supervision (Channel 13, July 7, 1978, McNeil-Lehrer Report), amounts to a violation of the Constitution. For two hundred years it was clear that the police had a "right" to use informers. After many years of gradual changes in the social and political climate, after many years' evolution of the interpretation of the Fourth Amendment, suddenly certain people found that the former interpretation was too narrow, although it has not been made clear what should be done to accommodate the social and individual interests, between the need for security and that for privacy, between the common good and legally protected civil rights.

Does that imply that meaning accepted during the previous stage was not objective? that it was erroneous? that it was defective in itself? No, the previous meaning was adjusted to the previous stage of evolution of the social conscience. The new stage requires new clarifications which will become "objective" thanks to the endless social, polical, dialectical, rhetorical discussions based on freedom of persuasion.

We argued that even without natural rights theories, one can deduce that every individual, society, nation, and all mankind have certain basic interests and values, which Hume defined as survival, stability, and security of property. The source of these interests is neither metaphysical nor mystical; the source is the mere existence of human beings as social entities who have an (innate) instinct for self preservation.

Political interests and ideals such as tolerance, liberty, or the right to vote are not as "basic" and "natural" as those enumerated above by Hume. Thomas Hobbes while recognizing the "right to life", rejected any assumption favoring democracy or republicanism. Based on logic and experience, he argued that it was absolute monarchy alone that could create conditions securing life, stability, and property. Hobbes's democratic opponents concentrated on the assumption that tyranny was dangerous to peace and therefore to life.

In the second half of the twentieth century the situation has drastically changed. Every despotism creates a clear and imminent danger to the life of whole groups of the population and, by pushing towards war, endangers the existence of nations. In this way the right to life can no longer be separated from democratic, human, rights; it has become organically connected with them. The right to life, as has already been mentioned, does not have to be deduced from any metaphysical premises.

The right to life in these new political and social circumstances can also serve as a justification for civil disobedience.

Lon Fuller argued that without acceptance of the concept of natural law, one cannot justify resistance against the state because law should not be resisted.[32]

Professor Samuel I. Shuman is right when he resolves Fuller's dilemma by arguing that favoring disobedience" does not imply that what is disobeyed is not law, any more than obedience implies that what is obeyed is law."[33]

Schuman's basic criticism is correct; there can be many reasons for obedience or disobedience of law (besides the moral or "legal.") Law influences many spheres of life, which cannot and should not naively be divided into two spheres: legal and moral. Political, economic, and aesthetic reasons can be regarded as being as good, valid, and convincing as the moral reasons for obedience or disobedience. The people may find that the economic and political consequences of obedience could be so harmful to the country that they would rather choose to disregard the law while still recognizing the given norms as valid law. Anyway, the decision whether to obey or disobey the rules promulgated by the existing authorities and called law by them must be made by the people and the problems for legal positivism are not—as Samuel Schuman once more correctly observed—different from those for any other theory about the nature of law, for example, natural law.[34] If one is a follower of an existentialist, phenomenological, or natural law theory, one has to make decisions within the framework of one's philosophy and the rejection of law in force must be justified *tant bien que mal* as such a rejection done by a juridical positivist.

Every rejection or acceptance of law implies a certain choice of values. All values are in competition, including the value of "domestic tranquillity," which has its special chapter in history. But, on the other hand, the value of international peace should not be identified with domestic peace or "internal security." Therefore, a criticism of this concept should not be applied automatically to international relations. Internal peace is not the highest value, which citizens must pursue at any price.

"I entirely agree with the view that the cases where men or associations oppose the will of the State should always be cases of last instance; I do not need to be convinced that peace is almost always better than conflict."[35]

Throughout the centuries there have been hundreds of writers who believed that internal peace constituted the highest value that governments pursue and defend. This attitude is at the same time political, juridical, and moral. It means, from the political point of view, that whatever the disadvantages might be of living under any form of government, they would still be outnumbered or rather outweighed by the advantages of domestic peace and order. The alternative could be civil war and disorder, which are allegedly always worse than the worst existing "peaceful" reality.

From the juridical point of view, "internal peace" is a very simple concept. It means that the status quo is legal and good, and whoever wants to change it using "illegal" means (a dictator would regard even the mildest criticism as illegal) should be punished according to the provisions of law. "Peace," incorporated in the legal status quo, is accorded juridical value, the purpose and the cause of law at the same time.

Thomas Hobbes was the first and the most eminent philosopher able consciously to combine this approach to the question of the preservation of peace. He identified the norms of morality with the legal norms and, vice versa, law was presented by him as a criterion of justice; the alternative of peace under the sovereign he depicted as a state of war of all against all.

His conclusions were presented in such a clear and categorical manner that he surpassed all his predecessors and successors: the worst peace, he argued, even genuine oppression (but "peaceful"), is still better than the state of *bellum ommium contra ommes*, in which life is nasty poor, mean, brutish, and short.

John Locke, one of the immediate successors of Hobbes in the sphere of political philosophy, also became the most eminent critic of the concept of peace as an "absolute value." The story of Cyclops, who detained Ulysses and his fellows in his cave, according to him, was an excellent example of despotic peace and order. Every day Cyclops used to eat one of Ulysses' companions; nevertheless, peace, law, order, and predictability prevailed in the cave.

Our conclusion is that "internal peace" is not a value that should be protected by the juridical system without any qualifications. The value of peace and order remains in competition with all other social values. The assessment of its value should always be made in an especially careful and critical way, because this concept is one of the most abused in political history.

All forms of totalitarianism, be they left or right, are in favor of "internal peace" and they are antagonistic to human rights. All attempts to defeat totalitarianism will be unsuccessful if criticism of any forms is neglected.

When Albert Camus wrote his *State of Siege*, Gabriel Marcel (1948) criticized him on the ground that the action of the play about totalitarian tyranny was laid in Spain instead of Eastern Europe. Albert Camus' reply is significant for the whole period following World War II. "Why Spain? Because there are some of us who will never wash their hands of that blood. Anticommunism, whatever reasons there may be for embracing it (and I know some good ones), will never gain acceptance among us if it indulges itself to the point of forgetting the injustice that goes with the complicity of our governments. I have stated as vigorously as I could what I thought of the Russian concentration camps. But they will not make me forget Dachau, Buchenwald . . . nor the dreadful repression that decimated the Spanish Republic."[36]

One could argue, Camus continued, that the crimes in Spain which were committed with the assistance of France were minor in comparison to the Soviet ones and that therefore there was no reason to start to shout. That is not so, Camus argued. And one should proceed forcefully in the West against the crimes committed in Spain: "That is the way, and absolutely the only way, we can maintain the right to protest against a reign of terror..." and further: "...you are willing to keep silent about one reign of terror in order the better to combat another one. There are some of us who do not want to keep silent about anything. It is our whole society that nauseates us."[36a]

Albert Camus' political philosophy can in this respect be reduced to the following maxim: the struggle against totalitarianism must be indivisible. One cannot defeat Lucifer with the help of Beelzebub—that is an old Polish proverb. Any limitation on the fight against the violation of human rights must inevitably be harmful to the whole war against totalitarianism. Fascism, and all kinds of right-wing totalitarianism cannot be genuine and efficient allies of democracy, which today is fighting desperately against its adversaries and against self-strangulation at the same time.

Almost thirty years have passed since the days when Camus made these arguments. In the meantime the situation has changed in one respect only: the Western democracies have started to collaborate with all types of totalitarian, inhumane, despotic, and feudal regimes. As long as collaboration is understood as a necessity, as long as compromise is understood as compromise, they do not endanger Western democracy or its ideals. The danger of collaboration becomes a real danger when such necessity is presented as a virtue. Then, and only then, the process of the degeneration of Western democracy and of the erosion of juridical ideals and human rights poisons the wellsprings of society.

About four centuries ago Sir John Harrington wrote:

"Treason doth never prosper. What's the reason?
Why if it prosper, none dare call it treason."

One of the characteristics of modern irrationalism is its attempt to present itself as a form of rationalism and logic. The rationalization of the irrational has taken on forms and dimensions unprecedented in history. The mere fact that irrationalism had to find a cloak beneath which to hide is the first decisive step towards its defeat. Hypocrisy is, as we have already quoted, the homage which vice pays to virtue. In the present world every political party, every statesman, every national and international institution attempts to win Reason for its causes.

We hope that the modernized theory of juridical positivism, augmented by a revived rhetorical tradition and human rights' concepts, can become a useful instrument in the struggle against myths of "internal peace," against creeping totalitarianism and pseudo-rationalism.

4. Kelsen's Pure Theory of Law — a Travesty of Juridical Positivism

Hans Kelsen is the philosopher of law who, more than anyone else, is responsible for the poor reputation of juridical positivism. Kelsen called his pure theory of law "consistent" positivism, by which he meant juridical positivism purified or cleansed of all ideological impurities. In the process of purification, however, Kelsen changed the basic elements of juridical positivism and indeed created a new theory which was only vaguely and superficially reminiscent of positivist legal philosophy.

Critics of juridical positivism, especially those representing natural law, confronted him with his own statements and uncritically—whenever they acted in good faith—regarded him the chief 20th-century spokesman for juridical positivism. Those criticizing Kelsen considered they were attacking juridical positivism. Kelsen's chief offense was that he had transformed juridical positivism into a straw man, thereby facilitating the task not only of his own critics, but also of those who criticized juridical positivism.

There are fundamental differences between Kelsen's "pure" theory of law and juridical positivism.

Kelsen announced that legal theory should be "liberated" from all sociological, ethical, political, and philosophical values. To him there were only legal norms which should be understood, interpreted, and applied in their purity. Legal norms declare what should happen, what "ought" to happen at a given moment after certain facts described by law take place. This "ought" is not a moral "ought" and has nothing to do with the notion of "ought" which at times is employed by natural scientists. This *"sollen,"* this "ought," is a juridical phrase which juridically describes "cause" and "effect." This legal concept, however, has nothing to do with cause and effect as understood in the natural sciences.

The concept of juridical *"sollen"* was combined by Kelsen with Adolf Merkl's *"Stufentheorie."* In Kelsen's interpretation the foundation of legal systems in every country forms a *"Grundnorm."* On this basis the highest authority, such as parliament, promulgates laws while other organs of government issue more concrete and less general juridical provisions. At the end of the system, as

Kelsen colorfully used to stress, especially in his lectures, is a guard who leads the prisoner to his cell and locks the door.

The basic difference between Kelsen and the positivists lies in Kelsen's view that the relationship between various steps (levels) in the inverted pyramid of the legal system is purely formal. There may be discrepancies between the various steps. To consider that legislators are always logical and never want any discrepancies in their legal system, according to Kelsen, is an act of faith based on ideology, not on facts.

All other assertions made by Kelsen are deductions from his description of law. Subjective rights are only ideological constructions, he taught, because they really do not exist. Having "real" existence are only provisions of law which in a general and vague manner describe how the provisions of law should be made and eventually executed.

The concept that the legislator must be limited by his own provisions of law was elaborated by Kelsen's countryman, George Jellinek. Kelsen also denounced and rejected this idea as ideological. A jurist, Kelsen wrote, cannot accept such a formula although it may be accepted by a politician or a moralist.

The positivist concept of legality, as the observance of the existing provisions of law and of the subjective rights of the citizens, was also denounced by Kelsen as inconsistent with his pure theory of law because once the existence of subjective rights had been denied, the concept of legality as the protection of the rights of the citizen also had to be rejected.

And lastly, the interpretation of law as the process of

defining the will of the legislator or, as other positivists used to write, of the "objective content inherent in law," also was rejected as ideological because, according to Kelsen, the provisions of law are so general that there is always the possibility of various interpretations. In this way Kelsen identified generality with vagueness. He equated various possibilities with unlimited possibilities.

The entire juridical system became a formal structure which in Kelsen's interpretation consisted solely of walls and pillars but no actual content. Obviously, this is not a theory of juridical positivism. According to juridical positivism, as we tried to point out through analysis of the writings of the classic proponents of this doctrine, and by presenting the theory of interpretation, the provisions of law have certain definite contents and are the source of rights. These rights can be created either by the constitution, in which case their content is very broad and general, or they may be created by the juridical norms issued by parliaments, or administrative or juridical organs, in which case their content is more limited, more particular and concrete.

According to juridical positivism, there is a hierarchy of juridical provisions. There are certain *"Stufen,"* or levels, the relations between which are not only formal but also conceptual.

Kelsen too obviously was influenced by the Kantian theory that an abyss separates *"sein"* and *"sollen"*! These notions are very important in Kantian philosophy; they are applied to the natural sciences and to the sphere of morality. One of the fundamental differences between Kant and the neo-Kantians is that

Kant had no doubt that "*sein,*" or the "thing in itself," really existed although it might have been unknown. Neo-Kantians usually try to get rid of the objective existence of the "thing in itself" and transform it into something which is subjective, whose existence is grounded solely upon our senses or perceptions. The neo-Kantians took a substantial step in formalizing the Kantain theory. The famous slogan, *"Zurueck zum Kant,"* was not indeed a return to the old Kant, but to the Kant who had been "processed" in a specific way.

Kelsen was under the influence of neo-Kantian philosophy. He applied certain neo-Kantian simplifications to the philosophy of law. According to the legal positivists a legal system is a true *Sein*. It is a reality which should be examined, made known and understood because it is not an unknown "thing in itself," but something which can become a *thing for us.* For Kelsen, a legal system is an unknown quantity which is symbolized by the fact that he regarded the *Grundnorm* as either a hypothesis or a fiction. Let us remember that the entire structure of law is based on the *Grundnorm.* If the basis is hypothetical or nonexistent, we live in an almost unreal world, in Vaihinger's world of "as if." We are very far from ascribing to Kelsen the neo-Kantians' version of subjectivism, but he inherited certain methodological arguments from them.

In previous chapters we have shown that juridical positivists believe in the existence of certain democratic and humanistic ideals which they seek to protect by provisions of law. Kelsen recognized this fact and therefore wanted to do away with these moral and humanistic values in his juridical, although not in his political, theory. In this way he distorted the very essence, the very nature, of juridical positivism as a theory of democratic order, of constitutional legality, as an instrument which protects the rights of "the man and the citizen." Juridical positivists developed their theory in order to protect and strengthen the democratic political system, whereas through his simplifications and formalization of the system of law, Kelsen presented it as a system which had equal value in an autocracy as in a democracy. Kelsen was specific to such an extent that he even mentioned that from the point of view of the pure theory of law there are no criteria to favor parliamentary constitutional regimes over fascist or Soviet ones. He admitted, however, that from the philosophical and political points of view, one might and should have preferences.

Kelsen's statements juridically equating democracy and Nazi dictatorship were truly shocking. Since his conclusion was said to have derived from juridical positivism properly understood, the contempt directed against Kelsen's theory was directed at juridical positivism as well.

Kelsen's "pure theory of law" probably produced more consternation among philosophers of law in the period between the two world wars than any other.

There is no doubt that subjectively Kelsen was a democrat as well as a great defender of the Western parliamentary system. He personally suffered when the Nazis seized power. He had to escape from Germany, settled in the United States, and his last books were published in this country. Although democrats must reject his pure theory of law, friends of totalitarian regimes are unable to be kind to him either. Kelsen's criticism of the Bolshevik theory of law made his name anathema to the Soviets. They considered him to have rejected not only liberal ideas, democracy, and legality but communism as well. The Nazis hated Kelsen for all his ideas, including his philosophical relativism.

It is one of the paradoxes of our times that a philosopher who undermined democratic ideas was unacceptable to the anti-democratic forces either. They could use his criticism of their enemies but they would have been the first to persecute him had they been able to lay their hands on him.

*

Kelsen twice published an essay on the value of democracy, once before and once after WW II. He presented himself as a consistent relativist and asserted that relativism constitutes the necessary and exclusive basis for democracy. Democracy is the rule of the majority, Kelsen wrote, and the majority may decide what is evil or good, useful or harmful. There are no objective criteria of justice or morality. Therefore, a consistent democrat must be a relativist and a relativist must agree that the decision of the majority at any time is the only correct one.

In order to dramatize this concept, Kelsen quoted the Gospel according to St. John. Pontius Pilate found himself forced to make a decision regarding whose life

---

*Hans Kelsen, Von Wert und Wesen der Demokratie (Tuebingen, 1929): Absolutism and Relativism in Philosophy and Politics, *The Am. Polit-Science Review,* vol. XLII, No. 5, 1948. The Metamorphoses of the Idea of Justice, in: *Interpretations of Modern Legal Philosophies* (New York, 1947).

to save, that of Jesus, or that of Barabbas, a murderer. As a Roman "democrat," Pilate decided to ask the crowd. The crowd opted for the murderer and Jesus had to die. Pilate accepted the verdict of the people and washed his hands.

According to Kelsen, Pilate behaved like a consistent relativist and democrat. According to him there were no "true" or "eternal" values in that situation which could have prevailed and swayed the scales in favor of Jesus. If we introduce other values and elements than popular preferences, democracy as a process will be destroyed. After all, Kelsen wrote, democracy is only a form whose contents are decided by the given majority. Kelsen therefore added that democratic decisions should be made by a normal and not a qualified majority. Such decisions should last only for a short time in order to permit a new majority to emerge and make its own decisions.

Kelsen argued that there was a difference, if not a gulf, between the position of a political democrat and a philosophical relativist on the one hand and his pure theory of law on the other. His preference for democracy was sociological, political, and moral, not in any way connected to his jurisprudence.

Nevertheless there is a very close link between Kelsen's political and juridical theory. This link is his philosophical relativism. In his theory of law and of politics, Kelsen examined only the form, but not the content. In reality, however, such a separation of form and content does not exist. The democratic form is determined by democratic ideas, not vice versa. A democratic form is necessary for the realization of the requirements which today are called human dignity, freedom, human rights, and the possibility of creative activities. Both political forms and legal norms are necessary in order to secure these values. There are many ways to interpret these values; they are interpreted at different stages of social and economic development. Nevertheless, these notions are never empty or vague. At particular periods in given nations these notions express certain qualities and quantities of values which are clearly understood by their adherents and adversaries alike.

When Kelsen rejected subjective rights, which today in certain circumstances may also be called human rights, he argued as a philosophical relativist. When he wrote that the majority can make any decision and any decision will be equally good, he also wrote as a philosophical relativist. A democracy which does not acknowledge certain human values and liberties is self-contradictory. Mankind needs democracy in order to represent and realize democratic ideals. We also need a theory of law which protects the same democratic ideals and values politically.

Juridical positivism was born in the tradition of the Western ideals of democracy and individualism. An attempt to divorce legal forms from their liberal, democratic content, does not purify juridical positivism, but creates an antipositivistic, indeed autocratic, theory of law under a misguided principle. Neither Pontius Pilate nor Shylock could be regarded as symbols of democracy and juridical positivism. Democracy cannot be symbolized by the washing of hands because its substance and form require an active participation by those who would preserve its political forms, institutions, and rights.

Kelsen's theory, on the other hand, may be regarded as a partial reflection of the new 20th century reality. There are more and more states and regimes in which democratic and human rights are but an illusion. Kelsen's theory reflects this fact. Constitutional proclamations exist, but they are meaningless. There are no logical, no real, no causal relationships between laws and administrative orders, between administrative orders and the actions of administrative personnel. There are discrepancies, and as Kelsen wrote, the sovereign legislator wants them to exist. From this point of view, the pure theory of law is a reflection of the antidemocratic, despotic, quasi-totalitarian reality existing in most countries.

Kelsen stated that the legal order is dynamic and unpredictable. To reach such a conclusion, however, one does not need to be a philosophical relativist and one does not have to reject democratic legal ideals contained in a theory of law. This conclusion can be reached by realists in the philosophy of law and politics.

5. Ronald Dworkin's Criticism of Juridical Positivism

In previous chapters we have concentrated on the positivist concept of the validity of law and the legitimacy of civil disobedience. We did not feel it necessary to consider other particulars of this theory because for the sake of our presentation, the idea that the positivists do not regard law as a value in itself was more important. They would not have subscribed to the infamous doctrine, "My fatherland, right or wrong." On the contrary, they regarded law as a social institution which should be examined and used just like other social institutions. A positive theory of law was for Bentham and Austin one of the pillars of their utilitarian philosophy and therefore they argued that law itself should be in conformity with the utilitarian principle of the greatest happiness for the greatest number of people. Law which does not conform to the principle is still law, but as they contended, its observance may be endangered by the attitudes and behavior of the people. We recollect these points in connection with Dworkin's criticism of positivism. Dworkin presented juridical positivism in an overly simplified way, and therefore he made his accusations not against the real theory of juridical positivism but against a straw man fabricated by himself.

Dworkin's basic indictment against juridical positivism may be narrowed down to the following: Juridical positivism acknowledges the existence of legal rules only; it has no place for standards or principles which are embedded in the legal system where they are not unequivocally expressed. Such principles should be given due weight.

The distinction between rules and principles was explained by Dworkin in his analysis of two N.Y. Court of Appeals cases: *Riggs vs. Palmer,* 1889, and *Henningsen vs. Bloomfield Motors, Inc.,* 1960[37] In the first case the court denied a legacy to a grandson who murdered his grandfather in order to collect it. According to a literal interpretation, the statue would have allowed the murderer to inherit; but then, as the court recognized, such an interpretation would have been too narrow, mechanical, and dogmatic. The court reasoned that interpretation and application of all law including contract law should be controlled by the fundamental maxims of the common law. One of the principles of the common law is that no one should be permitted to profit by his own fraud or reap advantage from his own wrongdoing.

In this case, as in other similar cases, that meant that no one should be permitted to acquire property by his own crime. (115 N.Y. 506, 22 NE 188, 1889).

In the second case, the court decided that limitations placed upon its own liability by an automobile manufacturer for its own defectively manufactured products should not be enforced by the court. One of the arguments used by the court was:

> In a society such as ours, where the automobile is a common and necessary adjunct of daily life, and where its use is so fraught with danger to a driver, passengers and the public, the manufacturer is under a special obligation in connection with the construction, promotion and sale of his cars. Consequently, the courts must examine purchase agreements closely to see if consumer and public interest are treated fairly. (32 N.J. 358, 161 A.Zd. 69, 1960).

Ronald Dworkin argued that the underlying principle by which the court was guided is as follows: The manufactuer is under special obligation to produce automobiles without defects because automobiles are such important means of transportation in America.

These two principles cannot be found in the statutes, according to Dworkin, but still they are an essential part of the legal system. By ignoring principles, juridical positivism impoverishes the legal system and reduces it to a set of commands and rules so that it cannot even develop an adequate theory of liability.

We have already mentioned that the founders of juridical positivism and those who were developing a theory of juridical interpretation for it did not regard a legal system as a Kantian "thing in itself," but as a part of the living social organism. Obviously, Dworkin's criticism does not pertain to genuine, but only to fictional juridical positivists. On the other hand, it is true that positivists did not write about "principles"; they used different terminology. But once they pointed out the connection between their theory of law and utilitarianism, they were by that very fact recommending that the provisions of law should be interpreted and applied in the light of "principles," using Dworkin's expression. Having introduced one or two general principles (utility, happiness) in the interpretation and application of the legal rules, there is no logical limit upon introducing further principles. And, indeed, the positivists realized that it would be impossible to interpret law without values and social and moral principles.

Dworkin created his notion of juridical positivism from arbitrarily selected elements and connected them with Montesquieu's ideal that a judge should merely be "mouthpiece of the law."

Juridical positivists are by no means impractical utopians. Although they wanted to apply the provisions of the law as strictly as possible, they knew that no system of law could function according to Montesquieu's ideal. They were too experienced to believe in such a fantasy.

Once we depart from Montesquieu's concept of judicial administration, we must introduce additional elements and they must necessarily be derived from experience, from various social ideas, concepts of justice, fairness, and finally, from the broad principles of equity, decency, and morality. Dworkin's assertion that juridical positivism does not recognize principles implies that juridical positivists do not understand the way a complex mechanism like a legal system functions; in brief they are not jurists, but pompous ignoramuses. As we know, juridical positivists were not only theorists, but also eminent practitioners. Their names are legion, and well enough known to the reader to need no identification.

That accusation leads Dworkin to a further attack on positivism. He writes that in order to apply the provisions of law, juridical positivism must inevitably depart from the legal rules and widen the sphere of juridical discretion. Therefore, he writes, juridical positivism is a doctrine which willy nilly justifies a situation in which the outcome of the juridical proceedings is undeterminate. According to Dworkin's theory, once we agree that principles are embedded in the legal system, then the outcome of any case would be predetermined, absent any mistakes. Neither Dworkin's propositions nor his reasoning are correct.

David Lyons observed ". . . Dworkin's assumption is false, and his conclusion that principles eliminate all indeterminacies cannot be fairly drawn. In order to eliminate all indeterminacies in the law, principles must cover all cases that might arise; they must have determinable weights; and the balancing process, in which principles are weighed against each other, must never be allowed an equal weight of principles on either side of a legal question. But we cannot assume that these conditions are satisfied."[38]

David Lyons correctly presented the issue. Every application of general rules to a particular, individual problem must be a creative act on the part of the jurist who interprets and applies the law. The specifics, particularities, and peculiarities of every case are infinite, but they must be encompassed and described by a lawgiver in terms which are necessarily general, because every legal rule must be general. There can of course be various degrees of generality, but still legal norms must be general. The principles which are referred to by Dworkin are also general; their content is usually even more controversial than that of the legal rules, and it would therefore be extremely difficult to determine which general principles should be brought to bear in any given case. Besides, nobody can provide a complete list of general principles which are embedded in a given legal system. Moreover, the principles which are brought into play are themselves constantly developing because the life of society is developing; the legal system is evolving as social ideas and values are constantly being reevaluated. There is no doubt that in the endless process of evolution and reevaluation, certain principles are rejected, certain are losing and others are acquiring "weight." Even principles which appear to be the same embrace new meanings which weigh more or less on the social and juridical scales.

The upshot of these considerations is that the application of every rule and principle must be a result of the process of argumentation which we described in a previous chapter. Although the result of the process of argumentation can be more or less reasonable, it cannot be predetermined, and therefore elements of uncertainty, unpredictability, and juridical discretion can never be eliminated from the life of the law any more than they can from that life which is reflected in the law.

Let us, finally, make one additional observation concerning principles. Every principle can be presented without difficulty in the form of a rule. For instance, the principle mentioned by Dworkin in *Riggs vs. Palmer* can be expressed as the following commandment:

Thou shalt not profit by thine own wrong.

The principle could have been expressed by the legislators themselves, and also in a general way, and not in the form of rules or "commandments." That was the approach adopted by the Polish legislature in the 1960's. The new Civil Code was preceded by an introduction in which were presented the general principles by which this Code should be interpreted and applied. Professor Rozmaryn, as already mentioned, even considered that the preface to the Constitution, which was not worded in the form of articles and paragraphs, also had normative weight which should be taken into account while interpreting the provisions of the Constitution. The same method was recommended in the Anglo-Saxon World by Coke and Kent—it was already mentioned above. This approach is also positivist!

The case of *Riggs vs. Palmer* was decided according to the positivist tradition, and positivist principles were strictly observed.

If we accept that every principle can be expressed in the form of a command or rule, then we might argue that this part of Dworkin's attack on juridical positivism is based on a linguistic misunderstanding or misinterpretation and not on the merits, but that issue leads beyond our discussion.

The criticism of Dworkin's theory presented above can appropriately be applied to his analysis of "hard" cases. David Lyons correctly observed that Dworkin does not explain what he means by hard cases. It seems that he might mean cases in which, as Lyons writes, "the law appears indeterminate because of vagueness, conflicting rules and the like; ... hard cases are those in which the decision goes beyond the holdings of past cases and beyond the literal import of established legal rules."[39]

Dworking argues that in order to resolve so-called hard cases the judge does not have to go beyond the legal system because he can accept his (Dworkin's) theory and apply established legal standards or principles. In this way the solution of even the hardest case will regarded as determined, if not predetermined, by the existing legal system encompassing rules and standards.

Let us observe that the classification into "hard" and "easy" cases is connected in one way or another with the Cartesian concept of truth. According to Cartesian philosophy, truth is what I see clearly and distinctly. We have already discussed various aspects of this concept.

When something is not clear and distinct, one must proceed according to the required pattern in order to make it clear. That is the famous Cartesian recommendation, but actually, nothing is ever clear or distinct when one starts interpreting and applying the law. Clarity and distinctness can and must be the result (and not a precondition) of the process of argumentation and of the search for truth. It cannot be a quality established at the outset. From the point of view of the theory of argumentation, which rejects the simplistic Cartesian notion of clarity, every case is "hard" and can become "easy" only after a process of argumentation and interpretation. In every case, as we have mentioned, the specific features must be embraced and expressed by general rules; afterwards, in the process of interpretation and application, the same general rules must be simultaneously expounded, narrowed down, and finally adjusted to the given particular case. Even at the first stage of interpretation and application, as every judge and lawyer knows, it usually turns out that what was regarded as simple and easy is a hard knot indeed.

These are the main theoretical reasons why Dworkin's concept of "hard" cases is without any philosophical justification.

It would not be easy to determine even the most important reasons behind the fallacy in the Dworkin's theoretical propositions. It seems, however that one of the causes of Dworkin's errors is that he himself is not sure about the relationship between law and liberty. Therefore in his essay, "What Rights Do We Have?" we find this statement:

> "This conception of liberty as license is neutral amongst the various activities a man might pursue, the various roads he might wish to walk. It diminishes a man's liberty when we prevent him from talking or making love the way he wishes, but it also diminishes his liberty when we prevent him from murdering or defaming others. These latter constraint may be justifiable, but only because there are compromises necessary to protect the liberty or security of others, and not because they do not, in themselves, infringe on the independent value of liberty."[40]

Dworkin's reasoning implies that the basis of the philosophy of freedom, including Democritus', Epicurus', Hegel's and John Dewey's contributions, had no impact on him. In our century, it has, after all, become almost a truism that freedom should not be interpreted as license, that freedom should not be regarded as the right propounded by Callicles, but is connected with reason, with developing social customs, and the standards of morality which slowly embrace more and more human values. One doesn't even have to be an adherent of Spinoza's, Hegel's, Marx's or Dewey's concept that freedom is comprehended necessity in order to agree with the thesis that the "right" to murder other people cannot be regarded as an element of individual freedom. Such "freedom" would endorse unlimited license of deranged people, of characters like the "Son of Sam," not to mention Dracula, or Jack the Ripper. Even barbarian tribes, whose way of life anthropologists were able to reconstruct and analyze, never included the wanton killing of others as part of their "freedom," (for they were familiar with elements of this concept). When they did kill it was based on some perceived necessity, like the struggle for survival or other reasons justifiable to their minds. Therefore, the concept that the law prohibiting certain types of behavior, especially murder, necessarily limits freedom is unacceptable and cannot be regarded as a basis for "taking rights seriously."

Dworkin writes further: "Bentham said that any law whatsoever is an 'infraction' of liberty, and though some such infractions might be necessary, it is obscurantist to pretend that they are not infractions after all. In this neutral, all embracing sense of liberty as license, liberty and equality are plainly in competition. Laws are needed to protect equality, and laws are inevitably compromises of liberty."[41]

Let us observe at the begining that Bentham wrote these famous words that every law is an infraction of liberty under very specific circumstances and in a particular historical context. He regarded law as a part of a governmental activity and according to him, as to every liberal in this period, everything the government did was evil in itself. Even if the purpose of the activities of government is the common good of the whole society, even if these functions are indispensable for the promotion of the greatest happiness and this evil as a matter of fact is necessary, still—argued Bentham—it is an evil nonetheless. It is in this sense and context in which every law is an infringement upon liberty, as the positivist Bentham wrote and the anti-positivist Dworkin repeats. But of course Bentham understood that law is for the human beings with *normal* human instincts and feelings, and therefore he did not regard every restriction upon behavior (thou shall not murder!) as a restriction upon human liberty.

Dworkin also observed that liberty and equality were plainly in competition; we will not write detailed comments on this remark, although it deserves a serious refutation. We regard this concept as one of the prejudices which have become popular in recent decades. Dworkin's general contention that law is needed to protect equality is strange, to say the least. Until now law has always protected existing inequalities, especially economic and social. It could happen that a social revolution or deep social reform could result in a change in economic and social relations and in the existing legal system and forms of equality. Whenever a new law introduces and protects the new equality, it always does it at the expense of old inequalities, and at the same time the new equalities are connected with the new inequalities. A correct *statement* concerning historical relationships between law and equality would be the following:

Existing legal systems have always been a result of existing economic and social inequalities; laws protected them. Sometimes law can become an instrument to abolish an old inequality, but, as has been mentioned, the new equalities are always accompanied by selected old inequalities and new inequalities besides.

The extent to which laws are compromises between equality and liberty, cannot be answered in one sentence. There is no doubt that the law can serve as an instrument for introducing political liberties, for protecting them and that it can also serve as an instrument for taking liberty away. We more often face the second alternative than the first. Therefore, it is very strange that Dworkin should assert that "liberty has been even more prominent in conservative service."[42] The reverse is the truth. History demonstrates that conservatives always defended privileges, implying limitations upon the liberties as well as the juridical equality of the less privileged. The latter always fought for their rights as they saw them, which they identified with their own ideas synonymous with the fight for equality, and vice versa. True, at every stage of history, in every nation, these notions had a specific, particular content. This fact does not deny the correctness of our general observation. In any case, the historical tendency described above it so well known and so generally acknowledged that there would be no reason to mention it except for Dworkin's distortions. It would be interesting, although not necessary to find out why Dworkin decided to deny obvious facts and how he thinks this denial serves his concept of law and rights. The full answer to this question would go beyond the framework of this book. It does seem that Dworkin could have presented his case more persuasively without adjusting history.

6. Legal Realism

During the first half of the twentieth century a new version of juridical positivism developed in the United States. It became known as legal realism. Wolfgang Friedmann wrote that pragmatism became a "new version" of positivism.[43] One may add that pragmatism became the philosophical basis of juridical realism.

At the time, many declared that the "new version" of philosophy, and the "new version" of legal theory only developed ideas of the past. There were many arguments, however, to demonstrate that the "new version" really did break new ground.

American legal realism of course has elements in common with juridical positivism. American authors, however, created their own theory in order to eliminate certain components of juridical dogmatism and legal conceptualism.

Endless discussions took place in which most of the partisans of the "realistic" ideas questioned whether legal realism was indeed new.

The students of the history of philosophy know that not many examples exist in which members of a given school openly admit adherence to it. It is a well known fact that in the dust of the battle one does not recognize one's own comrades-in-arms. The members of various schools of thought can justifiably quote Hegel's observation that the "owl of Minerva spreads its wings at dusk"; one starts to understand the real sense of events when the process of incubation reaches its maturity.

Nearly half a century has passed since the period of the great battles in American jurisprudence over the meaning of realism, over the mere existence of adherence to this school. Professor Edwin W. Patterson cautiously remarked in 1940: "Yet Garlan has produced persuasive evidence that the American legal realists have certain common objectives and that their concern is not alone with the law that is. They are also concerned with what the law ought to be, with the theory of justice."[44]

Professor Patterson himself did not wish to use the phrase "School of Realism," because of the decisive contention of Professor Llewellyn that there was "no school"[45] of American legal realism.

Today we see clearly that American realists founded a school and developed their own original philosophical ideas, whose value in the evolution of juridical theory should not be underestimated.

Legal realism, first of all, constitutes a reaction to the exigencies of juridical dogmatism. Juridical dogmatism, of course, is connected with juridical positivism, but it should not be identified with it. Juridical dogmatists regard law as an autonomous thing with a value in itself whose intrinsic purposes should be understood and respected. The juridical dogmatists apply to the legal system the famous maxims, *dura lex sed lex* and *pereat mundus fiat justitia*. They interpret these maxims in a rigidly literal manner, thereby contributing to the opinion that jurists are robots without hearts or feelings. Juridical dogmatism, indeed, is a malignant outgrowth of the system of law. The dogmatists are responsible for the divorce between juridical norms and the requirements of life, humanitarian feelings, and the common understanding of justice and equity. There were many reactions against juridical dogmatism, the most powerful of which came from the various proponents of natural law theories.

The traditional positivist school of legal interpretation is far removed from juridical dogmatism, although it takes existing juridical norms as its point of departure. On the other hand, it is true that the juridical positivists were unable to develop a theory of law and a philosophy of legal interpretation which would effectively combine an interpretation and application of law with the requirements of life and the complexity of human relations in our century. A reaction against this one-sidedness was inevitable.

At the beginning of the 20th century, two basic trends developed in the Western world against juridical positivism without however totally rejecting its premises. In Europe the reaction was represented by adherents of the Freie Rechtslehre. We use this term in its broadest sense, encompassing all those schools which wanted to liberate jurists from the rigidity of literalism without, however, embracing natural law.

The counterpart of these schools in America became legal realism. Here we will concentrate only on certain aspects of legal realism which have influenced the whole development of Western juridical thought in the twentieth century.

The classic presentation of the new elements of legal realism was done by Karl A. Llewellyn in his article on realism. According to Llewellyn, legal realism differs from previous philosophies in eight ways:

1. The realists analyze the law in flux as a changing juridical creation.

2. Law should not be regarded as an end in itself, but as a means to social ends. It should be regarded from the point of view of its purpose and actual effects.

3. Society should also be understood as being in flux and developing even faster than the law. Therefore, there always is a probability that certain portions of law need urgent re-examination in order to determine how well they still serve society.

4. One should temporarily dissociate the sphere of *is,* from the sphere of *ought*. This divorce, Llewellyn stressed, should be for the purpose of study only. Llewellyn realized that any study of reality is of course influenced by value judgments; nevertheless, he urged that during any inquiry into what *is*, an attempt be made to produce a description of reality without contamination, as far as possible, by the desires and wishes for what *ought* (ethically) to be. Llewellyn stressed that such a divorce between *is* and *ought* cannot be permanent, but is temporarily necessary, because without a true knowledge of *is* one cannot intelligently determine what *ought* to be.

5. Legal realism distrusts traditional concepts insofar as they are limited to descriptions of what the courts and people actually do. Realists are inclined to regard rules as general *predictions* of what courts will do, because they believe it is more important to analyze

rules as precepts (rules for doing) rather than *rules as actual activity or practice*. This point, of course, should be combined with point four. A sound prediction must be based on an analysis of present practices.

6. The distrust of traditional descriptive rules is accompanied by a distrust of the theory that existing legal rules largely determine actual judicial decisions. Indeed, many more elements determine the outcome of the deliberations of judges.

7. It is therefore better to group cases and legal situations into narrower categories than has been done in the past. Formerly, legal rules, at least in theory, were applied to many situations which were dissimilar but, "a realist tries to indicate explicitly which criterion he is applying in a particular instance."[46]

8. Realists insist on a reevaluation of every part of the law from the point of view of its effects. They are not satisfied even if the legal system "as a whole" works. They think it is worth while to find out the effects of each particular part.

None of the above ideas, Llewellyn stressed, is completely new. All can be drawn substantially from various orthodox legal books. New twists and combinations appear here and there. What is novel and characteristic for legal realism is a sustained and programmatic attack on the problems of law based upon these eight principles. There are many lawyers who pick up ideas which have been expressed; they play with them for a short time only and then they drop them. One should pick up these new ideas and "set about *consistently, persistently, insistently,* to carry them through ... Not hit-or-miss stuff, not the insight which flashes and is forgotten, but sustained effort to force an old insight into its full bearing, to exploit it to the point where it laps over upon an apparently inconsistent insight, to explore their bearing on each other by the test of fact. This urge, in law, is quite new enough over the last decades to excuse a touch of frenzy among the locust-eaters."[47]

The same ideas were expressed by many other realists. They introduced the distinction between law-in-books and law-in-action. They were the first to deliver a mortal blow to the remnants of the Kantian view that law-in-itself exists, that it can be understood as an autonomous entity divorced from other social phenomena. For the first time in history a forceful theory of the subject was consciously elaborated, namely that legal norms should be understood in a philosophical unity of thought and action, of expressed purpose and real effect.

We know that it is not true, as Lon Fuller alleged, that juridical positivism is characterized by the complete divorce between *is* and *ought*. Such a divorce is impossible in any event. At times, however, in the writings of juridical positivists one finds certain simplifications in this respect. Legal realists rather consistently hold that the beginning of *ought* already is intrinsically embodied in *is*, and therefore jurists should draw practical conclusions from this fact.

In order to accomplish this task a jurist should study not only law but also the needs of a society and the social conflicts within it. This is the meaning of the statement that law is a living instrument, not an end in itself but means to achieve socially desirable effects. Law is a living instrument of "social engineering."

At the beginning of this section we mentioned that

legal realism represents a new version of juridical positivism. In what followed we concentrated on the differences between legal realism and juridical positivism. In what sense, therefore, is there an affinity between legal realism and juridical positivism? Legal realists do not reject juridical norms established by legislators or by judges; they do not "negate" the existence of legal norms, but they want to enlarge the scope of their understanding, interpretation, and application.[48] They insist that one should examine what courts and people do so as to understand "generalized predictions." They want to know the legal material, truly to understand it. By insisting on "generalized predictions" they are in fact adhering to and elaborating positivistic attitudes: they want to know the *general* in order to know and predict the *particular*.

All legal realists agree with Holmes and Dewey that the application of formal logic was excessive and therefore its role should be reduced. The realists do not identify reasonable with logical as do juridical dogmatics. They have all outgrown formal Cartesian logic and they approach to rhetorical argumentation.

Legal realism constitutes a step along the road to the association of jurisprudence with the theory of argumentation founded on the *Rhetoric* of Aristotle and its revival in our century.

7. Does Antigone Need "Natural Law"?

Whichever theory of law we are inclined to adopt, we will never free ourselves from *Antigone's* dilemma. From the jurisprudential and ethical points of view, we must ask the questions which were asked by H.L.A. Hart:

> "In what way is it better, when faced with morally iniquitous demands, to think 'This is in no sense law' rather than 'This is law but *too* iniquitous to obey or apply'? Would this make men more clear headed or readier to disobey when morality demands it?"[49]

The answer to the question, in what way is it better, and more effective, was also provided by positivist realism, which in this respect only elaborates and specifies the answer given by H.L.A. Hart.

Hart wrote that people should be educated in order that they might more clearly realize what is morally at stake when disobedience is necessary. It is easy to agree with Hart that people should realize that mere certification of certain rules as legally valid should not be

> "conclusive of the question of obedience, and that, however great the aura of majesty or authority which the official system may have, its demands must in the end be submitted to a moral scrutiny. This sense, that there is something outside the official system, by reference to which in the last resort the individual must solve his problems of obedience, is surely more likely to be kept alive among those who are accustomed to think that rules of law might be iniquitous, than among those who think that nothing iniquitous can anywhere have the status of law."[50]

One of the most persistent of political, juridicial, philosophical, and theological myths is that there must be something "reasonable," and "moral" in every provision of law. This myth is indeed consciously fostered by governments, the most democratic and the most despotic. The social pressure to obey the laws without question, which has prevailed from time immemorial, has instilled a feeling of guilt in most people who decide to defy the law for social, moral, or even religious reasons. They do not find that the promptings of their conscience are sufficient, so they look for some other justification to excuse their disobedience.

The belief that obedience to law is a virtue in itself has given rise to another myth: that of natural law. This myth is needed to justify disregarding the belief all laws of the state must be obeyed. Since the emergence of state and law, the need for the myth of natural law has existed. After World War II this need emerged with enormous vitality, but has slowly and gradually started to subside, giving new forms of positivism an opportunity for attention. H.L.A. Hart is right to state that it is most important for citizens to be conscious of what is legal, despite the possibility that it contradicts either prevailing moral feelings or "critical morality." Anyway, the question has in the final analysis to be solved either by an individual or by a social group to which given individuals belong. If their decision is that obedience is immoral, they are confronted with the moral duty to disobey a law which is legally valid.

From the viewpoint of clarity, logic, and persuasiveness of reasonable thinking, it is even easier and more commendable to hold that the given (immoral) laws contradict the requirements of the Declaration and Conventions on Human Rights or the Helsinki Agreement, or that the particular law is incompatible with the democratic pronouncements contained in the constitution of the given country, and therefore one is not bound to observe them. That stand of positivist realism can indeed provide arguments that certain wicked norms are invalid even legally. The interpretation, however, will be based not on purely moral but on juridicial considerations. The norms will be rejected as not legally binding, not because of "something outside the official system," but because of something which is either implicitly and "officially" within the official system of law, or is connected with the official system of law in one way or another, because of the mere fact that a given state became a member of the community of the United Nations and voluntarily agreed to adhere to the principles laid down by documents adopted by that organization.

Hart is right to argue that the non-legalistic exclusion from the legal system of the rules which are "normally offensive" will indeed be detrimental to both morality and legality. Such arbitrary exclusion will only dissipate our effort to understand "the potentialities of the specific method of social control" to be seen in the legal system.[51]

All social norms affect social life to a greater or lesser extent. A legislator who wants to achieve his goals through the use of juridical norms has to bear this fact in mind, otherwise his legislative activity may fail. In order to assess all the causes of such a failure it is better to know exactly what law is, which norms are legal and whether they are really in force. This important idea, contained in his *Concept of Law,* H.L.A. Hart expounded and skillfully substantiated on many occasions.

Bentham, Austin, Mill, and others made their case after the fall of absolutism and they developed their theory of juridical positivism against the revolutionary tide of natural law theories. H.L.A. Hart elaborated his ideas after the fall of the fascist regimes and against a new wave of natural law philosophies. The historical similarities and the historical distance determine the similarities and distinctions in theoretical considerations and stresses put on various elements by each commentator.

Against various forms of contemporary positivism are invoked various concepts of natural law. With great skill, Prakash Sinha classified them into eleven categories. He defines his own theory of human rights as anthropocentric, normative, "the human rights imperative becomes the fulfillment of man's needs of his planetary existence with justice."[52] It is possible to agree with him provided that one interprets "human nature" as historically and socially formed, presupposing that the concept and content of human rights is also in a state of continuous development. Within such a framework the term "anthropocentric" can be extremely useful, indicating that in our epoch certain rights, liberties, and privileges became a part of civilized humanity.

In his discourse: *Legal Positivism: A Pragmatic Reanalysis* (Basel: World Congress on Philosophy of Law ans Social Philosophy, 1979) Professor Abraham Edel expresses an important observation: legal positivism as a theory is connected with a method generally characterized as "conceptual linguistic analysis" or the "analytic method."[53] Unfortunately there are numerous analytic modes. Legal philosophy should be free at anytime to use whichever method is more effective.[54] He recommends his own method which he calls "pragmatic reanalysis". The analytic method, Edel further observed, of which legal positivism was proclaimed a "custodian", is not fully elaborated or even strictly defined. One can emphasize either a formalistic construction or the more informal procedure of "ordinary language analysis."

It is not difficult to criticize juridical positivism and

its methodology by pointing out the alleged incompatibility of these two approaches within (or: in connection with) one theory of law. Such a criticism would be based, Edel observed, on the famous positivist tricotomy of fact, value, and logic (or in terms of the types of inquiry: science, ethics, and philosophical analysis). Pragmatic analysis, as recommended by Edel himself, undercuts the sharp distinctions among these triads and the two basic philosophies of law, natural law and positivism. He concludes that today the process of bridging the gap between certain aspects of juridical positivism and natural law theories has been well advanced and this assertion constitutes one of the fundamental premises common to Edel's "pragmatic reanalysis" and positivist realism discussed here.

Indeed the "sharp distinctions" between fact and value in legal practice never existed. The distinctions were exaggerated by the various philosophical schools[55] but practical jurists have always been aware of the hidden fragility of these legal philosophies. Pragmatic reanalysis and positivist realism take reality into account and they both construct their respective theoretical and methodological theorems accordingly. This is also the reason why positivist realism agrees with another observation of Edel:

"A systematic study of gaps, limits, permissions to legislate, permission to create law, the kinds of legal concepts that open the way to such processes, would thus be part of the fuller program of legal positivism".[56]

We have already argued that e.g. the concept of a gap in the legal system (not to mention the right of parties to create their own contractual legal rights and obligations) cannot be precise and given once and for all. The very existence of a gap is determined as much by philosophy and politics as by "formalistic" interpretation of the legal provisions.

The similarity between the approaches of positivist realism and Edel's version of pragmatic reanalysis, as illustrated by the example of lacuna in the law is not accidental, but is determined by important factors. They both agree that there is always, as Edel writes, a posibility to reformulate a non-moral problem as a moral issue. Values operate throughout any purposive selection, analytic task is to carry out a search for "value," built in the structure or processes of law, because these values (even when they operate unnoticed) must be deliberately selected to determine the outcome of the judicial case. "Such search is a retail, not a wholesale matter."[57]

Therefore positivist realism also agrees with Abraham Edel that the consideration of "once-and-for-all solutions is out of the line with the differentation of issues"[58] The result may depend among others "on the particular historical situation and whether the forces for anarchy or those for tyranny were more threatening"[59]—This approach is inseparably connected with the New Rhetoric.

Abraham Edel's pragmatic reanalysis moves in the direction of rhetorical methodology. No wonder therefore that he observed:

"Aristotle's *Rhetoric* can fruitfully be read as a curriculum for legal studies ... The close relation of the purposive, the factual, and the ethical, and the integration of concepts with contexts and purposes, are akin to the pragmatic mode."[60] The direction in which "pragmatic reanalysis" is moving is the point of departure of positivist realism. It uses consciously Aristotelian rhetorical traditions and absorbes its revived and elaborated form: the New Rhetoric. Pragmatic Reanalysis and Positivist Realism develop new, modern juridical methodology side by side; they overcome certain myths and obsolete dogmas. They both may lead toward a new systhesis or they can remain apart and produce a new proof of the inexhaustible vitality and pluralism of the philosophy and methodology of law.

*

Positivist realism tries to elaborate the famous remark made by Edward H. Levi:

> "A change of mind from time to time is inevitable when there is a written constitution. There can be no authoritative interpretation of the Constitution. The Constitution in its general provisions embodies the conflicting ideals of the community. Who is to say what these ideals mean in any definite way? Certainly not the framers, for they did their work when the words were put down. The words are ambiguous. Nor can it be the court, for the court cannot bind itself in this manner; an appeal can always be made back to the Constitution."[61]

Positivist realism takes into account a well established and reasonable hypothesis that the framers of any constitution or of any legal act may have intended the legal norms which they promulgated as a "growing instrument."[62]

Wherever and whenever the constitution and the positive legal norms enjoy great authority, the courts, administrators, and ordinary citizens can go back to the written document and quote it despite any previous interpretation and application. This fact constitutes a basis for freedom greater than a country could enjoy if no such documents existed.[63]

In this way positivist realism can overcome the burden of two theories: that a jurist while interpreting should look either for the intent of the legislator or for the objective intent or meaning expressed in the given text. There exists no reliable mechanism for a final and reliable determination what the legislators or the given text truly and once for all wanted to express or really expressed while using general and ambiguous (deliberately or out of necessity) words. Because of the nature of the legislative process there are many conflicting ideals to be found in every major legal document. It is only in the process of interpretation and confrontation with the new demands of life that the intent of the legislator or of the text is revealed, not as a *dictum* but as a process of elaboration and exposition.[64]

It is possible that two different situations can result in the same legal rules. One can also state that two general principles when applied can result in the same legal rule.[65]

How is that possible, theoretically? Answering this question Edward K. Levi quotes from Brett's opinion in *Heaven V. Pender* (11 L. R. Q. B. 503, 1883), who wrote that in such a case as described above there must be "some larger proposition which involves and covers both sets of circumstances . . . the logic of inductive reasoning requires that where two propositions lead to exactly similar premises there must be a more remote and larger premise which embraces both of the major propositions."[66]

The sense of this analysis when applied to the problem raised e.g. by Dworkin is that one can deduce from one general principle some less general (but still general) principles, and vice versa: a group of general principles presupposes the existence of a "more remote and larger premise." Finally we can invoke such most general principles as utility (mentioned by Cardozo in *The Growth of the Law*),[67] or love of one's neighbor, translated by Lord *Atkin* into a legal principle: you must not injure your neighbor—(both examples discussed by E.H. Levi).[68]

Needless to say that both principles—it does not matter whether philosophical or moral or theological—are so broad that one can draw from them an unlimited number of contradictory "general" and "specific" principles and norms. Who could deny that these principles are general, applicable, and in certain circumstances, juridical?

* * *

Professor Gray Dorsey has observed that once human will was admitted to be the origin of law, no lawmaking process "could escape the suspicion that it was guided by the interest of the legislator instead of objective wisdom."[69] Legislators always represent only partial will (or partial interests—it depends on the level of the social research whether one refers to law as an expression of will or interests) of the societies, because they are divided in various social strata, have various interests, and various perceptions of their interests. Law *nolens volens* represents either the most important common interests of the society or the interests of the most powerful group in the society at the given moment. Gray Dorsey's observation is indeed a persuasive argument against any natural law theory and against the simplistic reasoning that law *per se* must represent tendencies towards peace, justice, and equality. Mankind needs law to preserve certain basic values and interests necessary to assure its survival in a period of competition and diversification. Law can be important not because humankind is a sea of tranquility, but on the contrary: we need law because the life of nations is stormy and conflicts and antagonisms are "innate" and "ingrained" in them.

Therefore positivist realism agrees with Gray Dorsey's observation and his description of juridical positivism:

> "Positivist Law can and has looked to the experience of ordinary language, the inner order of social relations, history, community views of fundamental fairness and justice, the felt necessities of the time. Indeed, Natural Law theorists, beginning with Blackstone, have sometimes preferred to find the substantive meaning of principles and rules in experience in order to claim the prestige of being scientific."[70]

Positivist realism consciously takes this observation into account, regards "positivist law"[71] as a result of social and political relations and of the "felt necessities" of social and political relations and of the "felt necessities" of the time. Positive realism tries to update these "felt necessities".

This approach also explains why positivist realism attributes such importance to the social phenomenon which Gray Dorsey calls "jurisculture." He himself coined this word in order to indicate that ". . . jurisculture applies the evolutionary point of view . . . to the comparative, historical study of the processes of establishing and maintaining societies and legal systems."[72]

Positivist realism also regards legal provisions as being inseparable from the culture (in the broadest meaning of this term). We already quoted the Roman maxim: *si duo faciunt idem, non est idem*. In reference to the problems of jurisculture, positivist realism represents the point of view that the same juridical norms and institutions can have different meanings, applications and effects in different cultural environments. The understanding of law depends on the understanding of the social reality. Therefore the application of the provisions of law is influenced by the general culture of the society as well. The validity and effectiveness of any philosophy of law and of any system of law ultimately depend on their *authenticity*,[73] their adjustment to the given stage of the culture in the given society.

* * *

As we have indicated, the traditional antagonism dividing the natural law and positivist theories today is losing its previous validity and acuteness. This relative rapprochement constitutes a long process determined by a general evolution of our culture, by the process of modernization of the less developed societies, by the evolution of the international community, international law, and especially by the *positivisation* of the ideas of human rights.

This is the general atmosphere in which Professor Ota Weinberger (Graz, Austria) wrote his important discourse under the poignant title: *Jenseits von Positivismus und Naturrecht.*[74]

Ota Weinberger's point of departure is a theory which, according to the traditional terminology, could be described as positivism, but for the sake of analysis he presents his legal philosophy in a less traditional terminology. Law is for him a social reality, but it is very specific: it is an institutional fact. It is not sufficient to state "raw" facts in order to describe an "institutional reality." One must add practical notions also: ". . . *den*

Begriff der Handlung, den Begriff der praktischen Saetze (in Gegenüberstellung zu den Aussagesätzen), denn nur mittels solcher Sätze ist es moeglich, Sollen, Wertungen und teleologische Relationen auszudrücken."[75]

The upshot of this approach: the knowledge of law is at the same time the knowledge of reality and of the *"Sollen,"* ("ought") of the norms. The arguments *de lege ferenda* constitute, he argues, an inseparable part of jurisprudence, and legal practice is inseparable from concepts of justice. One should bear all these remarks in mind while reading Weinberger's definition of juridical positivism: a theory which regards law as an object of scientific knowledge.[76] The following elements belong to the system of positive law: all the general norms and the secondary norms, legal duties and rights *(Ansprueche)*, all kind of legal relations and *"Judikatur."*[77] And further:

> *"Zu den positiv institutionalisierten Momenten gehört auch die Rechtswissenschaft and die gesellschaftlich verankerte Interpretationsmethodik.* Zum System des positiven Rechts gehören auch die *Rechtsgrundsätze* und *der teleologische Hintergrund des Rechtssystems,* die teils als rationale *Abstraktionsprodukte* aus geltenden Rechtsvorschriften, teils als *institutionalisiertes Vorwissen* des Juristen in Erscheinung treten. Man könnte zwar einwenden, dass in diesem Falle wegen des Mangels einer expliziten formalen Quelle ein gewisses Moment der Ungewissheit ... auftreten kann, ich glaube jedoch, dass man auch diese Momente — da sie tatsächlich wirksam sind — als Bestandteile der rechtlichen Realität ansehen muss."*[78]

This concept of the sphere *(der Bereich)* of the positive law is very broad and obviously transgresses the traditional positivist notions. While elaborating on the traditional European positivist theory Professor Ota Weinberger is on the straight road towards American realism in jurisprudence. Here is another corroboration that realism is indeed an extended form of positivism. It is irrelevant to our consideration how far Professor Weinberger decided to depart from the letter of the European tradition in order to retain its essence. All the elements enumerated by him as constituting a part of a living organism of the system of law are indeed a part of the dynamic social reality; they constitute an element, as Goethe once expressed it, of the eternally green tree of life and practical activity.

Professor Weinberger uses his philosophical construction of the notion of law for a purpose which is most important from the viewpoint of our theory of positivist realism: he proves that juridical positivism rejects the simplistic concept ascribed to it that every *content* expressed by law could be uncritically accepted by the juridical positivists. Indeed juridical positivism denies that *"die freir Willkürlichkeit"*[79] could be approved by it.

In order to reject these accusations, one does not have to accept any natural law theory, including Hart's concept of the "minimum" of the natural law. The reasoning of Professor Ota Weinberger is so important that I have to quote him once more *in extenso:*

> Wenn *Hart* aus überlegungen über die anthropologische Rolle des Rechts Postulate über einen Minimal inhalt an Naturrecht aufstellt, kann ihm insoweit recht gegeben werden, dass ein Rechtssystem als institutionelles Gebilde gewisse inhaltliche Merkmale aufweisen *muß*. Diese inhaltlichen Bestimmungen können aber m.E. *nicht als Naturrecht* angesehen werden, sondern sie sind *definierende Merkmale des Rechtsbegriffes,* die dann zur Geltung kommen,

wenn man das Recht nicht nur strukturell, sondern auch von Standpunkt seiner gesellschaftlichen funktionen betrachtet.[80]

Law is law even if it violates certain moral and social postulates, but that does not mean that a person must obey these provisions. The natural law theorists argue that an immoral "law" is not a law and therefore, being a product of "naked power," is not binding. Indeed, in the struggle against power based on violence no theoretical considerations are even sufficient.[81]

> "Therefore I think that the positivist theory is in this respect more adequate, because it does not overlook the reality that in every society there exists a juridical consciousness which points out that force should not be the only element constituting laws."[82]

One can of course agree with the conclusion of the natural law theorists that law should guarantee freedom of speech and press and the opportunity to express truth. But one can also, as Professor Weinberger writes, argue that in order to function every society must communicate and have free access to the necessary information. From the social facts and needs one can deduce a postulate that one should speak the truth and should be given an unobstructed chance to do so[83], apart from the Biblical Commandments.

Finally, once we reject "absolute values" the shadow of absolute certitude will disappear and it will be replaced by "plausibility" and a "democratic search for consensus"[84]. Thus Professor Weinberger ends his considerations. Let us observe once more: the consistent, democratic, interpretation of juridical positivism, rationalistic and modernized, leads to the conclusion that any effective legal system and philosophy of law must be intrinsically connected with the "search for consensus," and this search can be successful by use of rhetorical argumentation and persuasion.

It would be irrelevant to discuss how far positivist realism could adhere to all the theses of Professor Ota Weinberger. But positivist realism agrees with his fundamental points of departure and with his method of reasoning and arguing. Positivist realist also agrees with Professor Weinberger's assertion that positivists must be more careful in the use of their argumentation and in the elaboration of their research programs, whereas the natural law theorists today, being less dogmatic and apodictic than their predecessors, should continue what they started; then they will more and more be aware that the decisive question in modern society should not be the problem whether "immanent" values exist and what their source is, but how values, more or less generally accepted, should be incorporated into the existing positive law systems, how interpreted, and observed.

It becomes more and more important for both juridical schools to accept certain historically and socially evolved common values and unite their efforts to realize them than to give up cooperation in order to continue the endless philosophical disputes concerning the origins of values. In the world in which democracy, freedom, and human rights are endangered, threatened by all kinds of despotism, real totalitarianism or *creeping* totalitarianism, the meaning of certain philosophical divisions becomes less important, whereas the bonds uniting the followers of liberty are becoming more and more important and meaningful.[85]

*

Let us quote at the end of this section the famous dialogue between Napoleon and Laplace, as it has come down to us:

Napoleon: I see no place for God in your system, Mr. Laplace.

Laplace: Sire, I have no need of that hypothesis.

The answer of Laplace could be used as our reply to the question posed at the beginning of this section of our book: *Does Antigone need "Natural Law"?* . She no longer needs that hypothesis at the end of this century.

X.
CONCLUSIONS: TOWARD POSITIVIST REALISM

We live at a time when a new concept of law is evolving, although it has not been theoretically assessed. One may call it positivist realism.

Positivist realism can be described as a philosophical amalgam of juridical positivism and American jurisprudence, international and municipal norms on human rights, and the philosophy and methodology of the New Rhetoric.

Positivist realism emerges as a theory of law adjusted to the new social conditions and political realities of the end of the 20th century. It encompasses the traditions of the Western philosophy of law and the experience of all kinds of modern societies. It is a theory of law that explains the nature of law and can aid the perennial struggle for democracy and peace, social order and human rights, international cooperation and sovereignty. This notion, like the Hegelian essence, tries to penetrate into the depth of important relationships hidden under the surface; positivist realism is not just a study of phenomena, whether they take form of juridical norms or the behavior of lawyers. It studies phenomena as a first step toward understanding the substantial relationship between norms, morality, and behavior on the one hand

and social, economic, and political relationships on the other.

Virtually all states today (there are a few temporary exceptions) are members of the international community symbolized by the United Nations. They have all accepted the Charter of the United Nations as a valid legal document. A majority of them also signed the Universal Declaration of Human Rights. All of them voted for the Declaration on Principles of International Law (1970). Almost half of the world's nations joined the International Covenants on Human Rights (1966). The provisions concerning human rights, as expressed in the Charter of the United Nations and in other documents are binding in various ways on the governments of all countries. It does not matter what a given government thinks about the relationship between international law and internal law; whether it considers that international law becomes part of internal law by its own authority or through some domestic legislative transformation, is irrelevant for our further conclusions. The norms of international law as well as the general and specific provisions of the constitutions and other general legal acts, even of dictatorships, are a source of immunities, liberties, and subjective rights which cannot morally, if not legally, be denied or ignored.

Nobody today may claim that he adheres to the principles of due process of law while regarding democratic freedoms and subjective rights as empty and void. Rights and duties can, of course, be more or less general or specific. General legal provisions which are embodied in constitutions create very broad notions of rights which can be specified in legal acts of lower rank. They can be made more or less real, they can be expanded or abridged, but they cannot be cancelled, liquidated, interpreted as being empty, rendered null and void. Whenever the authorities try to curtail or nullify democratic liberties and rights, their attempts or acts are illegal because they violate the provisions of higher, basic, fundamental, legal acts and guarantees to which they themselves have adhered.

In non-democratic states, particularly in the totalitarian ones, the facade of relatively democratic and progressive legal norms are all that exist as the last hope, the last life preserver that the oppressed citizens may look to. In totalitarian countries, constitutional and juridical pronouncements are almost like propaganda. The security police can violate these safeguards, liberties, and rights without fear of immediate retribution. But the virtue of a legal positivist attitude is evident here: the victim knows his rights and can claim them; the oppressor knows that he has violated the law; he must hide his violations, must consider public opinion, the weakness of his political regime, and the possibility of future punishment, which has not been evaded by much more powerful violators than he.

It is a modern paradox that the citizens of non-democratic countries can afford to ignore the law on the books even less than the citizens of traditional democracies can. They must stick to the traditional interpretation and application of positive law (including constitutional law), because any deviation from the letter of the law will be held against them and not against the powerful authorities.

Positivist realism as a philosophy of law is the theoretical foundation for the concept of the famous legalism elaborated in the 19th century, of the true *Rechtsordnung* and *Rechtsstaat* in the best meaning of the terms.

We have made no effort here to analyze all aspects of American realism. There are specialized studies devoted to this subject. Our contention is that being basically positivistic, American juridical realism introduced new dimensions in legal theory, which influenced the way of thinking of all philosophers of law in the 20th century. Sometimes non-American philosophers do not even realize how greatly their approach to legal theory has been changed.

From the sociological viewpoint, American legal realism is a product of a society which contains more legal and political safeguards to protect the rights of the individual than any other, although still too few. American society, with such a deeply ingrained juridical culture (apart from well known and publicized abuses and inconsistencies in legal and political practice), can afford what the realists proposed and what Bentham called a liberal interpretation of law. It would be difficult to imagine that this "liberalism" could be transformed, under normal American circumstances, into license and a disregard of the Constitution, and of the basic principles of common and statutory law. The general package of guarantees includes an independent press and selfgoverning political, social, professional, and even religious organizations.

By no means could American methods and experience be mechanically transplanted to another soil. From the very beginning, apart from specific concepts of the individual authors, legal realism was meant to be a theoretical corrective of the exigencies of traditional narrowly

Conclusions: Toward Positivist Realism

interpreted, juridical positivism. Legal realism tried to direct juridical positivism toward a concept of justice which could finally be free from the danger expressed in the words *summum ius, summa iniuria.*

But finally it is the New Rhetoric which enables us to connect the two doctrines: realism and positivism, regarded until now as intellectually divided.

A study of the writings of American legal realists as a whole leads to the conclusion that these American thinkers devised no new anti-positivistic philosophy of law, but rather a development within positivistic philosophy, a tendency to assure maximum justice within a legal system which, according to Llewelyn, is in constant flux within the society, while the society itself is always changing too.

Even if, in their rebellion against traditional conceptualism, some "legal realists" rejected the traditional "philosophy of positive law," that does not mean very much: a person's description of himself is not necessarily accurate.

The further the legal realists go from allegedly dogmatic, schematic, juridical positivism, the nearer they are to a non-dogmatic positivism, one which is more modern, more rhetorical, more grounded on experience, and less on syllogistic logic.

Let us reconsider at least one example and compare the social and political conditions in the USA at the end of the last century when the Supreme Court legalized the concept of "separate but equal" with the political climate in the 1950's when, in *Brown v. Board of Education,* the Supreme Court finally reversed itself, turning toward integration.

The Supreme Court struck down the principle "separate but equal" when an important part of the nation had become mature enough to ask for and to accept racial integration. The justices mature although not simultaneously with society; they are influenced by the new attitudes, feelings and ideas of their society. If the law to a certain extent is what the courts decide, it is important to remember that the courts do not decide capriciously as in a social or logical vacuum. The decision of the Court in *Brown v. Board of Education* was free in the sense that nobody physically or mentally compelled the justices to do what they did. They were free because they had chosen freely but only between given possibilities; they understood the potential power of social expectations, upheavals, and the increasing activity of the underprivileged. Their views were influenced by their perception of the existing circumstances and social needs. Thus, the maxim, "law is what the courts decide," can have a deep social, moral, and political meaning when one understands the two-way mechanism of determinism and freedom, of objectivity and subjectivity, of necessity and chance.

Feelings, emotions, perceptions, as well as individual understanding are also determined by the existing bonds, by social solidarity and antagonisms, by the moral climate, and by countervailing passions, ideology, and mythology.

The more free and independent the Court is, the more predictable its decisions will be. When freedom of thought and the depth of the juridical reflections are even better secured, the decisions of the justices will be even less arbitrary, less capricious, more deeply analyzed, and more clearly formed.

All these considerations and conclusions are applicable only to the jurists (Courts) in a democratic country where the system of justice is free of all official, hidden or open, administrative pressures, prejudgments, invisible springs, and visible corruption. A system of justice and law in itself can exist only in a country in which freedom of interpretation and application exists. Whenever and wherever the courts are denied the right to interpret and apply the law freely the result is more arbitrariness, more capriciousness, more unpredictability (or perhaps more predictability based on the expectation of overwhelming immorality and terror), more violations of reason, logic, and justice, and more cases when the victims wonder whether the court is ashamed of what it is doing.

Positivist realism can finally overcome the recurrent mythology of natural law theories; nevertheless, we must say that these two basic theories of law which have provoked such strong mutual antagonism, have served to feed one another. Each of them survived because of the weaknesses of its rival. Every step forward of one theory would inevitably be followed by a new development of the other, and vice versa.

The criticism of the 18th century version of natural law was followed by the triumph of juridical positivism. But at the end of the 19th century and the beginning of the 20th, new natural law theories enjoyed a revival.

The juridical positivists usually underestimated in the dust of the battles, the progressive implications of the natural law theories represented by Locke, Rousseau, and their American counterparts, but they pointed out that these theories were not scientific, that they suffered from fundamental logical defects, that life was changing so quickly and profoundly that it was nonsense to assert that perennial unchangeable rules could regulate ever new social phenomena.

The concept of a "natural law with changing content" had been provoked by the charges of rigidity and unchangeability on the part of the norms. But Stammler's remedy is worse than the sickness itself. The concept of "something" firm, eternal, unchangeable, being a foundation of stability and certainty, constitutes the whole *raison d'etre* of the schools of natural law; they cannot give up these premises without ceasing to be what they are. The logical flaws of these theories were already shown by Petrazhytsky; there is no need to repeat his arguments that "natural law with changing content" is a contradictio in adiecto.

On the other hand, although juridical positivism represented a tremendous step forward in the development of the juridical sciences, it too was limited by its own program. The narrow concept that legality exclusively depends on the will of the legislator and the observation of his rules could only dismay decent people familiar with government-sponsored terror and massive repression, and unfamiliar on the other hand with the true origins and traditions of juridical positivism. If an obvious injustice is legal, down with such legality! If the violation of human dignity is legal, according to the jurists of the establishment pretending to be juridical positivists, then reasonable people should look for another philosophy of law not so blatantly antagonistic to elementary human feelings.

What could that other philosophy be? It would be simple to answer: let us return to the philosophy of natural law! But an unscientific answer cannot be an effective medicine to cure political and social deficiencies.

Conclusions: Toward Positivist Realism

The weakness of a narrowly interpreted juridical positivism has been overcome only recently by combining juridical positivism with the positive expression of human rights and broadened by the new theory of argumentation.

Positivist realism which is expounded in this volume is not a timeless theory of law. It presents the latest legal developments in their most general form.

It is a philosophy of law for a period when state-enforced law "pervades" the life of nations to a degree incomparably greater than during the period of Bentham, Austin, Mill, Ihering, Jellinek, and their colleagues. It is a period when the norms of international law and morality are becoming more and more multifarious, permeating deeper and deeper into everyday life. It is a philosophy of law for a period when states of various political and social structures coexist on this globe and cooperate with one another despite their basic differences and antagonisms, and it supplies instruments for cooperation.

The last but not the least aspect of the philosophy of positivist realism is that it is a theory of the period when more and more educated jurists realize that legal norms do not constitute a solid body and are not a fluid in a jar either; they do not have a fixed consistency, but are being "expounded," are something "living," and can be enriched or impoverished by the new requirements of life. What is being expounded, however, is law, a genuine positive law, that must be as real as the American Constitution, about which John Marshall made the immortal observation, "... *it is a Constitution we are expounding* ..."

REFERENCES

Chapter I.

1. Cicero, *De Legibus*, Book 1, VI. (Quoted from: Morris R. Cohen and Felix S. Cohen, *Readings in Jurisprudence and Philosophy*, Boston-Toronto: Little, Brown and Co., 1951), p. 376.
2. *Ibid.*, p. 400.

Chapter II.

1. David Baumgardt, *Bentham and the Ethics of Today,* (Princeton: Princeton University Press, 1952), p. 5.
2. Karl Marx, *Capital*, (Chicago: Charles H. Kerr & Co., 1921, vol. 1, ch. XXIV, p. 668): "Bentham is a purely English phenomenon . . . With the dryest naïveté he takes the modern shopkeeper, especially the English shopkeeper, as the normal man. Whatever is useful to this queer normal man . . . is absolutely useful . . . Had I the courage of my friend, Heinrich Heine, I should call Mr. Jeremy a genius in the way of bourgeois stupidity."
3. Jeremy, Bentham, *An Introduction to the Principles of Morals and Legislation* (London: The Athlone Press, 1970) p. 14.
4. *Ibid.*, p. 14.
5. *Ibid.*, pp. 14-15.
6. *Ibid.*, p. 15.
7. David Baumgardt, *Bentham and the Ethics of Today*, (Princeton: Princeton University Press, 1952), p. 3.
8. Jeremy Bentham, *An Introduction to the Principles of Morals and Legislation* (London: University of London: The Athlone

Press, 1970), p.282, ch. xvii, para. 2.
9. *Ibid.*, p. 282, para. 3.
10. *Ibid.*, p. 294, ch. xvii, para. 23.
11. *Ibid.*, p. 302-304.
12. *The Collected Works of Jeremy Bentham*, ed. J.H. Burns. *Principles of Legislation and Of Laws in General*, ed. H.L.A. Hart (London: The Athlone Press, 1970), p. 1.
13. Jeremy Bentham, *An Introduction to the Principles of Morals and Legislation* (London: The Athlone Press, 1970), p. 299.
14. *Ibid.*, p. 290.
15. *Ibid.*, p. 281; ch. xvii, para. 1.
16. Jeremy Bentham *Pannomial Fragments* in *The Works of Jeremy Bentham*, ed. John Bowring (New York: Russell and Russell, 1962), vol. III, p. 211. Bentham did not complete this work. The last fragments are dated June 1831.
17. Jeremy Bentham, *Pannomial Fragments* in *The Works of Jeremy Bentham*, vol. III, p. 212.
18. Bentham asks: what should be the object of any debate: Should it be *to win over* the opponent without humiliating him? "So to shape his discourse, that, on return to it, the adversary shall, for the avoidance of a still more afflictive humiliation, submit to the humiliation of coming over to his side." How could this delicate purpose be achieved? Bentham presents the Aristotelian method in his own interpretation and starts to explain — in contrast to this method — the Socratic method of disputation. Here the manuscript ends abruptly with the note: "Go on explaining the mechanism" —Jeremy Bentham, "Essay on Logic" op. cit., vol. VIII, p. 237-238.

    One can assume that Bentham wanted to elaborate on the Socratic method as sometimes more adequate or more fruitful than certain parts of Aristotelian logic, but he did not have a chance to return to this problem. He wrote the last parts of his "Essay on Logic" when he was already in his eighties.
19. Jeremy Bentham, *An Introduction to the Principles of Morals and Legislation*, p. 241, ch. xvi, para. 42.
20. *Ibid.*
21. *Ibid.*
22. *Ibid.*
23. *Ibid.*
24. One element by Bentham quoted above requires further clarification: why does he write about right as a "fictitious en-

tity?" In this respect the nominalistic limitation of Bentham's philosophical methodology and theory come to the surface. Whatever is not *corporeal*, in the strictest Baconian sense, is a fiction for Bentham, a product of the mind created for the purpose of expediency.
25. David Baumgardt, *Bentham and The Ethics of Today* (Princeton: Princeton University Press, 1952), p. 124.
26. Jeremy Bentham "General View of a Complete Code of Laws" in, *The Works of Jeremy Bentham*, vol. III, p. 209.
27. *Ibid.*, p. 158.
28. Jeremy Bentham "Pannomial Fragments" in *The Works of Jeremy Bentham, op. cit.*, vol. III, p. 211.
29. Jeremy Bentham "General View of a Complete Code of Laws" in *Complete Works of Jeremy Bentham,* vol. III, p. 209.
30. Jeremy Bentham "General View of a Complete Code of Laws" in *The Works*, vol. III, p. 209-210.
31. *Ibid.*, pp. 33-34; 40.
32. *Ibid.*, p. 33.
33. *Ibid.*, p. 209.
34. *Ibid.*, p. 210.
35. *Ibid.*, p. 210.
36. *Ibid.*, p. 210.
37. *Ibid.*, p. 210.
38. *Ibid.*
39. Jeremy Bentham "On the Liberty of the Press and Public Discussion" (first published in 1821) in, *The Works of Jeremy Bentham*, ed. John Bowring (New York: Russell & Russell, Inc., 1962), vol. II, p. 277.
40. See below Chapter VIII: Human Rights: Philosophical and Juridical Problems.
41. "Compare the results in states in which the publications of ideas has been restrained, and in those where freedom of thought and of speech has been permitted. You have, on the one hand, Spain, Portugal, Italy; on the other, England, Holland, North America. Where do we find greatest happiness? Where the highest standard of morals? Where is society most agreeable, where people most secure?" *A Bentham Reader*, "Indirect Legislation," p. 176. (New York: Pegasus, 1969) ed., Mary Peter Mack.
42. *Ibid.*, p. 177.
43. *Ibid.*

44. A censor, for instance, " . . . risks nothing by prohibition, but everything by permission. In doubtful cases, it will be not he that suffers; it will be the Truth." *Ibid.*, p. 177.
45. *A Bentham Reader*, ed. Mary Peter Mack (New York: Pegasus, 1969) p. 176.
46. "What is a censor? He is an interested judge, . . . who proceeds in secret, condemns without a hearing, and decides without an appeal. Secrecy of procedure, that greatest of abuses, is absolutely essential." *Ibid.*, p. 176.
47. Jeremy Bentham "On the Liberty of the Press, and Public Discussion" (first published in 1821) in, *The Works of Jeremy Bentham*, ed. John Bowring (New York: Russell and Russell, Inc. 1962) vol. II, pp. 277-278.
48. *Ibid.*, p. 279.
49. *Ibid.*
50. *Ibid.*, p. 279.
51. *Ibid.*, p. 279.
52. *Ibid.*

Chapter III.

1. No substantial monographs exist on Austin's theory.
2. John Austin, *Lectures on Jurisprudence or the Philosophy of Positive Law*, ed., Robert Campbell, vol. I (New York: James Cockcroft and Company, 1875), pp. 5-6.
3. *Ibid.*, p. 6.
4. *Ibid.*, p. 3.
5. *ibid.*, pp. 12-13.
6. *Ibid.*, p. 13.
7. *Ibid.*, p. 14.
8. *Ibid.*, pp. 18-19.
9. *Ibid.*, pp. 19-20.
10. *Ibid.*, pp. 107, 178.
11. *Ibid.*, pp. 106-107.
12. *Ibid.*, p. 107.
13. *Ibid.*, p. 108.
14. *Ibid.*, p. 108. Not so, Kelsen. See chapter IX, para. 4.
15. *Ibid.*, p. 3-12.
16. In the review of Lon L. Fuller's book, *The Law in Quest of Itself,* Professor Myres S. McDougal observed: "We have all

been brought up to drub poor old Austin and his 'sovereign.' But in his defense against the kind of attack to which Professor Fuller subjects him, it must be said that any key symbol, any top abstraction in a system of social analysis must leave many particulars of the system unexpressed. The important focus of attention for a critic should be on the subsequent specification of those particulars." Myres S. McDougal. "Fuller v. American Legal Realists. An Intervention." *Yale Law Journal*, 1941, reprinted in Morris R. Cohen and Felix Cohen, *Readings in Jurisprudence and Legal Philosophy* (Boston-Toronto: Little Brown and Co., 1951), p. 661.

17. John Austin, *op., cit.,* p. 153.
18. *Ibid.,* p. 153.
19. *Ibid.,* p. 155. Compare also para. 249.
20. *Ibid.,* pp. 155-156, para. 252.
21. *Ibid.,* p. 155, para. 252.
22. *Ibid.,* pp. 156-157, para. 254.
23. *Ibid.,* p. 157, para. 254.
24. *Ibid.,* p. 157, para. 254.
25. *Ibid.,* p. 157, para. 254.
26. *Ibid.*
27. *Ibid.*
28. *Ibid.,* p. 166, para. 264.
29. *Ibid.*
30. *Ibid.,* p. 167, para. 264, (footnote). Nonetheless, observed Austin, the expression became famous, and one of the reasons for its popularity is the fact that it became "a great favorite with shallow scoffers and buffoons."—*Ibid.*
31. *Ibid.,* p. 167, para. 264.
32. *Ibid.,* pp. 173-174, para. 273.
33. *Ibid.,* p. 174, para. 273.
34. *Ibid.,* p. 175, para. 273.
35. *Ibid.,* p. 174, para. 273.
36. *Ibid.,* pp. 173-177, paras. 273-277.
37. *Ibid.,* p. 20, para. 32.
38. *Ibid.,* p. 20.
39. *Ibid.*
40. *Ibid.,* p. 77, para. 123.
41. *Ibid.,* p. 78, para. 123.
42. *Ibid.,* pp. 72-73, paras. 113-115; pp. 77-78, paras. 123-124.
43. *Ibid.,* p. 73, para. 117.

44. *Ibid.*, p. 73-74, para. 117.
45. *Ibid.*, p. 74, para. 117.
46. *Ibid.*, p. 75, para. 120.
47. *Ibid.*, p. 75, para. 118.
48. *Ibid.*, p. 75, para. 120.
49. *Ibid.*, p. 174, para. 273.

Chapter IV.

1. See Joseph H. Drake, Editorial Preface to the English translation of *Der Zweck im Recht*, p. XVII in Rudolf von Ihering, *Law as a Means to an End* (New York: The Macmillan Co., 1924).
2. "Law is the sum of conditions of social life in the widest sense of the term, as secured by the power of the State through the means of external compulsion," Ihering, *Law* . . . , *op. cit.*, p. 380. This definition is more sociological than "purely" juridical. Obviously the "conditions of social life in the widest sense"—are historico-sociological.
3. *Ibid.*, p. 380.
4. *Ibid.*, pp. 239-240, ch. VIII, para. 10.
5. *Ibid.*, p. 241. "The criterion of all legal norms is their realization through coercion by the *State authorities* appointed for the purpose . . . Considered from this point of view all law presents itself as a system of coercion enforced by the State." *Ibid.*, p. 251.
6. *Ibid.*, p. 240, ch. VIII, para. 10.
7. *Ibid.*, p. 241, ch. VIII, para. 10.
8. *Ibid.*
9. *Ibid.*, p. 251, ch. VIII, para. 11.
10. *Ibid.*, p. 252.
11. *Ibid.*, pp. 253-254, Ch. VIII, para. 11, vol. I.
12. *Ibid.*, p. 230.
13. *Ibid.*, p. 181.
14. *Ibid.*, p. 182.
15. *Ibid.*, p. 184.
16. *Ibid.*, p. 184. Also p. 190: "Force both knows what it is and feels it; it demands the same regard from law as law from it."
17. *Ibid.*, p. 184.
18. *Ibid.*, p. 184.

19. *Ibid.*, pp. 242-243.
20. *Ibid.*, pp. 234-235.
21. *Ibid.*, p. 235, ch. VIII, para. 9.
22. *Ibid.*
23. Rudolf von Ihering, *The Struggle for Law* (Chicago: Callaghan and Co., 1915), p. 2.
24. Ihering is obviously under the influence of the political economy of Adam Smith who developed the idea that labor is the source of the wealth of nations. Karl Marx admitted that his theory of value was based on Smith's work and that he himself added to it only the concept of surplus value. There is no doubt that Hegel's dialectic also influenced Ihering's way of thinking, as will be demonstrated in the subsequent paragraphs.

    "Only through a lasting connection with labor can property maintain itself fresh and healthy. Only at this source is it seen, clearly and transparently, to the very bottom, to be what it is to man." (*Ibid.*, p. 52). "Communism thrives only in those quagmires in which the true idea of property is lost." (*Ibid.*, pp. 53-54).
25. *Ibid.*, pp. 5-7.
26. *Ibid.*, pp. 10-12.
27. Ihering, *Law as a Means to the End*, op. cit., p. 386.
28. *Ibid.*
29. *Ibid.*, p. 383.
30. *Ibid.*, pp. 170-172.
31. *Ibid.*, p. 382-383.
32. *Ibid.*, p. 383.
33. Ihering showed a good measure of his political naïveté when he recommended the return to Roman traditions in order to defend "individual independence" (Ihering, *Law, op. cit.*, p. 383), reminding his readers that the Roman guarantees of private rights that were analyzed by him in *Geist des Roemischen Rechts auf den verschiedenen Stufen seiner Entwicklung* (Leipzig, 1852-1854, vol. II, pp. 133-218), should be regarded as examples to be followed.

Chapter V.

1. Possibly a special school of the *Freie Rechtslehre* separate from the sociological, or the *Interessenjurisprudenz,* did not exist

because the four schools mentioned above and other similar theories represented various trends with one denominator: the *"Freie Rechtssprechung,"* or *"Rechtsfindung."*

One can also argue that the various schools of the *"Freie Rechtslehre"* represented a general reaction against the exigencies and ideals of juridical positivism and its traditional method of interpretation.

At the turn of the century it was Eugen Ehrlich, a sociologist and jurist, who either popularized or introduced the terminology *"Freie Rechtslehre"* into university lectures and literature, especially in the article (1888) and later in a pamphlet: *"Freie Rechtsfindung and Freie Rechtswissenschaft"* (1903). Heck in *Das Problem der Rechtsgewinnung* (1912), makes the following characteristic observation:

"Als Vertreter der Freierechtsbewegung bezeichnen sich Forscher verschiedener Anschauung ... Im Interesse der Klarheit empfiehlt es sich, die urspruengliche, dem Wortsinne allein entsprechene Bedeutung beizubehalten. Die Freirechtsbewegung in diesem Sinne ist somit durch die Tendenz charakterisiert den bisherigen Einfluss des Gesetzes de lege ferenda oder de lege lata, allgemein oder unter bewissen Bedingungen zu Gunsten richterlichen Ermessens zurueckzudraengen." (p. 25).

2. The same sociological analysis can be applied, *mutatis mutandis*, to the Austrian-Hungarian monarchy which was also a prison of its nations even though the Austrian absolutism was *"gemildert mit Schlamperei"*—as the popular saying characterized that regime. The oppressed minorities, including the Czechs and the Poles in Austria-Hungary, also fought for their rights and "true legality."
3. Friedrich K. Savigny; *System des Heutigen Roemischen Rechts,* I, 1840, vol. I, p. 211.
4. George F. Puchta; *Vorlesungen ueber das Heutige Roemische Recht,* 1873.
5. Belime, *Philosophie due Droit,* 1881, p. 490.
6. Wurzel, *Das Juristische Denken,* 1904, p. 28.
7. Shershenevitch, *Kurs Grazhdanskovo Prava,* 1901, Vol. I, p. 7.
8. Professor Eugeniusz Waskowski: *Teoria Wykladni Prawa Cywilnego* (Theory of the Interpretation of Civil Law) Warsaw, 1936, p. 57.
9. *Ibid.,* p. 170-207.
10. *Ibid.,* p. 5.

11. *Ibid.*, p. 7.
12. *Ibid.*, p. 12.
13. *Ibid.*, p. 5-6.

Chapter VI.

1. Leszek Kolakowski in a speech delivered in London, January 26, 1976, for the Assembly of the Polish Students and graduates in Great Britain. Published in Aneks, Uppsala, No. 11, 1976, p. 11.
2. I discussed these problems in my book: *The Activity of the Socialist State,* Warsaw University Press, Warsaw, 1957.
3. *Theory of Law and State*, collective work, Moscow 1955. The Polish translation of this definition is based on the edition from 1949 (Warsaw, 1951, p. 188ff).
4. Kazimierz Opalek-Witold Zakrzewski, *Z zagadnien praworzadnosci socjalistycznej*, Wydawnictwo Prawnicze, Warszawa, 1958, pp. 5-6, 35-36.
5. *Ibid.*, p. 7.
6. *Ibid.*, pp. 13-15.
7. *Ibid.*, p. 20.
8. *Ibid.*, p. 26.
9. *Ibid.*, p. 31.
10. *Ibid.*, p. 206.
11. *Ibid.*, p. 216.
12. *Ibid.*, p. 218.
13. *Ibid.*, pp. 237-245.
14. *Ibid.*, p. 119.
15. *Ibid.*, p. 120.
    Professor Leon Lustacz proved that the normative acts in Poland were so numerous and inflated that the process of issuing the legal provisions got out of hand, reaching unreasonable proportions (*State and Law*, Warsaw, No. 2, p. 294).
16. *Ibid.*, pp. 142-44.
17. *Ibid.*, p. 246
18. Stefan Rozmaryn: (1) *Konstytucja jako ustawa zasadnicza Polskiej Rzeczypospolitej Ludowej* (The Constitution as the Basic Law of the Polish People's Republic), Polish Scholarly Publishers, Warsaw, 1961. The book will be referred to as "The Constitution..." (b) *Ustawa w Polskiej Rzeczypospolitej Ludowej* (The Law in the Polish People's Republic) — the

publisher as above. Warsaw, 1964. The book will be referred to as: "The Law . . ."
19. *The Constitution*, p. 35.
20. *Ibid.*, pp. 17-18.
21. *Ibid*, p. 21.
22. *Ibid.*, pp. 23-24.
23. *Ibid.*, p. 26.
24. Maurice Duverger observed that in order to correctly understand political ideas and institutions one also should examine against whom they directed: See: Maurice Duverger, *Introduction à une Sociologie des régimes politiques*, in Traité de Sociologie, ed. by G. Gurvitch, Paris, 1960, Vol. II, p. 19.
25. *Ibid.*, pp. 35-36. Cf. D. Kerimov: *Zakonodatielnaja diejatielnost sovietskogo gosudarstva* (Legislative Activity of the Soviet State), Moscow, 1955, p. 68.
26. *The Constitution*, pp. 71-72.
27. *Ibid.*, pp. 74-78.
28. *Ibid.*, pp. 260-261.
29. *Ibid.*, p. 262.
30. *Ibid.*
31. *Ibid.*, p. 263.
32. Carl Schmitt, *Verfassungsrechtliche Aufsaetze*, Berlin, 1958, pp. 217ff and 387. In this book was reprinted his pre-war essay *Grundrechte und Grundpflichten*, 1932.
33. *The Constitution, ibid.*, pp. 285-286.
34. *Ibid.*, pp. 285-286.
35. *Ibid,*, p. 291.
36. *Ibid.*, p. 292.
37. John N. Hazard, *Settling Disputes in Soviet Society* (New York: Columbia University Press, 1960), p. 481.
38. Professor John N. Hazard in his pamphlet *Modernization and Codification* (New York: Russian Institute, School of International Affairs, Columbia University, 1968) writes: "To a jurist trained in the traditions of the Ango-American common law, it is intriguing to meditate on the possibility that the common law method of developing law slowly through the individual decisions of the judges is out of date in the latter part of the twentieth century." (p. 72).

John N. Hazard, "Unity and Diversity of Socialist Law" *Law and Contemporary Problems,* vol. 30 No. 2, Spring, 1965.

John N. Hazard, "Modernization and Codification," *Revue*

Roumaine des Sciences Sociales. Série de Sciences Juridiques, Vol. 12, No. 1, 1968.
39. Professor John N. Hazard writes: "As between the People's Democracies of Europe and the U.S.S.R. there is greater variation, but a common approach has been preserved. Since acceptance by Soviet communist leaders of the fact of resistance, evidenced by Tito's disaffection and the 1956 events in Hungary and Poland, there has been less pressure from the Soviet side for conformity to Soviet models in textual detail." John N. Hazard, "Unity and Diversity in Socialist Law," *Law and Contemporary Problems,* vol. 30 No. 2, Spring 1965 (New York: Russian Institute, School of International Affairs, Columbia University, reprinted from the symposium on Unification of Law, published as the Spring, 1965 issue of *Law and Contemporary Problems,* Duke University School of Law, Durham, N.C.), p. 289.
40. Professors D.A. Kerimov ("Liberty, Law and Legality in the Socialist Society," Moscow 1960, p. 15) and Nora Ananieva, Bulgarian Academy of Sciences, stress the same point concerning the "mirror reflection" in law. Professor N. Ananieva writes: *"Je tiefer und gruendlicher der Gesetzgeber die Wirklichkeit und ihre objektiven Entwicklungsgesetze erkannt hatte, desto hoeheren Freiheitsgrad wird er im Rechtsschaffen erreichen, und mit einem groesseren Effekt die Rechtsregulierung der gesellschaftlichen Beziehungen verwirklichen ..."*

Professor Nora Ananieva, *"Recht, Widerspiegelung, Demokratie."* A paper written for the IX *Weltkongress fuer Rechts- und-Sozial-philosphie,* Basel, 1979. Translation: The more deeply and completely the legislator comes to know reality and its objective developmental laws, the higher will be the degree of freedom he will achieve in the work of law and the greater will be the effect of regulatory law conjoined with its social relations.

She continues: *"Die passende Widerspiegelung der Wirklichkeit im Recht ist eine Voraussetzung fuer die Effektivitaet der Rechtsregulierung und fuer die Freiheit des Subjekts auf Rechtsschaffen.* (P. 2). Translation: The adequate reflection of reality in law is a precondition for the effectiveness of regulatory law and for the freedom of the subject in working in the law.

What happens if the "reflection" is distorted, as every mirror reflection must be? What mechanism is there to improve or

clarify it? That is the true essence of the problem.
41. Adam Lopatka "The Concept of Socialist Law," a paper presented at the Congress in Basel, p. 1.
42. Professor Anna Michalska (University of Poznan, Poland) is one of the few authors in the communist bloc who has presented this point quite clearly: "In the definition of law accepted in socialist science there is included an element—the establishment of law by the State—which puts it among the definitions based on positivistic concepts . . ." (P. 93).

"The element putting the Marxist definition of law among the positivistic definitions is contained in the genus of this definition . . ." (P. 104).

She adds: "This is, however . . . not the classical positivistic definition, in virtue of its further elements: class character of law and the dependence of its content on social and economic relations." (P. 96). *Contemporary Conceptions of Law* (Warsaw: Polish Academy of Sciences, Institute of State and Law, and Polish Section of International Association of Philosophy of Law and Social Philowophy, 1979). Anna Michalska, "The Positivistic Element in the Marxist Definition of Law and its Evaluation," pp. 93-107.
43. Dehangir Kerimov, *"Die Marxistische Auffassung vom Wesen des Rechts", Probleme Der Modernen Welt* (Moskow: "Gesellschaftswissenschaften und Gegenwart," Akademie der Wissenschaften der UdSSR, 1979), p. 9.
44. *Ibid.,* p. 13.
45. Vladik Nersesjanz *"Das Verhaeltnis von Recht und Gesetz: Die Geschichte der Rechtslehren und die Gegenwart," Probleme Der Modernen Welt* (Moscow: "Gesellschaftswissenschaften und Gegenwart," Akademie der Wissenschaften der UdSSR, 1979), pp. 73-82.
46. *Ibid.,* pp. 79-80.
47. *Ibid.,* p. 82.
48. Vladimir Tumanov *"Naturrecht Und Juristischer Positivismus in der Einschaetzung des Marxismus," Probleme Der Modernen Welt* (Moskow: Akademie der Wissenschaften der UdSSR, 1979), p. 19.
49. *Ibid.,* pp. 19-20.
50. *Ibid.,* p. 24.
51. Adam Lopatka, "The Concept of Socialist Law," a paper presented at the World Congress on Philosophy of Law and Social Philosophy, Basel, August 27-September 1, 1979, pp. 8-9.

52. *Ibid.,* p. 9.
53. *Ibid.,* pp. 13-14.
54. John N. Hazard "Unity and Diversity in Socialist Law," *Law and Contemporary Problems,* Vol. 30, No. 2, Spring 1965, Duke University School of Law, p. 289.
55. John N. Hazard, *Settling Disputes in Soviet Society* (New York: Columbia University Press, 1960), pp. 489-490.

Chapter VII.

1. Oliver Wendell Holmes, *Collected Legal Papers* (New York: Peter Smith, 1952), p. 50.
2. *Ibid.,* p. 312.
3. Gompers v.U.S., 233 U.S. 604, 610 (1913). In *The Holmes Reader,* (Dobbs Ferry, N.Y.: Oceana Publications, Inc., 1964), p. 205.
4. Holmes "The Path of the Law," *Collected Legal Papers,* p. 170.
5. *Ibid.,* p. 181.
6. *The Holmes Reader,* p. 209.
7. Holmes, *Collected Legal Papers,* p. 191.
8. *Ibid.*
9. *Ibid.,* p. 181.
10. John Dewey, *Philosophy and Civilization* (New York: Minton, Batch and Co., 1931), p. 130.
11. *Ibid.,* p. 131.
12. This sentence is one of the first to appear in the book by Holmes, *The Common Law.* Later one reads: "The felt necessities of the time, the prevalent moral and political theories, institutions of public policy, avowed or unconscious, even the prejudices which the judges share with their fellow-men, have a good deal more to do than the syllogism in determining the rules by which men should be governed. This embodies the story of a nation's development through many centuries and it cannot be dealt with as if it contained only the axioms and corollaries of a book of mathematics." (Cambridge: The Belknap Press of Harvard University Press, Mass., 1963), p. 5.
13. John Dewey, *op. cit.,* p. 132.
14. *Ibid.*
15. *Ibid.,* p. 133.

16. *Ibid.*, p. 136.
17. *Ibid.*, p. 139.
18. *Ibid.*, p. 140.
19. *Ibid.*, p. 136.
20. *Ibid.*, p. 138.
21. *Ibid.*, p. 139.
22. *Ibid.*, p. 136.
23. *Ibid.*, p. 139.
24. John Dewey, "Afterword" in *The Public and its Problems* (Chicago: The Swallow Press, 1954), p. 223-224.
25. Chaim Perelman, The New Rhetoric: A Theory of Practical Reasoning, in *The Great Ideas Today* (Chicago: Encyclopaedia Britannica, 1970). Reprinted in *The New Rhetoric and the Humanities* (Dordrecht-London: Reidel Publishing Co., 1979), p. 8.
26. *Ibid.*
27. *Ibid.*, p. 9.
28. *Ibid.*
29. Cf. Stephen Haseler in *Commentary*, vol. 64, No. 2, August, 1977, p. 80.
30. Perelman, Dialectic and Dialogue, in: *Hegel-Jahrbuch*, 1970, ed. Wilhelm R. Beyer (trans. by W. Kluback), p. 12. Reprinted in *The New Rhetoric and Humanities, op. cit.*, pp. 76-80.
31. Chaim Perelman, Eugene Dupréel, L'homme et L'oevre, in: *Revue Internationale de Philosophie*, N-83-84, 1968 (trans. by W. Kluback); (Bruxelles, Editions de l'Institut de Sociologie, 1968, p. 230.
32. Dupréel wrote a classical essay on the unclear idea and its methodological significance. It was written as a fundamental critique of Descartes' concept of the clear and distinct idea.
33. *Ibid.*, p. 231.
34. *Ibid.*, p. 236.
35. *Ibid.*
36. Perelman quotes and analyzes this statement of Descartes in "Disagreement and Rationality" in: *The New Rhetoric and Humanities* (Dordrecht, Reidel, 1979), pp. 111-116.
37. Chaim Perelman, A Theory of Practical Reasoning, *op. cit.*, p. 30.
38. *Ibid.*
39. Cf. Mikhail A. Bakunin: "To him (the revolutionist) whatever

aids the triumph of the revolution is ethical; all that which hinders it is unethical and criminal"—*Catechism of the Revolution*, Article 4.
40. Chaim Perelman, A Theory of Practical Reasoning, *op. cit.*, p. 30.
41. Cf. Perelman: "The Rational and the Reasonable" in: Rationality Today, Ottawa University Press, 1979. Reprinted in *The New Rhetoric and the Humanities* (Dordrecht, D. Reidel Publishing Co., 1979), p. 117.
42. *Ibid*.
43. *Ibid*.
44. *Ibid*., p. 118.
45. *Ibid*.
46. *Ibid*., p. 119.
47. *Ibid*., p. 123. There is, incidentally, a link also between the dialectic of the reasonable and the dialectic of justice and equity.
48. C. Wright Mills, *Power, Politics and People*, ed. Irving Louis Horowitz (New York: Oxford University Press, 1974), p. 393.
49. *Ibid*., p. 402.
50. There are conservatisms which officially are based on irrational ideas, but the modern Western and Eastern conservatisms present themselves as rationalistic social movements.
51. C. Wright Mills, *op. cit.*, pp. 603-610. By the way, Mills refers the same characteristics to the communist "realists" and "rationalists."
52. Leonard G. Miller, Moral Scepticism, *Philosophy and Phenomenological Research*, 1961, vol. XXII, pp. 239-245. Cf. Chaim Perelman, The Justification of Norms, in *Justice, Law and Argument* (Dordrecht, Reidel, 1980), p. 107.
53. Chaim Perelman, The Justification of Norms, *op. cit.*, pp. 108-112.
54. *Ibid*., p. 108.
55. *Ibid*., p. 109.
56. Chaim Perelman, Legal Reasoning, in *Justice, Law and Argument, op. cit.*, p. 126.
57. *Ibid*., p. 127.
58. *Ibid*.
59. *Ibid*., p. 129.
60. *Ibid*., p. 132.
61. *Ibid*., p. 133.
62. *Ibid*., p. 135.

63. Perelman, Law and Rhetoric in *Justice, Law and Agreement, op. cit.*, p. 123.
64. *Ibid.*, p. 124.
65. Perelman, *Disagreement and Rationality* in *The New Rhetoric and the Humanities*, 1979, p. 116.
66. Chaim Perelman and L. Olbrechts-Tyteca, *The New Rhetoric* (Notre Dame-London: University of Notre Dame Press, 1969), p. 17.
67. *Ibid.*, p. 19.
68. *Ibid.*, p. 21.
69. *Ibid.*, p. 23.
70. *Ibid.*, p. 25.
71. "... not every appearance would be true; for an appearance is an appearance to someone, so he who states that all appearances are true makes things relative." Aristotle, *Metaphysics* (Bloomington-London: Indiana University Press, 1966, trans. by Hippocrates G.Apostle), 1011a 19-21, p. 69.
72. *Ibid.*, 1011b, 25-20, p. 70.
73. *Ibid.*, 1012a, 3-5, p. 70.
74. *Ibid.*, 1028b, 20-29, p. 158.
75. *Ibid.*, 1051b, 3-5, 6-8, p. 158.
76. Chaim Perelman and L. Olbrechts-Tyteca, *op. cit.*, p. 67.
77. *Ibid.*, pp. 67-68.
78. *Ibid.*, p. 68.
79. *Ibid.*, pp. 68-69.
80. *Ibid.*, p. 69.
81. Heraclites, Fragments 46, 47, in: Milton C. Nahm, *Selections from Early Greek Philosophy*, (New York: Appleton-Century Crofts, 1964).
82. *Ibid.*, Fragments 46, p. 71.
83. *Ibid.*, Fragments 55, 51-115, p. 71-75.
84. *Ibid.*, Fragments 83, p. 73.
85. Hans Kelsen, *Von Wert und Wesen der Demokratie*, Tuebingen, 1929.
86. Perelman-Olbrechts Tyteca, The New Rhetoric, *op. cit.*, p. 415.
87. Adolf Hitler, *Mein Kampf* (Boston: Houghton Mifflin Co., Sentry Edition, 12th Printing), pp. 240-241.
88. *Ibid.*, p. 242.
89. *Ibid*.
90. *Ibid.*, p. 180.
91. *Ibid.*, p. 179.

92. *Ibid.*, p. 180.
93. *Ibid.*, p. 181.
94. *Ibid.*, p. 184.
95. *Ibid.*
96. *Ibid.*
97. *Ibid.*, p. 185.
98. *Ibid.*
99. The art of instigating the emotions only, without any appeal to reason, is a corruption of rhetoric, it is demagoguery.
100. Hegel, *Lectures on the History of Philosophy.* (London: Routledge and Kegan. New York: The Humanities Press, 1974, vol. 1), p. 358. By the way, rhetoric cannot and should not be reduced to oratory; oratorical elements nevertheless are an important part of the theory of argumentation.

Chapter VIII

1. Kazimierz Opalek, in his fundamental monograph, *Prawo Podmiotowe* (Warszawa: Panstwowe Wydawnictwo Naukowe, 1957, p. 6) elaborates on F. Somlo's concept *(Juristische Grundlehre,* Leipzig, 1917, p. 52). Opalek indeed was philosophically impressed by Somlo's oratorial comparison.
2. Prakash Sinha pointed out: "The traditional doctrine of natural law gives a permanently valid formulation to the essential structure of man and sets up permanently valid standards of human conduct. Thus, the doctrine fails to take into account the historicity of man or the historical character of his nature. An adequate theory of human rights must not ignore the historicity of man." S. Prakash Sinha, "The Anthropocentric Theory of International Law as a Basis for Human Rights," *Journal of International Law,* Vol. 10, Spring 1978, p. 977.

    In this book I do not intend to present the history of the human rights' concepts and their transformation into a "positive" international law, because the number of monographs in this respect is almost unlimited. Especially important are the works of Louis B. Sohn, e.g.:

    "A short history of United Nations documents on human rights," in *The United Nations and Human Rights* (New York, 1968).

See also: Sohn and Buergenthal, *International Protection of Human Rights* (New York, 1973).
3. In his book, *The Rights of Man Today*, Louis Henkin wrote: "The transformation of natural rights into positive legal rights took an additional and different step with the development of an international law of human rights. The international law of human rights is higher positive law, binding on states that adhere to it regardless of their own constitutions or other laws (p. 22). And further:

"Although in some countries domestic courts will apply domestic law even if it is inconsistent with an international norm or obligation, that puts the state in default on its international undertaking." (p. 152).

Henkin's monograph *The Rights of Man Today* (Boulder, Colorado: Westview Press, 1978), is the most precise presentation and substantiation of the thesis that international law of human rights has been transformed into a higher (not in Kelsen's meaning, see ch. IX, para. 4) positive law and therefore any state which violates it, acts illegally. The expression, elementary human rights, is very often encountered. This expression can be understood as the catalogue of human rights, which may be interpreted more or less broadly. The differences are political and philosophical, but the adherents of various human rights views agree that some elementary, generally acknowledged, rights exist, such as the right to life, freedom from torture, and freedom of conscience. The word "elementary" can also be replaced by the words, basic, or fundamental. But all these words are restrictive in regard to a broad understanding of the popular term, human rights, so often used and abused. We will be using the expression, "elementary," "basic" or "fundamental" human rights only in specific contexts, because today the mere notion of human rights is usually *eo ipso,* identified with the generally accepted elementary rights of individuals and nations.

Martin P. Golding observed: "The terminology of rights pervades so much of our everyday moral and political discourse that it is virtually inconceivable to us that such discourse could ever have gotten along without this terminology. We meet with the language of rights whenever we open up the daily newspaper." Martin P. Golding, The Concept of Rights: A Historical Sketch, in: *Bioethics and Human Rights*, ed. by E. and B. Bandman (Boston: Little, Brown and Co., 1978), pp. 45-46.

One should also agree with the Golding's following observation: "Perhaps we have had an inflation in our moral economy, an inflation in demands put in terms of rights, to the point that the concept of rights is beginning to lose its value as moral tender. We seem to need a new concept . . . But what could this new concept be?" (*Ibid.*, p. 50).

There is no doubt that this XXth century conception of human rights is much broader than the concept of natural rights developed against political absolutism and feudalism. Louis Henkin characterized this phenomenon in the following way:

"Within nations, even socialism now acquiesces in limitations on government and cannot resist all claims for political-civil rights, and capitalist-bourgeois-libertarian states are irrevocably committed to economic and social welfare for all as of right." (Louis Henkin, *The Rights of Man Today*, op. cit., p. 30).

The best theoretical and the most comprehensive comparative analysis of the problem of "welfare-rights" in the Anglo-Saxon world (USA and the British Commonwealth) one can find in the book of essays, *The Impact of American Law on English and Commonwealth Law*, edited by Jerome B. Elkind (West Publishing Co., St. Paul, Minn., 1978). Especially important are two essays by Jerome B. Elkind ("Race Relations-Repeated Intervention"; "Overview and Conclusion") and an essay by David V. Williams ("Constitutional Law-Reception and Impact").

4. Jerome Hall, *Foundations of Jurisprudence* (New York: The Bobbs Merril Co., 1973), p. 2.
5. A. Baumgarten, *Die Wissenschaft vom Recht und ihre Methode. Kasuistik und zusammenfassende Methode* (Tuebingen: 1922), p. 642. See also Kazimierz Opalek, *Prawo Podmiotowe* (The Subjective Right) *op. cit.*, p. 7.
6. Czeslaw Martyniak, *The Foundations of Law and the Teaching of St. Thomas Aquinas* (Lublin: Katolicki Uniwersytet Lubelski [Catholic University in Lublin], 1947).
7. Wesley Newcomb Hohfeld, *Fundamental Legal Conceptions as Applied to Judicial Reasoning* (New Haven: Yale University Press, 1923), p. 49.
8. *Ibid.*
9. Oliver Wendell Holmes, *The Common Law* (Cambridge: The Belknap Press of Harvard University Press, 1963), p. 169.
10. *Ibid.*

11. Wesley Newcomb Hohfeld, *Fundamental Legal Conceptions as Applied to Judicial Reasoning, op., cit.*, p. 42.
12. *Ibid.*, p. 48.
13. *Ibid.*, pp. 36-37.
14. *Ibid.*, p. 37.
15. *Ibid.*
16. *Ibid.*, p. 50.
17. *Ibid.*, pp. 50-56.
18. Wolfgang Friedmann, *Legal Theory* 5th Edition, (New York: Columbia University Press, 1967), p. 310.
19. *Ibid.*
20. Kazimierz Opalek, *Prawo Podmiotowe, op cit.*, p. 460.
    Martin P. Golding in his essay "The Concepts of Rights: A Historical Sketch" (*op. cit.*, supra) elaborates his own original theory about the origins and evolution of the notion of rights and analyses the distinction between what he calls *option rights* and *welfare rights*. (Compare also: Martin P. Golding, *Towards a Theory of Human Rights, Monist*, 52:521, 1968.)
    Golding's distinction may be theoretically fruitful.
    We could not analyse this approach too closely in this book, but the bases of our philosophies are compatible and rather complimentary.
    One should especially agree with Golding's contention:
    ". . . just as the classical idea of right needed to be supplemented in the late Middle Ages by the idea of rights, so too did option rights eventually need to be supplemented by another type of rights: welfare rights." (p. 49).
21. George Tapley Whitney and David F. Bowers, eds., *The Heritage of Kant* (New York: Russell & Russell, Inc., 1962), p. 257.
22. *Ibid.*, p. 257.
23. *Ibid.*, p. 253.
24. Nathan Rotenstreich, *From Substance to Subject* (The Hague: Martinus Nijhoff, 1974), p. 34.
25. Immanuel Kant, *Critique of Pure Reason*, trans. by Norman Kemp Smith (New York: St. Martin's Press, 1965), p. 312.
26. *Ibid.*
27. Hegel,*Philosophy of Right,* trans. by T.M. Knox (Chicago: Encyclopaedia Britannica, Inc., 1952), p. 16.
28. Georg Wilhelm Friedrich Hegel, *The Philosophy of History*, trans. by J. Sibree (New York: Dover Publications, Inc., 1956), p. 19.
29. *Ibid*, p. 23.

References

30. Karl Marx, *On Freedom of the Press and Censorship*, trans. and ed. by Saul K. Padover (New York: McGraw-Hill Book Company, 1974), p. 142.
31. Marx & Engels, *Basic Writings on Politics & Philosophy*, ed. by Lewis S. Feuer (New York: Doubleday & Company, Inc., Anchor Books, 1959), p. 360.
32. Frederick Engels, *Anti-Duehring*, C.P. Dutt, ed., trans. by Emile Burns (New York: International Publishers Co., Inc., 1970), pp. 309-310.
33. Karl Marx, *Selected Writings in Sociology & Social Philosophy*, eds., Bottomore and Maximilian Rubel (New York: McGraw-Hill Book Co., 1964), p. 95.
34. John Dewey, "Philosophies of Freedom," in *Philosophy and Civilization* (New York, N.Y.: Milton, Balch & Co., 1931), p. 291.
35. *Ibid.*, p. 277.
36. John Dewey, *Individualism, Old and New* (New York: Capricorn Books, 1962), pp. 36-38.
37. *Ibid.*
38. *Ibid.*
39. John Dewey, "Philosophies of Freedom," *op. cit.*, p. 278.
40. Thucydides, *The Peloponnesian War* (Baltimore: Penguin Books, 1965), p. 117.
41. *Ibid.*
42. Samuel D. Warren and Louis D. Brandeis, "The Right of Privacy" *Harvard Law Review,* Vol. 4 (1890), pp. 193-195 (emphasis added).
43. Thomas E. Emerson, *"The System of Freedom of Expression"* (New York: Random House, 1971), p. 545.
44. *Ibid.*, pp. 546-547.

Chapter IX

1. Robert Campbell, Introduction, *John Austin: Lectures on Jurisprudence, or the Philosophy of Positive Law* (New York: James Cockcroft & C, 1875), p. XVII.
2. W. Jethro Brown, *Austinian Theory of Law* (London: John Murray, 1926), p. 334. In the polemics against the thesis that there were periods when aboriginal Australians observed the law because of their faith in the enforcing power of the supranatural

authority, W. Jethro Brown writes that a jurist and a philosopher should bear in mind a reality of profound importance: in our life, there is such a thing as State-enforced law!
3. In this respect one should remember the remark of Salmond *(Jurisprudence,* p. 54, quoted by Brown, p. 339): "There may have been a time in the past when a man was not distinguished from an anthropoid ape, but that is no reason for now defining a man in such wise as to include an ape."
4. Various natural law theories have been used to justify: Roman rule over the world, feudal hierarchy, the superiority of church power over state power, absolute monarchy, colonialism, and even slavery and racism.
5. See Nicholas Capaldi, *Clear and Present Danger. The Free Speech Controversy* (New York: Pegasus, The Western Publishing Co., 1969) p. 74.
6. *Ibid.*
7. H.L.A. Hart, Positivism and the Separation of Law and Morals, *Harvard Law Review,* Vol. 71, No. 4, 1958, p. 593. (Reprinted in *Introduction to Law,* Selected essays reprinted from *Harvard Law Review,* ed., Arthur E. Sutherland, Harvard Law Review Press, Cambridge, Mass., 1977, p. 101).
8. Roscoe Pound wrote: "Roman law in its decadence... confined the judge, when questions of law were in issue, to the purely mechanical task of counting and of determining the numerical preponderance of authority ... I have referred to mechanical jurisprudence as scientific because those who administer it believe it such. But in truth it is not science at all. We no longer hold anything scientific merely because it exhibits a rigid scheme of deductions from *a priori* conceptions." Roscoe Pound, Mechanical Jurisprudence, *8 Columbia Law Review,* 1908. Reprinted in: Morris R. Cohen and Felix S. Cohen: *Readings in Jurisprudence and Legal Philosophy* (Boston: Little, Brown and Co., 1951) p. 537-538.
9. Quoted after James Reston, "The Blood and the Mule," *The New York Times,* April 6, 1977.
10. *Minnersville School District v. Gobitis, 310 US 586 (1940).*
    See Alan Barth: *Prophets with Honor* (New York: Alfred A. Knopf, 1974). Answering the question of whether it was constitutional to compel school children to salute the flag, Justice Franfurter wrote:
    "The precise issue, then, for us to decide is whether the legislatures of the various states said the authorities in a thousand

counties and school districts of this country are barred from determining the appropriateness of various means to evoke that unifying sentiment without which there can ultimately be no liberties, civil or religious." There is a "wisdom of training children in patriotic impulses ..." (p. 114-115).

Louis Levene observed in the *Cornell Law Quarterly*, (26, December, 1940) in connection with this decision that "there has come the danger that patriotism will degenerate into a popular fetish" *(Ibid.,* p. 119).

The New Republic (No. 102, June 24, 1940) wrote in an editorial that the court itself says in effect that "we must imperil religious liberty in the interest of the American state, which is worth preserving because it guarantees religious liberty ..." *(Ibid.,* p. 121).

11. Ernst Cassirer, *The Myth of the State* (New Haven: Yale University Press, 1946). See especially in Part One the following paragraphs: The Structure of Mythical Thought; Myth and Language; The Function of Myth in Man's Social Life. Compare also: M.F. Ashley Montagu, Cassirer on Mythological Thinking in: Paul Arthur Schilpp (ed), *The Philosophy of Ernst Cassirer* (Evanston: The Library of Living Philosophers, Inc., 1949) pp. 361-377.
12. Thomas Paine, *Common Sense and Other Political Writings* (Indianapolis-New York: The Bobbs Merrill Co., Library of Liberal Arts, 1953) p. 32.
13. C.K. Ogden, *Betham's Theory of Fiction* (London: Kegal Paul, Trench, Trubner and Co., 1932) p. 150.
14. Quoted by Charles A. Beard in the Introduction to the book: John P. Frank: *Mr. Justice Black. The Man and His Opinions* (New York: Alfred A. Knopf, 1949) p. xiv.
15. *Ibid.*
16. Wolfgang Friedmann, *Legal Theory* (New York: Columbia University Press, Fifth Edition, 1967), p. 86-87.
17. *Ibid.* p. 261.
18. Ch. Perelman, "L'interpretation dans le droit," *in Archives de Philosophie du droit,* Tome XVII, 1972, (Translation by William Kluback, p. 29).

Chaim Perelman writes that Eyken's book "was considered, in Belgium, during the half of a century, as a classic."
19. "Saleiles himself formulates the difference with French elegance" ... Wolfgang Friedmann, op. cit. p. 262.

Cf. also Francois Geny: *Méthode d'interprétation et source*

du droit privé positif, Paris, 1932, p. xxv. R. Saleiles: *Le code civil et la méthode historique* (Le Code Civil. Livre de Centenaire), Paris, 1904.
20. Roscoe Pound and Theodore F.T. Plucknett, *Readings on the History and System of the Common Law* (Rochester: The Lawyers Co-operative Publishing Company, 1927), p. 263.
21. *Ibid.*
22. *Ibid.*
23. *Ibid.*
24. Jerzy Wroblewski's observation is correct: one who agrees with the principle that it is the legislator who knows best what he wanted to express, will "automatically accept the static theory of interpretation, which constitutes ... an ideological background of the whole construction," Teoria Wykladni ..., op. cit., p. 114.
25. B. Nutting, *The Ambiguity of Unambiguous Statutes, Minnesota Law Review,* 1940, vol. 24, p. 516. See also J. Wroblewski, Teoria Wykladni ..., op. cit., p. 105.
26. Chaim Perelman, "L'interprétation dans le droit," in *Archives de Philosophie du Droit,* Tome XVII, 1972, (translation by William Klubak, p. 30).
27. *Ibid.,* p. 31.
28. *Ibid.*
29. Rudolf von Ihering, *Law as Means to the End,* op. cit., p. 248.
30. *Ibid.*
31. *Ibid.,* p. 249.
32. Lon Fuller: "Human Purposes and Natural Law," *Journal of Philosophy,* No 53/1956, p. 655-656.
33. Samuel J. Shuman: *Legal Positivism* (Detroit: Wayne State University Press, 1963), p. 196.
34. *Ibid.*
35. Harold J. Laski: *Studies in Law and Politics,* (London: George Allen a. Unwin Ltd., 1932) p. 253.
36. Albert Camus, *Why Spain?* (A reply to Gabriel Marcel), printed in *Combat,* 1948, quoted after Albert Camus, *Resistance, Rebellion and Death,* (London: Hamish Hamilton, 1961) p. 58.
36a. *Ibid.,* p. 60.
37. Ronald Dworkin: *Taking Rights Seriously,* (London: Gerald Duckworth and Co., 1977) p. 23-31.
38. David Lyons: *"Principles, Positivism, and Legal Theory,"* in *The Yale Law Journal,* Vol. 87:415, 1977, p. 421.

References

I agree with the line of criticism adopted by Professor Lyons in his article and I follow his reasoning below.
39. *Ibid.*, p. 427.
40. Dworkin, *op. cit.*, p. 267.
41. *Ibid.*
42. *Ibid.*, p. 266.
    To what extent the concept about the "competition" between equality and liberty became obsolete especially in the XXth century see also Louis Henkin, *The Rights of Man Today*:
    "The twentieth century adopted equality and liberty as basic rights and expanded and deepened the eighteenth-century connotations of equality ... The twentieth-century synthesis, then, perhaps became possible only when and where economic class lines blurred and both classes (upper or middle class and lower—M.M.) participated in political power" (Louis Henkin, *The Rights of Man Today*, Westview Press, Boulder, Colorado, 1978), p. 25.
43. Wolfgang Friedmann, *Legal Theory, op. cit.*, p. 30-32, 293-295. Columbia University Press, 1941), foreword by Edwin W. Patterson, p. VIII.
45. Karl A. Llewellyn expresses this contention in his famous article: "Some Realism about Realism—Responding to Dean Pound," 44 *Harvard Law Review* (1931), 1222-64.
46. Edward Allen Kent, *Law and Philosophy. Readings in Legal Philosophy.* (Englewood Cliff, N.J.: Prentice Hall, Inc. 1970) p. 63.
47. *Ibid.*
48. *Ibid.*, pp. 64-65, 70-72.
49. H.L.A. Hart: *The Concept of Law* (London: Oxford University Press, 1972), p. 205.
50. *Ibid.*, p. 206.
51. *Ibid.*, p. 205.
52. S. Prakash Sinha: "The Anthropocentric Theory of International Law As a Basis for Human Rights" (*Journal of International Law*, Vol. 10, Spring 1978), p. 501.
53. Abraham Edel, *Legal Positivism: A Pragmatic Reanalysis* (Basell: World Congress on Philosophy of Law and Social Philosophy, 1979, paper #117), p. 1-2.
54. *Ibid.*, p. 2.
55. "The present philosophical tide is running against the sharp trichotomy," *Ibid*, p. 9.

56. *Ibid.*, p. 4.
57. *Ibid.*, p. 13.
58. *Ibid.*, p. 17.
59. *Ibid.*, p. 17.
60. *Ibid.*, p. 31.
61. Edward H. Levi, *An Introduction to Legal Reasoning* (Chicago-London: The University of Chicago Press, 1974), p. 58-59.
62. This expression was used by Edward H. Levi, *op. cit.*, p. 59.
63. Edward H. Levi, *Ibid.*
64. If one ever accepts the premise that the statutory laws express the will of the legislator (consent in this respect seems to be universal), one does not have to accept the theory that the purpose of the interpretation and application of law must be the finding of the subjective will (intent) of the legislator and not of the "objective" meaning of the norms. Of course, as we already mentioned, the latter theory does not solve all the philosophical questions of judicial interpretation, either.
65. *Ibid.*, p. 17.
66. *Ibid.*
67. N. Cardozo: *The Growth of Law* (New Haven: Yale University, Benjamin Press, 1924), pp. 40-41, 76-78.
68. Levi, op. cit. p. 23-25.
69. Dorsey Gray: *Towards World Perspectives of Philosophy of Law and Social Philosophy*. A paper submitted for the opening session of the World Congress on Philosophy of Law and Social Philosophy, Basel (Switzerland), 1979, p. 20.
70. Dorsey Gray, *op. cit.* p. 22.
71. The expression "positivist law" is used here in the same sense as it was used by Dorsey Gray: "Positive Law became Positivist Law because the success of positivism in the new physical sciences inspired the attempt to use the same method with respect to social and legal phenomena."—Dorsey Gray, *op. cit.* p. 18-19.
72. Gray Dorsey, *op. cit.* p. 2-3; cf. p. 31.
73. Gray Dorsey, *op. cit.* p. 32.
74. Ota Weinberger, *Jenseits von Positivismus and Naturrecht*, World Congress on Philosophy of Law and Social Philosophy, Basel, 1979.
75. *Ibid.*, p. 2.
    Translation: One must also add practical notions: ". . . the notion of an action, the notions of practical propositions (in con-

trast to affirmative propositions) for, only through the use of such propositions is it possible to express the ought, values, and teleological relations."
76. *Ibid.*, p. 5-6.
77. *Ibid.*, p. 6.
78. *Ibid.*, p. 6-7.
    Translation: "To the positive institutionalized factors belong also jurisprudence and the methodology of interpretation which is grounded in society. To the system of positive law belong also legal principles and the teleological underpinning of the system of jurisprudence which appear in part as rational abstractions of valid legal provisions, in part, as institutionalized foreknowledge of the jurists. One could object of course that in this case, due to the lack of an explicit formal source, an instance of uncertainty ... can occur to a certain extent. I believe, however, that these factors also—since they are actually effective—must be viewed as legal reality."
79. *Ibid.*, p. 7 (Translation: "unlimited license")
80. *Ibid.*, p. 7.
    Translation: "When Hart, due to considerations of the anthropological role of law, sets up postulates concerning a minimal content of natural law, he can be proven right in so far that a system of law *must* exhibit certain characteristics with regard to its content. The extent of these stipulations *cannot*, however, be regarded as *natural right*, but as *defining characteristics* of the *concept of law* which then will come into play when law is regarded not only structurally, but also from the *standpoint* of its social functions."
81. *Ibid.*, p. 9.
82. *Ibid.*, p. 9.
83. *Ibid.*, p. 12.
84. *Ibid.*, p. 12.
85. Louis Henkin in *The Rights of Man Today* expounded one of his crucial theses that the twentieth century has been "both escaping and bridging the dichotomy of natural and positive law" (Louis Henkin, *The Rights of Man Today,* Westview Press, Boulder, Colorado, 1978) p. 23.

    And therefore: "In positive law today, it is human rights that are national and international law, not the laws of Hitler or some other 'jurisprudence of terror' " (p. 27).

    Positivist realism embraces Henkin's thesis that the rejection of a "jurisprudence of terror" today should and can be based on national and international law without any reference to "natural law."

The Charter of the International Military Tribunal (London, Aug. 8, 1945) is an example of the transformation of the requirements and norms of justice and equity into positive international law, including international criminal law, concerned with the rights of individuals. The concepts of "crimes against peace," "war crimes," and "crimes against humanity" were developed from the previously accepted norms of international law and from "the dictates of public conscience," as it was worded by the American delegation preparing for the Nuremberg Trial of the Nazi criminals. See: Bradley F. Smith, *Reaching Judgement at Nuremberg* (London: Andre Deutsch Limited, 1977) p. 51.

The dictates of public conscience (one can use many names to express the same concept of the conscience of mankind outraged by the unprecedented enormity, cruelty, monstrosity, and bureaucratic pedantry of the crimes committed by the states) prompted the transformation of the rudimentary ideas of crimes against peace, humanity, the laws and customs of war, into a notion of a crime as defined by the positive international criminal law.

The Nuremberg Military Tribunal stated in one of its opinions ("The Justice Case," 1951):

> In declaring that the expressed determination of the victors to punish German officials who slaughtered their own nationals is in harmony with international principles of justice, we usurp no power; we only take judicial notice of the declarations already made by the chief executives of the United States and her former Allies.—quoted from: Wolfgang Friedman, Oliver J. Lissitzyn, Richard C. Pugh: *International Law* (West Publishing Co., St. Paul, Minn., 1969) p. 236.

Here the Tribunal noted another aspect of the "positivisation" or transformation into legal norms of certain ideas: one takes *"judicial notice"* of existing juridical facts. The *"law in making"* becomes *the law* in *life* and in *books* at a certain moment in time and it can be applied immediately.

The next step in the process of the "positivisation" of the principles concerning crimes against peace, humanity, and the customs and the laws of war was done by the General Assembly of the United Nations when it unanimously affirmed "the principles of international law recognized by the Charter of the Nuremberg Tribunal and the judgement of the Tribunal" (Dec. 11, 1946).

A special problem facing the application of "the right of Antigone" fighting her oppressors is the shelter used by all tormentors: "I acted under orders." This excuse was used by the Nazi criminals, most notably Adolf Eichmann in Jerusalem. In this connection Gideon Hausner, the Attorney General of Israel, observed:

> Let Eichmann invoke his 'superior orders.' Their execution was in any case illegal, since they were contrary to the universal principles of ethics and the rules of civilization.—Gideon Hausner, *Justice in Jerusalem* (New York: Harper and Row Publishers, 1966) p. 301.

The concept that the execution of the illegal orders (or voluntarily assumed duties which are *contra legem*) is *ipso iure* null and void, is generally accepted by the legal systems of all civilized nations. These principles were transplanted after WWII from the sphere of municipale law into the sphere of international criminal law. The International Military Tribunal clearly declared that the Nazi criminals cannot be regarded innocent because Hitler assigned them their tasks, *if they knew what they were doing!* Gideon Hausner correctly stated that the defendant knew or should have known what he was doing when the assigned tasks were contrary to "the universal principles of ethics" and "the rules of civilization."

In the process of the realization of law certain principles of ethics and civilization are "promoted," "advanced," "lifted," or "raised" to the rank or level of legal principles whose application is socially urgent and important. In the modern bureaucratic world in which more and more people work within "a disciplinary framework" (expression of Gideon Hausner, *op. cit.*, p. 395), the problem of "obedience" and loyalty is becoming more and more complicated and important from the social, political, and ethical viewpoints.

"It had been recognized that the principle of blind obedience would ultimately undermine discipline itself" (Gideon Hausner, *op. cit.*, p. 395). Today more than ever it has become a moral and sometimes a legal duty to disobey certain orders, recommendations, and "advice."

The oath of loyalty has its limits. As Justice Musmanno stated in the *Concentrations Camps* case:

> Each and every person who took his oath surrendered his personality, gave up his right of individual judgement and self-criticism . . . and exposed himself to the winds of moral irresponsibility . . . This oath of loyalty by itself is an act of sacrilege and a base crime and cannot serve either as a justification or an explanation for the crimes which were perpetrated by virtue of this alleged loyalty. (quoted by Gideon Hausner, *op. cit.*, p. 393)

This judgment is more and more topical; the tormentors of Antigone cannot find a legal shield behind their oath of loyalty. Loyalty ceased to be a virtue in itself! Today its scope is not only morally but also legally limited.

Many pertinent aspects of the question of the "superior orders" are discussed by Telford Taylor, *Nuremberg and Vietnam: an American Tragedy* (New York: A New York Times Book, 1970) pp. 42-57.

A milestone is the transformation of "natural" and/or "human" rights into a positive legal system in Europe was embodied in the *European Convention for the Protection of Human Rights and Fundamental Freedoms* signed in Rome on Nov. 4, 1950. Between the years 1952-1966 five additional Protocols were signed and in 1969 the *Agreement relating to Persons participating in Proceedings of the European Commission and Court of Human Rights* was signed.

The *Court of Human Rights* was established in 1959.

The provisions of law and the machinery created in Europe to protect human rights are analyzed by A.H. Robertson, *Human Rights in Europe* (Manchester, University Press, 1977).

INDEX

Adams, 253
Amin, 242
Ananieva, 383
Aquinas, St. Thomas, 244, 391
Aristotle, 5, 19, 166-167, 197, 207-208, 210-211, 220-221, 351, 388
Austin, 14, 39-67, 74, 94, 165-166, 279, 328, 348, 351

Bacon, 140, 238
Bakunin, 386
Balzac, 10
Barth, 394
Baumgardt, 13, 373, 375
Baumgarten, 239, 391, 395
Beard, 296, 395
Bentham, iii, v, 9-40, 42, 47, 50, 67-68, 72, 94, 140, 165, 328, 337, 348, 371, 373, 395
Bergbohm, 121
Belime, 380
Beria, 134
Beylis, 112
Black, 395
Bonaparte, 119
Bowers, 392
Brandeis, 274, 277, 311, 393
Brown, 393-394
Burda, 130-131
Burgenthal, 390
Byron, 102-103

Campbell, 279, 393

Camus, 316-318, 396
Capaldi, 394
Cardozo, 165, 167, 309-310, 354, 398
Cassirer, 288, 395
Cave, 252
Celsus, 44, 107
Churchill, 229
Cicero, 5-7, 373
Cohen, F., 377, 394
Cohen, M., 377, 394
Coke, 302, 333
Comte, 167
Creon, 1, 282

David, i
Democritus, 5
Descartes, 186, 204, 238
Dewey, 165, 167, 172-176, 178, 231, 257, 268-269, 257, 268-269, 336, 345, 355, 385
Dorsey, 354-355, 398
Drake, 378
Dumont, 9
Dupréel, 180-182, 184-185, 211, 245, 386
Duverger, 382
Dworkin, 301, 328-329, 331-336, 338-339, 353, 396-397

Edel, 349, 350-351, 397
Ehrlich, Eugen, 98, 380
Ehrlich, Stanislaw, 130
Ehrenzweig, ii

Eichmann, 401
Elkind, 391
Emerson, 274, 393
Engels, 118, 120, 122, 160, 265-266, 268, 393
Epicurus, 295
Eyken, 301, 395

Frank, John, 395
Frankfurter, 394
Frege, 178
Friedmann, 254, 297, 339, 392, 395, 397, 400
Feuchtwanger, 275
Fuller, 313, 376, 396

Gaius, 44
Geny, 98, 224, 301, 395
Godwin, 190
Goethe, 9, 23
Golding, 390-392
Gorgias, 211
Granet, 10
Grotius, 249
Gsovski, ii

Hall, 238, 391
Harrington, 318
Hart, 286, 346-348, 394, 397, 399
Haseler, 386
Hausner, 401, 406
Hazard, viii, 149-150, 163, 382-383, 385
Heck, 380
Hegel, 10, 74, 88, 152, 156, 221, 231, 245, 257, 263-264, 269, 336, 340, 389, 392
Hemingway, 121
Henkin, 390-391, 397, 399
Heraclites, 211, 388
Hitler, ii, 216, 388
Hobbes, 39, 140, 231, 315
Hohfeld, 224, 247, 252-253, 391-392
Holmes, 165, 167-173, 224, 247-248, 285-286, 291, 311, 345, 385
Hugo, 74

Hume, 312

Ihering, 67-82, 84-85, 88, 90-93, 224, 371, 378-379, 396

Jackson, 252
Jacobins, 60
Jellinek, 320, 371
Jodlowski, 130
Jourdain, 302

Kadar, 125
Kafka, 191
Kant, 32, 71, 239, 251, 257-260, 262, 268, 321-322
Kantorowicz, 98
Kelsen, ii, 148, 212-213, 224, 236, 318-327, 376, 388
Kent, 302, 333, 397
Kerimov, 143, 154-157, 382-384
Kluback, 386, 395-396
Khrushchev, 125
Kolakowski, 128-129, 381
Kollataj, 249-250
Kuntz, ii

La Rochefoucauld, 223
Laski, 396
Lenin, 118, 122, 138
Levene, 395
Levi, 352-354, 398
Lieberman, 123
Lindley, 250
Lippman, 287-288
Lissitzyn, 400
Llewellyn, 340, 342-343, 397
Locke, 42, 237, 270, 315, 369
Lopatka, 130, 153, 162, 384
Louis XIV, 17
Lucretius, 295
Lustacz, 381
Lyons, 331, 334

Mably, 104
Mackelday, 246

Index

Maneli, ii, v, vi, viii
Mansfield, 46
Marshall, 148, 371
Martyniak, 243, 391
Marx, ii, 9-10, 13, 117-122, 140, 156, 158-160, 257, 264-272, 336, 373, 393
McDougal, 376-377
Merkel, 285
Michalska, 384
Mill, 39, 67, 72, 94, 99, 106-107, 348
Miller, 194, 386
Mills, 192, 194, 307, 387
Montagu, 395
Montesquieu, 33, 45, 97, 330
Musmanno, 402

Nersesjanz, 157-158, 384
Nixon, 155
Nutting, 306, 396

Ogden, 395
Olbrechts-Tyteca, 179, 185, 388
Omar, 293
Opalek, 129, 131, 134-138, 255-256, 381, 389, 391-392
Orwell, 180

Paine, 54, 237, 245, 289, 295, 395
Pashukanis, 117
Patterson, 340
Perelman, vii, 165, 167, 175-178, 180-182, 184-185, 187, 190-192, 195, 300, 306-308, 386-389, 395-396
Pericles, 273, 277
Petrazhytsky, 111, 137, 370
Pilate, 324-326
Plato, 132, 260
Plucknett, 396
Pollock, i
Pope Leo XIII, 159
Pope Pius XII, 234
Pound, 394, 396-397
Protagoras, 211
Puchta, 74, 85, 104-105, 380
Puffendorf, 249

Pugh, 400
Pushkin, 102-103, 149

Rabel, ii
Rejsner, 117
Reston, 394
Rheinstein, ii
Robertson, 402
Roguin, 299
Roosevelt, 229
Ross, 254
Rotenstreich, 392
Rousseau, 54, 60, 63, 119, 154-156, 234, 237, 275-276, 369
Rozmaryn, 131, 139-149, 381
Russell, 19, 261

Saleiles, 224, 301, 395
Savigny, 24, 74-75, 104, 106, 380
Schmitt, 147, 382
Seidler, 130
Schuman, 313-314, 396
Shershenevitch, 105, 380
Sinha, 349, 389, 397
Smith, Bradley F., 400
Sneed, 252-253
Socrates, 195
Solon, 25
Somlo, 108, 227, 389
Sohn, 380, 389
Spinoza, 49, 336
Stalin, ii, iv, 116, 118-120, 122-123, 128, 133-134, 256, 270-272
Stammler, 243
Stendhal, 14
Story, 7
Strong, 252
Stuchka, 117

Taylor, 402
Thrasymachus, 39
Thucydides, 393
Timasheff, ii
Toreno, 22
Tumanov, 159-161, 384

Ulpian, 44-45

Vaihinger, 322
Voltaire, 23, 33
Vyshinsky, iv, 117-119, 121, 124, 135, 157, 232

Warren, 274, 393
Waskowski, 100-102, 106, 110, 380
Wedderburn, 10-11
Weinberger, 356-360, 398-399

Whitney, 392
Williams, 391
Wilson, 229
Windscheid, 224
Wright, 296
Wroblewski, 129-130, 396
Wu, ii
Wurzel, 380

Zakrzewski, 134-138, 381
Zawadzki, 130